MW00944190

Dear Tanya,
There are creepy crawlies laughs and lessons! Hope you like them all.
Melanie J. Marshall
February 2012

LADYBUG

Melanie L. Marshall

© Copyright 2006 Melanie Marshall.
Except for use in reviews, to reproduce or use a portion or all of this work by any means, in any form, without prior written permission from the author is prohibited.

All of the stories in this book are born of childhood memories. Except for the author's, her family, public figures or entities, all names have been changed to protect the identity and privacy of those whose influence shaped and inspired her to give them life in print.

Editors: Victoria White, The Virtual Writer and Joyce H. Sexton

This book is printed on recycled paper.

Book design by Melanie L. Marshall

Note for Librarians: A cataloguing record for this book is available from Library and Archives Canada at www.collectionscanada.ca/amicus/index-e.html
ISBN 1-4122-0219-1

Printed on paper with minimum 30% recycled fibre.
Trafford's print shop runs on "green energy" from solar, wind and other environmentally-friendly power sources.

TRAFFORD
PUBLISHING™

Offices in Canada, USA, Ireland and UK

Book sales for North America and international:
Trafford Publishing, 6E–2333 Government St.,
Victoria, BC V8T 4P4 CANADA
phone 250 383 6864 (toll-free 1 888 232 4444)
fax 250 383 6804; email to orders@trafford.com
Book sales in Europe:
Trafford Publishing (UK) Limited, 9 Park End Street, 2nd Floor
Oxford, UK OX1 1HH UNITED KINGDOM
phone +44 (0)1865 722 113 (local rate 0845 230 9601)
facsimile +44 (0)1865 722 868; info.uk@trafford.com
Order online at:
trafford.com/04-1616

10 9 8 7 6 5

To my dearest friend and sister, Catherine Denise Marshall-Landsley. Her unconditional love, encouragement, enthusiasm and support have made me a better person and nurtured me all of my years.

Melanie L. Marshall

In loving memory of my mother,
Ella Catherine Powell Marshall,
my friend, my confidant,
my champion.

MELANIE L. MARSHALL

LADYBUG

MELANIE L. MARSHALL

NEPAL

Twinkling, winkling, night bright stars—skies of truest blue.

Kathmandu. Precious love and peace.

MELANIE L. MARSHALL

For Some Time Apart

The year I got my stomach pumped was the year we were supposed to leave Kathmandu, Nepal. The thought of leaving home was not a welcome one, and I began to worry. Welcome or not, worried or not, leaving was real. Mother said we were returning to the United States of America on "home leave." I asked her why we had to leave home and she said, "Don't worry, baby." I tried not to, but it was difficult. I didn't understand why we couldn't stay in Nepal forever. Thinking about it, despite what mother said, did worry me.

When I got my stomach pumped, everything happened so fast I do not remember if I had time to worry. From the moment I told mother I had eaten all the tiny candies in the little bottle from the high shelf in her closet, we were on our way to the mission infirmary. Once there, I was put on a freezing-cold metal table and got poked and prodded, which made me squirm and jump even though I was supposed to lie perfectly still. I didn't like it. I liked it even less when the doctor uncoiled a long, thin, snake-like plastic tube and waved it in the air like a wand before pointing it at me. I knew about snakes; some were dangerous and some were not. I wasn't afraid of snakes—why be afraid of the plastic tube? I didn't know better, that's why.

That long, thin plastic tube went into my throat, down and down and down. By the time most of it had disappeared inside me, I understood it was a kind of snake, maybe even the dangerous kind. The plastic snake had its fangs in me, it held me tight. I was pinned to the cold, hard table like a butterfly on a display board, too busy getting my guts sucked clean to have worries of any kind in my head. I clung to my mother's hand and kept my eyes closed. Even so, the heat from the bright overhead light bulb burned yellow-orange onto my face and into my eyelids. I think I wondered if the light might stain my eyelids and look the way iodine did on my skin when I got cuts disinfected. I hoped not. I just didn't know.

I focused on mother's soothing, gentle voice and I tried not to cry; I tried to be a good girl. The menacing gurgling, clicking, humming, spitting, burping noise of the snake in my stomach frightened me so that I lost my battle with tears. When it was over, I knew I'd never look at pills in a bottle and think of them as candy again. Not ever.

As bad as the stomach pumping was, I was afraid leaving Kathmandu was going to be worse. I realized there were many things I didn't know and millions more I didn't understand, and this home-leave business was something I didn't understand. Another thing I didn't understand was what mother meant when she told me that, when we returned to Washington, D.C., my father would have to be debriefed. I had never heard that word before and I didn't like the way it sounded.

De plus another word meant minus something important so de-briefed sounded very serious to me. Scary-serious, like a visit to the dentist where I imagined my teeth would get pulled out if they had cavities! I'd be de-teethed, and my gums would bleed buckets from the deep holes the pulled out teeth left and later food would get stuck in the holes and it'd rot and the rot would spread to my other teeth…

What I really wanted to know was if my father's debriefing was going to hurt? I told her it sure sounded like it ought to. Would he have to come home in an ambulance? Probably not, she said. Well, didn't de-bunked mean you got kicked out of the top of a bunk bed and that's a long drop, it'd hurt wouldn't it, the fall and the kick, right?

And, de-feathered meant you got your feathers plucked out and that must hurt too. The only birds I knew about getting de-feathered were the chickens in our yard and they were dead when we plucked them. Mother put her hand on my head and looked at me for a long time. Her eyes searched my face. I think that was how she read my mind. She was able to do that all the time, she said it was a mother's gift.

After father's debriefing, mother explained, we would go to visit her mother and other relatives. I never heard the rest of what she said because I was stuck on the fact that my mother had a mother! Of course, it made sense. I understood about parents and babies; I was my mother's baby. I knew horses had foals and cows had calves and hens had baby chicks when their eggs hatched. I just didn't realize my mother had a mother too. This was very important, exciting information, but I just didn't know where to put it when my head was full of worry and my heart was loaded with sadness.

Even with this exciting new information, the only real thought in my head was how, in the whole wide world, could I leave Kathmandu? Home was Nepal, and even though I had learned that we, as a family, went wherever my father was assigned, leaving home was not something I looked forward to. Thinking about it made my insides tumble.

My insides didn't tumble the way they had with the stomach pumping. They didn't gurgle and burp the way they had when a tapeworm was eating me down to skin and bones and my stomach made hungry noises all the time. With the tapeworm, my stomach bucked and pitched and rumbled, but the feeling was not the same.

One year, on Christmas Eve, my insides rolled and boiled and skipped when Santa smiled at me as he put gifts under our Christmas tree. And once, I took one of mother's long, black, shiny hairpins to use as a car key. I turned it in the ignition of my father's Jeep, and it started with a jolt. My insides hadn't tumbled the same way those times either. No, the dread of leaving didn't feel like that; it was a heavy weight, sort of like an earthquake-danger kind of feeling.

I knew that kind of feeling because we had had an earthquake. My insides got jumbled and queasy while it shook our world. I knew the earthquake situation was serious because earthquakes could maim and injure and kill, not to mention obliterate entire villages. During our earthquake, mother's voice was calm, but her hands shook. I knew she was anxious but she wore a brave face. I was worried because mother had on her brave face, and that was very serious. It meant she didn't have to say things to me twice. I knew I was to be a good girl—I was to do whatever she said, even if I was afraid.

During our earthquake, I'm not certain what upset me more, the earthquake or the fact that mother's hands shook. I knew neither was a good thing, and my insides bubbled like water over a dam of stubborn sticks. The brave face mother wore was much the same as all her other faces; the expression in her eyes was the key. She spoke to me with her eyes faster than with words.

Mother's eyes? They usually smiled and laughed or twinkled at me. Sometimes, just sometimes, her eyes sighed. They rarely shed tears that I ever saw, and then only tears of happiness and joy. Her eyes were my barometer; and I think they were how she read my mind. When I saw how worried they looked during our earthquake, I wanted to cry, but before I dared to, the danger had passed.

As mother helped me prepare for bed the night before we were scheduled to leave, I wondered how long it would be before my stomach settled. I said my prayers and mother told me that when we returned to Kathmandu after home leave, we would move into a new house where I would have my own room. She kissed me good night. The image of our suitcases on the floor—with the clothes we would wear the next day folded neatly on top—woke up my insides. They wouldn't be still or quiet. I was afraid they'd talk all night, and that was the last thing I thought before I fell asleep.

Morning arrived, as it does, and we went to the airport. This trip was the first time we would all travel together. I didn't remember having flown in an airplane, but my brothers and sisters did. I stayed close to mother and looked around the terminal. It was full to brimming with our fellow travelers, as well as many people who had come to say farewell. We got ready to board the plane, but at the last minute we got to stay!

The plane roared down the runway and took off without us. It climbed sharply into the bright blue sky and we waved until it was out of sight. Then we left the airport and returned home. Hours later, we learned that the plane we were to have been on had crashed over the mountains and that there were no survivors. I didn't know how such a thing was possible. All the people I had seen get on the plane were gone—they were never coming back. Mother said not to worry. People went to heaven when they died; they didn't hurt or have any problems. I did know a little something already about heaven, I lived there. I didn't quite understand the heaven the plane crash people would be in. I wondered if their heaven was half as beautiful my own? If it was, I thought that would be very good.

In Nepal, the dead were burned on huge funeral pyres on the river. If the fire was not hot enough, or if there was not enough fuel, then some people did not get completely burned up. I knew that sometimes bits of burnt dead people got washed up on the riverbanks. I thought unburned people pieces were creepy, but I knew that was how the funeral ceremony worked. Before I could think about the plane crash and wonder anymore about all the lost people, mother kissed me awake, and I learned I'd been having a nightmare.

I told mother all about it, and she said I had a very active imagination. She said I had to learn how to turn it off. She said to remember how it felt when I found Santa putting gifts under our Christmas tree. Think about how my insides felt then, she said; they tumbled then too, right? Yes, that was true. I remembered that I'd been surprised to see Santa putting gifts under our tree. Not afraid-surprised; amazed and happy-surprised! Santa ate three of mother's sweet spice shortbread cookies and winked at me. Then he gave me a big hug and said to be a good girl. He smelled like my father's Old Spice aftershave and his long white beard tickled my face.

It was thrilling-exciting then, not scary-exciting the way it had been when we'd had the earthquake that ate one of the backyard trees by our well. The tree disappeared into the angry maw of Mother Nature that showed itself as a jagged crevice in the earth. Mother Nature ate that tree right up! Then, several hours later, the earth closed up again as though the tree had never even been there. All that remained was a line in the earth, and that line smoothed away to nothing after the first hard rain.

My nightmare was very frightening; it left me shaken. I told mother my insides felt like an earthquake about my nightmare. I had trouble separating it from reality because even though I was no longer sleeping, I still thought the plane crash people were gone from the sky in the same way the tree was gone from the backyard of our old house. I told mother I knew I could not live if anything like that ever happened to her. She kissed me again, smoothed the worry lines from my forehead and said to remember that all my imaginary plane crash people would go to heaven.

Mother reminded me that heaven was a very good place and, should something like that ever really happen, the families here on earth needed my prayers. I could pray for the families to remember their love, to have fond memories, and to cherish their loved ones. She said love and memories kept us together no matter where we went. Whether we were parted for a long time or a short time, memories we had of family and friends were the ties that kept them close to our hearts. Love and memories sustained us; we had to hold on tight to them.

I snuggled under the covers and considered what she'd said while I waited for sleep to come and carry me up into the high mountain midnight where the wind danced and the stars sparkled in quiet peace. I thought about what mother said and knew it was important. I told myself I had to always remember mother's love for me. I knew I had to keep her love close. I told myself to always remember my love for her and I knew I had to cherish her in my heart should we ever be, for some time, apart.

A Poppy for Friday

I made a promise to mother. And I promptly broke it. Well, no. I never promised. I knew what promises were and knew the importance of keeping them. And even at the age of four I knew you could never break a promise. I also knew you could not be held to a promise if you made it with your fingers crossed behind your back. I forgot to cross my fingers behind my back. I lied to mother.

On this particular day, there was some sort of hubbub brewing. I heard wisps of conversation between my parents. Along about midday, mother pulled me aside to talk about my eating habits. Nothing too major. For example, when I made mud pies, I ate them. They were best after a morning rain. I'm sure it was something special in the rich soil of Kathmandu Valley.

Freshly turned soil was the most delicious by far. Then, perhaps, rice-paddy dirt with bits of kernels for an added crunch. Food was good! I ate most everything willingly except liver and okra. Liver tasted like cow dung mixed with river mud. Okra looked like slugs, and felt like them too.

It was no secret that I ate dirt. I ate things people have nightmares about, like crickets, ants, and earthworms. I liked all foods, and sometimes my love of food got me into trouble. Any time I ate dinner at Susie Vail's, I got into trouble for eating all my vegetables. If I ate all my vegetables, she and her brother Stephan had to eat theirs too. I really loved vegetables, so I always ate them. Susie kicked me under the table as a signal to stop. Her kicking didn't stop me, and neither did Stephan's pinches!

One day a story aired over the BBC about a child who ate unwisely and died. Mother impressed upon me the dangers of eating things at random. She told me that was probably how I got my tapeworm—did I understand? I understood. Getting the tapeworm hardly slowed me down, though. I remember that it made me stay thin for a long time, but otherwise I felt fine. I was certain that mother knew I was a connoisseur of all growing things. Wasn't I an epicure of edibles and a garden gourmet too?

I knew a lot about the flowers growing in our garden. Mother said that plants were called flora and that animals, like our horses and chickens, were called fauna. Bambi was a fawn, a baby deer. The two words—fawn and fauna—sounded almost the same, but they meant different things. The begonias I liked were called flora. Begonia flowers tasted good; they were tart and tangy. Geraniums were flora too. I knew their milk was poisonous so I was careful about them.

I knew Rose petals tasted the way they smelled and marigolds were so stinky that I never ate one. Pansies, like violets, melted on the tongue and would stick to the roof of your mouth if you let them. Yes, I knew quite a bit about the garden flowers. I knew some other things too. I knew how to count on my fingers and toes, but I didn't know how to count money. Mother said I could absorb a wealth of information if I paid close attention and listened well.

Mother knew everything! She had to. She had to know everything in order to make her heavenly delicious apple pies and her died-and-gone-to-heaven buttermilk bread and melt-in-your-mouth butter horns. Oh, and she made wish-there-was-more peach roll pies, too. She had to know everything to do all that!

I paid close attention when I tasted the flowers in mother's garden. I liked some better than others. Snapdragons were springy, like egg noodles. They tasted like the milk skin you get on your hot chocolate when it is chewy and bland and has not totally dissolved. I didn't care for milk skin or snapdragon flowers.

Mother said dandelion greens were good. I didn't know this firsthand because I never ate them. I did like to blow off their feather-fuzzy heads. Mother wanted me to show her what I planned to eat before I ate it. Stop snacking for Show and Tell? I think not. And, I remember wondering, most impatiently, why she was telling me this.

Mother looked at me expectantly and repeated, "Okay, Ladybug?" I nodded in response, thinking, Yes, yes, yes—okay, okay! Now may I please be on my way? That is what I yelled back in my mind because I wouldn't have dared to yell out loud. I had mud pies to make and pretty bright flowers and fresh green plants to harvest and eat. Maybe today I would find a special treat.

I was finally free from mother's scrutiny. I raced outside to play. Pretty red flowers caught my eye. A rose on Sunday, begonias on Monday, corn on Tuesday, sugar cane on Wednesday, sweet peas on Thursday, why not a poppy for Friday? I ate one. The petals were fine, powdery. They tingled, stained my fingertips, and curled up quickly when I plucked them from the solid center part of the flower. They were slightly sweet on the tip of my tongue, tangy on the edges. The luscious red petals folded around my tongue, enveloping it like a cocoon. They melted slowly in my mouth.

That solid center part was encased in a tough green skin. When the skin was peeled away, there was dense, silky hair inside, just like corn silk, only white instead of yellow. The inner core was pitted, like a fig with all its seeds. The poppy center had black seeds. It was sour smelling and far too chewy. Inside was a pasty white liquid that was somewhat sticky. The liquid was sour smelling too, but not enough to keep me from putting a big glob of it in my mouth.

When the liquid began to dry on my fingers, it took on a texture of chalkiness. It was not the tastiest specimen in my garden of delights. I decided then that poppies were not the best. Although the petals were very good, the green bulb center was not. I would not conduct any further taste tests as far as that flora was concerned.

Sitting on the high stone wall that encompassed our yard and mother's garden, I looked up and up to where cotton-white clouds choo-choo-chugged across the cerulean sky. I sat this way for what seemed like hours. My eyes wandered around the compound and jumped around in their sockets too. I noticed because I didn't know before then that eyeballs could jump.

I noticed how the black crows hippity-hop-hopped on the orchard wall while the bees buzzed to the beat of a water buffalo's bellowing bass notes from the rice fields across the road. I think the chickens clucked along in time. And there, in the garden, each individual blade of grass sang to me. Butterflies waltzed in and out and around the poppies, flashing stained-glass colors with each flap of their wings. I thought I felt the earth move. My head was at once empty and heavy, filtery clear and stewy thick.

I remember looking out at row upon row of the brilliant red-headed poppies. I watched them sway back and forth, and forth and back on slender green stalks, each one inches from the next. They waved slowly in their well-dressed beds. I catalogued the event—poppy petals were good. They wrapped around my tongue like a warm winter blanket. The poppy centers that anchored the petals were stinky and hairy. They were full of seeds, chewy and bitter.

When at last I climbed down from the high stone wall, I felt more than a little sick. My head had a mind of its own, and my brain and body were not cooperating with each other. I could not hold my head up because my neck didn't work anymore. The climb down the garden wall and the walk to and through the side patio door saw me bent double, my head next to my white, lace-trimmed socks tucked into navy Keds. I wore my favorite, powder-blue, smocked sun suit.

The wide yard stretched away like an ocean. I wobbly-waded across it like a drunken bumblebee. I stumbled like a bobby pin in a three-legged race. Abandoning my Ked-clad feet, I crawled up the cool marble steps at the back of the house on my hands and knees. I got myself into my little corner room and onto my bed tucked snug at the back of the house. The high valley sunshine streamed through the big window and watched me fall asleep.

Vestiges of memory tell me that I flew that day. I flew low over the Kathmandu Valley. I looked down and saw the Light of Peace from Swayambhunath Stupa shine brightly from one side of the valley to the other. I flew even higher into the summer night sky—far up and up, and over the hills into the snow-capped Himalayas! I cruised on thermal air currents.

Hairy mountain yaks grazed on tumbling, brush-strewn prairies of brown and tan and gray and green. I saw curling vines of silver smoke sway skyward from squat round yurts anchored to the dusty ground of the arid plains. I saw the Yeti. Was it a dream or was I really there? I do not believe it was a dream.

Later, I learned that I slept through dinner that night and through the entire next day. No fever, no chills; just a deep, very deep and abiding slumber. Mother said she and my father had been puzzled, but not overly concerned. They decided that if I needed to sleep, they would let me. It was summer after all, and I was quite an adventuress. No doubt my adventures had worn me out, and no wonder. I was outside from sunup to sundown, and they reasoned that it was about time I caught up on my sleep.

I told mother the truth when I was home on summer break one year. She remembered that Day of the Deep Sleep and said it had been very curious. However, it had ceased to matter when I woke up ravenously hungry. The truth, when I told it, simply horrified her. She said, if she had known it at the time, she would have turned completely gray from worry.

What prompted the memory? Mother asked if I still ate begonias. Yes, I do.

Never Touch Fire

Our backyard was a wondrous place. One small part of it was mother's gigantic vegetable garden. Other parts were an orchard, a chicken coop, stables, and mother's flower garden, which sprouted snapdragons, geraniums, petunias, poppies, pansies, and my personal favorite—begonias.

I had an entire world of flora at my disposal for hours each day to play in and to examine. I loved to make mud pies and have tea in mother's flower garden. I put my tea and bake ware sets to use on these occasions. I made all kinds of delectables.

Sometimes it was a pound cake of orchard mud garnished with rose petals atop a cookie-cutter design. My specialty was mud pies. They were best with tangy begonia buds just after a gentle rain, before the air got too dry and while the digging was easy. I shaped and molded my dainty mountain mud pies with the ease that comes from practice.

This fresh-air baking activity kept me in plain sight from anywhere on the upstairs balcony that wrapped around the house. It kept me in plain sight but didn't necessarily keep me out of trouble. Still, I often baked in the garden for hours and reluctantly gave up the joy of this activity to go inside for meals for which I, of course, had no appetite. Why should I eat indoors when I had already consumed one or two tasty mud pies in the sweet summer sunshine of the Kathmandu Valley?

One sunny morning I raced outside to sit on the wall high above the poppy beds. It was a favorite spot of mine. I was not yet allowed outside the compound by myself. The walls were the boundaries I could not cross. I could stand on them, walk on them, and sit on them, but I was not to go beyond them. I didn't mind. My two favorite walls were the ones that surrounded mother's flower garden. I could stand on one of these and just see over the back orchard wall into the palace guard barracks.

The other wall was the outermost wall, the boundary beyond which I was not allowed alone. It seemed quite daring to sit and walk on this wall, testing mother's apron strings. I was adept at trotting atop the wall after butterflies. I had no net, just my unbridled curiosity. It was a ten-foot plunge down either side, but I never thought of jumping off. Dallying along, high up on the wall, I often felt I was on the verge of discovering something monumental.

On this particular day, I was delighted to find the most intriguing creature I had seen in ages. It was a star-bright, albino-white, two-inch-long, plump and hairy caterpillar. It fascinated me. I had learned about worms and caterpillars from the picture encyclopedia.

I knew the difference between slugs, caterpillars, leeches, and worms. I could appreciate their usefulness in the garden. I knew worms turned the soil and were sometimes in my mud pies. Slugs were gross and slimy. They ate up the garden and left trails of glistening goo.

Slugs oozed slick when you stepped on them. They could make you slip and fall if you were not careful. Besides all that, they looked like boiled okra and felt like it too. Leeches looked like bits of raw chicken liver. They were soft, blood-sucking blobs. When you went swimming, you and a buddy had to check all over each other's body to be sure those blobs had not latched onto you somewhere. If they had, you sprinkled salt on them so they curled up and dropped off.

Caterpillars were chameleon-like in that they crawled into the fork of a tree branch, spun themselves into cocoons, and later emerged as butterflies. This caterpillar was as white as the snow-capped peak of Annapurna. It was the most beautiful crawler I had ever seen. I watched closely as it inched its way along the top of the stone wall. I carefully delayed its progress with a strategically placed twig to turn it in the opposite direction. This exercise helped me to better study the way it moved.

The sun was bright above us, not hot, but certainly helpful in illuminating the segments in the caterpillar's body. The sunlight sparkled on the tiny crimson dots above the joint of each leg. There were hundreds and hundreds of snow-white hairs that moved the way tall rice in a field moves in a gentle breeze—the way the long leaves whisper and sigh when they sing just before harvest.

The caterpillar crept along the wall at a steady pace, undulating like mother's fresh-washed, white cotton sheets when they billowed and waved in the Kathmandu blue-sky mountain breeze. When the sun shone in just the right spot, the caterpillar looked like a furry, fat bristle brush on a bed of deep red rubies.

The sun was high in the sky, and before too long, I reluctantly answered mother's call to come in to lunch. I do not know what I ate that day. I only know I could hardly wait to get back outside. I told mother of my glorious find up on the crest of the garden wall and she cautioned me. She reminded me that some things beautiful could be harmful as well. I made a mental note, quickly finished eating, and hurried outside, irresistibly drawn as by a magnet.

The caterpillar had not made much progress since I had left it to go inside and eat. I was happy to see it again. The wall was much warmer than earlier, and there was no ready shade. Thinking perhaps that the furry crawler might need shade, I grasped it between the index finger and thumb of my left hand. It was then I felt the little beastie's sting. It had given me two fingers full of piercing quills, leaving great gaps in its formerly abundant white feathers of fur.

The fascinatingly beautiful caterpillar, and the object of my absorption, had bitten me! The brilliant-white, feathery hair was a defense. Just as a porcupine ejects its quills, the caterpillar had shot its arrows into my fingers. The two affected fingers began to swell and swallow up the fine slivers almost immediately. The crawling leaf-eater had shot me with poison. The quills soon disappeared into the swelling in my fingers. They stung like wicked shards of glass.

Before I could scramble down from my perch on the wall, my left hand inflated to twice its normal size. It burned with pain. I hurried inside for help. Mother administered first aid. She sat me on the wide lip of the sink in the small, second-floor bathroom and soothed the worst of the swelling to a dull throb.

And, while I watched from my seat on the sink, a big black crow swooped down near the wall where I had left my attacker. He hopped and bobbed and trotted along the wall. Then, with an effortless spread of his wings, the crow soared away. I secretly hoped he had taken the caterpillar to have for dinner.

A Clean Heart

I discovered one day that I had beauty marks. I didn't really know what it meant to have beauty marks. Mother said they were different from warts and different from moles too. I had a wart on my knee sometimes. I could find no moles though. I felt uneasy about the idea of moles because I knew they were rodents, like rats and mice, and I didn't know how they could be on a person as well.

I knew that rats and mice often carried disease and wondered if moles did too. The thought unsettled me, so I set it aside until a time when I could understand it better. That happened sometimes when I encountered new ideas or words. I had to ponder them; I had to understand how they fit, not only in my head but in my heart. And if they didn't fit, I learned early on to put them away. I knew that I might understand later—or that I might never understand.

I didn't think my beauty marks were beautiful. I knew mother was beautiful; I could see her beauty with my own eyes. She sometimes said that beauty was in the eye of the beholder. I guessed this meant that how to think of my beauty marks was up to me. To me they just looked like ink dots. One was pinpoint size and all the others were pinhead size. They were all dark dots to me and I didn't see any use for them. I put them from my mind. All of them except one.

The one mark, the pinpoint one, looked like a beauty mark, but I knew it was not. If I hadn't known how it got there, I might have thought it was a beauty mark. Maybe. Well, except that I did know how it got there. It was more than a beauty mark, and it was important. This mark was one that mother said I was not to be given, but it was given to me anyway. My pinpoint mark was a symbol, perhaps a talisman. A hint of a whisper of a mark—an indelible kiss, said Ayah Lemah. She said I carried the kiss of the Light of Peace.

Ayah Lemah said I wore the light of peace of Kathmandu Valley on my very person. She said I was a person, not just a little girl. I liked thinking about it that way. My memories of that nurturing paradise valley of green, the substance of which filled my soul in its infancy and planted the seeds of my essence, are filled with the joy of life and the promise of a life well lived. That very same substance grew me; I am myself because of it.

My strongest memories are of the love and protection of all the adults who surrounded me in Nepal. No matter where I went, no matter whom I met, the people I knew were considerate and kind and treated me with a most gentle tenderness—so too, my Ayah Lemah. She was gentle, like mother, with a voice as sweet and a touch as tender. Ayah Lemah was my nanny.

When I missed mother, it was Ayah Lemah, and only she, who thoroughly comforted me. She tickled me under my chin and smoothed my worry lines, or held me on her hip and distracted me with lovely, soothing songs. She fed me slices of mother's heavenly buttermilk bread with butter or cinnamon sugar.

Not enough good can be said of those who love and care for tiny, tender souls. No amount of thanks would be enough for those special people who sow hope and safety. Surely it is they who lay the strongest foundations upon which young roots anchor and are sustained.

My very best memories have to do with mother's love and her trust in my Ayah Lemah and my trust in both of them. My clearest memory of a visit to a house other than a relative's is of a visit with Ayah Lemah to hers. At her house, the fire was an open pit in the middle of the floor. It was a shallow hole ringed by sturdy stones that had been found right outside on the ground. The ashes in the pit were white hot. I was not to touch!

Ayah Lemah boiled water and made us thick, sweet chai. The blend of tea and spices was her own recipe that she had perfected as a young girl. A simple whiff of her chai, she said, told her husband that it was neither his mother's nor his mother-in-law's, but his wife's. This is what young girls must learn, she said, to make what is common into something special in order that it touches others in a vibrant and unique way. She talked to me like that, as though I was a big girl and could understand.

I did understand in my own way. I understood how life was clouded with circumstances that were the same no matter where you lived. I understood how Ayah Lemah's chai tasted different when she made it for me at her house than when she made it for me at my house. In that difference, I understood that Ayah Lemah poured her love for me into the tea whether she brewed it on the clean, hard dirt floor of her home or in the cool tile kitchen of mine.

In Ayah Lemah's tea I tasted warm coriander and strong, blunt black earth, sweet honeycomb, goat's milk fresh from the teat, and a pinch of salt to bring out the green-growing fullness of the high mountain valley. Ayah Lemah's tea was like mother's bread—you could drink and drink and eat and eat, but you would never get enough.

I understood love to be as good as mother's bread and as good as Ayah Lemah's tea. Although they existed in the same frame—my frame—I also understood that being with Ayah Lemah was not the same as being with mother. I thought my love was as great for both, but I knew there was a difference, like the difference between tea on the floor and tea in the kitchen. Both were delicious and comforting, both gave me a wholesome feeling of satisfaction, but only one belonged to me. The other was borrowed.

My borrowed time with Ayah Lemah was ours and ours alone. I learned to lay the perfect kindling for a near-smokeless fire. I learned that flames didn't have to lick the air for a fire to be plenty hot. I learned to hold the thick stick—kept on the wide flat stone beside the fire—with both hands to lift the whistling kettle from the hot ashes.

I learned that patience had to be cultivated like the fields in which the cane sugar and black tea grew. I knew when I was with Ayah Lemah that she would protect me and wash and feed me, and I didn't have to know what I ate. All I needed to know, and I did, was that it would not harm me since it came from her. That is how I got the tiny little mark between my eyebrows.

It was a special blessing day. All young children were to be blessed and to be given protection from harm. Some children didn't live long enough to get the blessing. Many children died before they turned five years old. I was almost five; my birthday was only a few months away. Mother said I could have any kind of cake I wanted for my birthday. I already knew it would be her 1-2-3 cake. I could hardly wait.

On the blessing day, I went with Ayah Lemah in the late morning. We walked down to the main road. Ayah Lemah carried me on her hip. There were many people going the same way. Some sold trinkets; some sold food. All of us waited for the procession to come along. We brought flowers from the garden to throw as offerings. We stood along the road, Ayah Lemah and I, two among hundreds.

We watched the priests walk down the center of the road. They chanted and struck gongs whose sounds hung in the air for a long time. Pilgrims followed the priests. They came from the many villages the priests had passed on their long journey down into the Kathmandu Valley. The hand-woven cloth robes of the priests were the color of a midsummer sunset tinged with touches of gold from the bright-shining sun.

The priests traveled on foot from their monastery perched high up on the steep face of the Himalayan foothills. The procession came slowly down the narrow mountain road. Each side was lined with people holding out children to be blessed by the priests. They were on their way to Swayambhunath Stupa on the other side of town.

I had been to Swayambhunath Stupa many times. We called it Monkey Temple because monkeys lived there and were sacred. The monkeys were bold and unafraid and I think I was a little afraid of them. At times they had bitten people, but whenever I was there they did no more than screech and beg for food. Even with the monkeys, the Light of Peace was my favorite place to visit. There were no monkeys on the side of the road.

A thousand sticks of incense lent fragrance to the air. It smelled different on the road than in the temple. The smell of marigolds in the temple was overpowering. On the road, the marigold fragrance was not as strong, their scent mingled with those of the raw earth, sweet honey, sweat, dung, and the sharp tastes of a new season. It was the season of blessings.

Each child got a tika, which is a small dot of indelible dye in the space between the eyebrows. Mother had told me and Ayah Lemah to be sure I didn't get one. When the priest stopped to bless me, Ayah Lemah held me high. I got a garland of orange and yellow marigolds and a tiny black tika. I let her get me one because I understood. Within my small self, I understood that she needed me to. Ayah Lemah explained that the tika told anyone at a glance that I was renewed.

Being renewed meant that I began again. This beginning was ordered by my own karma, and the dot was my beacon into this world of new beginnings. The dot between my brows was also my past lives watching the life I now lived. The way was lit so that I might not stumble.

What Ayah Lemah said sounded very important. I thought about it. I could have told her there was no need for me to wear any exterior marking of my faith. I already knew that God was in me and that Jesus had died for my sins. I already knew that the Lord was my light and my salvation and that his death on the cross had created in me a clean heart and a renewed spirit. That is what mother told me, and I knew what mother said to be true.

And, I knew too, that mother knew that Ayah Lemah loved me. So, with my young heart clean and with my renewed spirit, I accepted the blessed eye of the Light of Peace. Ayah Lemah and I went back home. We came into the house through the kitchen and I hugged mother's legs hello. Her hands were deep in dough. She smiled a big hello back at me.

Mother was making her heavenly buttermilk bread. I knew I would get an end piece when the loaf was just cool enough to cut. Sometimes I had a warm slice with butter or cinnamon sugar. Or both. I liked it best just plain. Since my tapeworm, I had been skin and bones. The butter and cinnamon sugar slices were supposed to put more meat on my bones so I would not be stick-thin anymore. I loved her bread.

Cook said my garland was almost bigger than I was. I gave it to him to hang over the door. It would keep the evil spirits at bay. He pulled off a flower and tucked it into my hair. I ran off to find Ayah Lemah. She was shelling peas in the garden shade. I sat with her and shelled peas too. She said I was a little pea like those in the pods because I was a sweet pea. I asked her if ladybugs liked peas. She said to shell enough peas for a mouthful. I did.

Ayah Lemah smiled at my fat cheeks. When I had swallowed my mouthful of peas, she asked whether I liked them. I did. We laughed together. After a while, I ventured out of the shade. Ayah Lemah said to stay where she could see me. I imagined the food goddess, Annapurna, smiled upon me as I chased the young chickens around the dirt yard bathed in the rays of the gentle valley sun until it was time for supper.

Bumble-Lena

I think it can be said that I was rather curious as a young child. Nothing was too ordinary to catch my attention. I lived in a wonderland of entomological treasures. I was always trapping some small insect to keep for a day or two of study. After I studied my finds, I freed them again near the spot where I had caught them. I liked to dig in the soil and watch the bugs scurry out of the light too.

All life was sacred, and reincarnation was fact, not fairy tale. Two-Ton, the bull that lived in the middle of the road to Monkey Temple, had once been someone's husband, mother, sister, or some other relative. He was so huge he didn't often move. Some said he could not move. He was tended to with compassion and respect by people who watered and fed him each and every day.

I had no personal pets. In our compound were chickens for eggs and Friday night dinner, a goat or two for curry or stew, and the odd lamb or duck for very special occasions. As children, we shared the two horses as well as the dogs that belonged to my father. He took the dogs with him on his many field trips, which was a good thing because most of my father's dogs barely tolerated the rest of us, even in his presence.

I wanted a pet of my own, so I decided to catch one. The day of ownership came one spring morning when the sky was a clear, sharp blue and the air was fragrant with the scent of flowering plants and fresh horse manure on the compost pile. I wandered around our spacious yard looking, ever looking, for a pet to adopt and call my own.

Thus I chanced upon a beautiful black and yellow bumblebee. She was shiny-black like my Sunday patent leather shoes and boldly yellow like the fruit of a freshly peeled, perfectly ripe mango. The bright orange-yellow was the exact same color as one of my brother's crayons and looked to be as soft as brushed velvet.

I followed the flying beauty as she harvested in mother's flower garden. She didn't dally among the marigolds, but she stayed a long while among the poppies. While she was hard at work on the snapdragons I took the chance of stealing away to find a container in which to house her. I was a little worried that she might fly off over the garden wall and be lost to me upon my return. I had to hurry.

As luck would have it, she was still there when I returned. She would have been hard to miss. She was so big that the tiny matchbox I had pilfered for her new home was clearly too small. So I caught her in my two hands, cupped together, fingertips touching, with plenty of space inside for her to buzz around. She was plush and furry and looked to me to be bigger than my thumb!

Sheee-bee was not pleased that I had contained her. She began to batter the fleshy walls of her prison and I realized that she might sting me. I knew that some insects lost their stingers after using them and then died. I wanted her to live so I carefully put her into my left pocket. I held it closed while I searched for a more suitable container.

I found one in the kitchen. It was a jumbo-sized matchbox. It was perfect. I emptied it of the fire sticks with one hand because I still had to keep my pocket closed so beautiful Bumble-Lena, Beelena for short, would not escape. Into the jumbo matchbox she went, buzzing loudly. Just then Cook came in, and Beelena's brand-new home was promptly confiscated with her still in it.

I barely had time to explain to Cook why I needed the matchbox. I held it to his ear and we both heard her buzzing loudly in her new home. Cook went into the pantry and returned with a small jar for me to use. I liked the matchbox better, but I knew it was not to be. I transferred my beautiful Beelena to the jar, and Cook supervised as I poked small air holes into the lid with the shiny metal can opener. Cook wanted me to let the sheee-bee free and I wanted Cook to just let me be!

Once I asked Cook if he had a real name. He said his given name was Namit Paranambunamya. I asked why we called him Cook if his name was Namit Paranambunamya. He told me to say Namit Paranambunamya three times fast. I tried to but my tongue had trouble. We laughed and laughed about how funny it sounded. I asked if might call him Babu Cook, or Babu Namit, the way I called Mr. Shamraya Babu Shamraya. "You may," he said, "but 'Cook' suits me just as 'Babu Shamraya' suits him, should it not suit the Ladysbug as well?"

Ladysbug. That is what Cook called me, not Ladybug, as mother did. When I asked him why, Cook told me I had to be Ladysbug because I was my mother's, the "Lady's," little bug.

He also reassured me that Cook was a good name. He had studied over many years to prepare all foods. He said that Cook was the name he liked best.

I didn't argue, but I didn't agree either. My parents said I was to address adults as Mr. or Mrs. and also that I was to do as I was told. I would call Babu Namit, Cook, as he said to. After all, I disliked my given name so much that sometimes when mother used it I cried. I decided that if Namit Paranambunamya wanted me to call him Cook, I would call him Cook.

Bee and I left the confines of the kitchen and the watchful eye of Cook for my little bedroom at the back of the house on the second floor. Once there, I put Beelena on my windowsill and watched her crawl around in her circular confines for what could have been hours. I was so thrilled to have a pet, and such a beautiful one too. Mother came to the doorway and called me down to dinner.

Dinner was an inconvenience because I would rather have been with Beelena. When I was finally freed from the dinner table I raced back to my room to visit with my dear charge. Beelena was very still in the jar, and this alarmed me. But there was no reason for alarm; she was just resting.

After my bath it was bedtime already, and I had to wish Beelena good night. It was then I remembered that I had not given her anything to eat. When I explained this to mother, she allowed me to go downstairs and into the kitchen and prepare a bit of sugar water for Beelena.

That done, I returned quickly to my room, and mother was waiting there with an eyedropper! She cautioned me against putting in too much; Sheee-bee only needed a very little. I unscrewed the lid to the jar and carefully squeezed out two drops of food for my dear velvet-vested bumblebee. I said my prayers and went to sleep with a happy heart—I had a pet all my own.

Sometime in the night I climbed out of bed and checked on Beelena. I thought it might be kind to give her another bit of food. When morning came I awoke with joy, knowing I had a pet to love and care for. I scrambled out of bed and to the windowsill. There was Beelena. Unmoving—sleeping, surely—in a glass house all her own.

I picked up the jar and tapped the lid, and my Sheee-bee didn't stir. I shook the jar gently at first, then more vigorously. Beelena didn't crawl or fly. She floated. Just as understanding dawned on me, mother came into the room. I didn't have to tell her; she knew at once what had happened.

I had a heartfelt cry for the short life in captivity of my beautiful Bumble-Lena. I prayed she was buzzing and carefree in bee heaven. I knew I had shortened her life, however inadvertently. That made me cry all the more.

Being held tight in mother's loving arms fortified me and gave me the strength to provide Beelena a proper burial. I wrapped beautiful Bumble-Lena in my best white linen handkerchief. Then, under a sun as bright as the yellow in her bumblebee coat, I dug a hole in the rich brown earth. I put her to rest in the red poppy beds, wishing her forever-sweet dreams under their swaying red heads.

Well-Dressed Windows

I got stabbed once, in the chest. It was a couple of years before I went to school, and my brother was still home with me and mother. On occasion we played together. Generally, he was too rough-and-tumble for me and I played by myself. I liked my own company just fine. On this day we were getting new curtains. Mother was in her loft, sewing them in the sweet morning sunshine. I sat on the window seat and watched the machine needle peck into the fabric faster than I could see.

I tried counting how many times the needle jumped up and down into the fabric but it was impossible because it jumped a million times a second and I only knew how to count to one hundred. I was happy to watch and learn. I knew that the needle was part of the sewing machine and that I was not to touch it on my own because it was very sharp and could be dangerous. Mother showed me how thread went through the tiny eye of the needle.

Up until then, I hadn't known needles had eyes—but it made sense that they had to have eyes in order to see their way into threading the fabric pieces together. They had to be sharp, those needles, sharp like the kitchen knives that Cook drew across his whetstone. I was not allowed to touch those knives either. I could look and watch, and learn and see, and that is what I did.

I looked at how the sewing machine grabbed the fabric and pulled it from front to back; I watched how the stitches ran straight and tight. I learned that it was important to guide the fabric, not pull it, because the machine had traction and there were tiny metal teeth under the smooth plate where the needle went in. Those tiny teeth pulled the fabric automatically. Well, yes, I could see how it worked. The needle marched through the fabric with a tat-tat, tat-tat, similar to the noise my brother's cap gun spit out when he fired it in rapid succession.

Mother said the traction from the metal teeth kept the fabric moving as fast as the needle pulled the thread through it. Traction. My little brain filed the information away. When I didn't understand things, I found a place to put them in my head. I knew from experience that the information popped out later when I could understand it better. I sat on the window seat and watched as mother made the curtains. She was going to make sets for all our rooms, and my brothers were to get theirs first.

My two brothers shared a room, and my two sisters did too. They were all older than I. I had my own little room at the back of the house, a short hallway across from my parents. I was not getting curtains that day, but I wondered aloud why the other rooms had to have them. Mother said it was important for windows to be well dressed. The curtains, or sheers, filtered the light so it would not be too hot or too cool. The drapes were made of a heavier fabric, and they kept the heat in and the cold out.

I liked the sunshine coming in my windows during the day, and I loved the silver, twinkling stars blinking and winkling at me during the night. I didn't think I wanted curtains or drapes on my windows. Maybe it would be okay, though - I would get to open and close them, open and close them, open and close them. I liked doing that, but nobody liked me doing it, so I knew that curtains and drapes at my own windows would keep me, and them, plenty happy if I had my own curtains and drapes to play with.

Lunchtime was an hour away, and mother had finished the things for the boys' room. They had drapes of heavy madras cotton in a striped pattern of orange, gold, blue, brown, red, and yellow with matching bedspreads and pillow shams. Mother had made the spreads and shams first. Now my brothers had beautifully dressed windows to match. When I went to tell mother how wonderful the windows looked, she was not at her sewing machine.

Although I was curious about the sewing machine, it frightened me enough that I stayed away from it when mother was not near. I found her in the room my sisters shared. She was up on a step ladder measuring the big front window that overlooked the roof of the guardhouse at the entrance to the compound.

I didn't go into my sisters' room very often. They were busy mostly and did girly things that I didn't have the patience for, like curling their hair and putting on makeup for hours and hours. Being in their room without them, with just mother, was different. I wanted to climb the ladder when mother stepped down, but she said not to climb the ladder, so I didn't.

There were curtain rods from all over the house on the floor. They were not all the same size, and mother had gathered them together to properly match them with their mates. For my sisters' big front window, mother said she would need three rods. She had two, and she showed me what to look for so I could help her find the third to match.

I looked around for the third rod. I didn't find it, but I did find a shorter rod that was just the right size for a hobby horse. I turned out to be no help to mother, but she didn't seem to mind. I had a horse without a head, but I could pretend. I said giddy-up and rode my new pony. A little while later, my brother came into the room. Soon he found a rod to ride and galloped out. I followed him out of the room and we rode around the house in our bare feet on our shiny curtain-rod horses.

We played racehorse, and since he was ahead, of course my brother won. I didn't care, I was riding a horse in the house! We were swashbucklers, like in the pirate movies in which people said: "Ahoy there," "matey," "aye," "captain," and "forsooth." It didn't matter that pirates didn't travel on horseback. Pirates hunted for treasure, and someone always wore an eye patch or walked the plank. Or both.

I closed one eye. It was harder to see that way, so I didn't do it for long. We rode through the hallways and said "en garde" before putting our horses to use as swords. We clanged and clashed and then raced down the stairs.

When we got to the ground floor, my brother went into the kitchen pantry. He held up a package of grape Kool-Aid, and I knew what that was all about. We would ask mother if we could have Kool-Aid mixed with sugar without the water. It was an expensive snack, because we had to buy Kool-Aid from the PX and it was not something we could have all the time. I was very excited—I think I liked Kool-Aid and sugar better dry than with water.

My brother and I both knew we had to ask mother's permission. He raced on ahead of me back through the kitchen and out the dining room door. It was a swinging door. As I followed close behind, my head filled with the prospect of a sweet-and-sour snack, I raised my rod in front of me in a wave of triumph just as the dining room door to the back stairway swung in toward me.

The force of the impact smacked me back against the dining room table. I stood there motionless. I didn't breathe. The curtain rod was in my chest just below my breastbone. I brought my hands up and touched it. The rod was rooted in my chest, pointing straight ahead, and parallel to the floor. I watched as blood welled around the edges where the rod went in. It seeped out slowly, turning my white T-shirt red. I took a deep breath and the blood stopped.

When I exhaled, blood welled up again and began to dribble. It made a red trail down my chest. I watched it creep from under the hem of my T-shirt and slide down bare skin to pool into my belly button. The hole filled up, and then, all at once, the blood pulsed out of that shallow cavity and spread in a rush down the curve of my belly.

I stood watching, waiting. Red ribbons of blood soon rolled down my legs. I bled into the dining room carpet. But that is not what I was thinking. I was thinking that if mother said we could have Kool-Aid and sugar and I didn't get upstairs, my brother would make it up and not give me any.

It was the thought of no sweet-and-sour snack that told me to turn my back and push out the dining room door. I held the curtain rod to keep it from swaying. It really hurt when it swayed. I took slow and careful steps up the cool marble back stairs. I used the wall to steady myself. Scarlet prints smudged the wall wherever I touched it. I walked down the long side hallway toward my sisters' room. I could see the doorway—it was not far now.

My brother rushed out of the door only to stop abruptly when he saw me. He ran forward and looked at the rod in my chest and then looked at my face. I was trying not to cry. My brother ran back into my sisters' room. I was at the door before he could say anything to her. She was sitting on one of the beds. She had found the third curtain rod and had pieced it together with the other two. Now it would fit the big front window fine.

I walked into the room and mother looked up. I thought I saw her face turn gray. She shot up off the bed and came to me. I had my hands around the curtain rod. It was pulling down, and the pressure made my throat back up. It felt like my insides were being pushed up into the back of my mouth. I didn't think that was a good thing. I barely managed to tell her about it. She didn't think it was a good thing either. My brother just watched, as though if he moved in any way he would miss the best part of the show.

By this time I was beginning to feel cold. After all the running we had done, I thought I should have been hot. I was not hot, and my teeth chattered. I stood in the sunlight streaming in through the big window of my sisters' room. I stood in a shallow pool of my own blood. It ran warm and red down my chest. And, just as it had before, it caught for a heartbeat, dipped into my belly button, and ran into the waistband of my shorts. There it welled and disappeared for a moment, then streamed down my shaking legs to the floor.

I watched how the dark red ribbons curved around the inside of my knees and ran down the side of my calves to my ankles. The blood puddled on the floor behind my heels. I watched how it welled and eased around to trace the outside of each foot. I wondered: if I lifted my feet, would I see a bright red outline? It was fascinating how the ribbons of blood running down my legs were almost identical and how they pooled at the back of each heel in almost the same exact place. My eyes got blurry and my head seemed to want to float away.

Mother wanted me to sit. I was afraid to bend my knees because I felt as though my insides were fighting to pop up out of my mouth. I think by then I did not dare to talk, but I know she understood. She let me stand. She had a clean towel in her hands and was trying to wrap it around the base of the rod. I was beginning to tremble, and I didn't want anyone to touch the rod. Not even mother. It hurt.

Mother told me to hold the towel against my chest. I did, and that fast, she pulled the curtain rod out! The end that came out of me was slick with blood. A small, round piece of what had been the white cotton of my T-shirt covered the open end of the rod. A single filament dangled by a thread. As I watched in a trance of fascination, a plump and glossy droplet of blood swelled and then fell off that piece of T-shirt onto the floor.

Ssspplaat. It spread on the floor like a fallen snowflake. Only it was red—red around the edges and lacy inside. I imagine that no two splats would have been alike, but I saw only the one. Mother told me to hold the towel tight against my chest. I did, and before I knew it, I was sitting on my own bed wrapped in a blanket. I do not know how I got there. I think I knew it didn't matter, and I didn't ask.

Mother prepared to bandage my wound and I tried not to think about the damage caused by the curtain rod. Because the end of the curtain rod was hollow, and extremely sharp, it cut clean through, creating a cylindrical plug. The mark it made was perfectly round, about the circumference of a Lincoln-head penny. But the hole was an odd plug that was about an inch deep. I felt compelled to touch it. I am sorry I did. The top of the plug felt just like the end of a Vienna sausage. Up until then I loved Vienna sausages. To this day I cannot think of them without remembering the pain of the impact or the cold, fat, rubbery, sausage plug in my chest.

Mother bandaged my wound carefully. I watched. She cleaned it with the sterilized cotton from the blue box with the red cross on it. She dipped the cotton into a small glass bowl of warm soapy water and added a tiny drop of Clorox. After my wound was clean, she put cotton—sandwiched between gauze squares—on top of it. Then, she wrapped me around with an Ace bandage to hold everything in place.

The Ace bandage had a shiny metal fastener shaped like a blunt-ended figure eight. It had a pair of curved teeth at each end to catch the bandage and hold it taut. The teeth of the fastener lay exactly over my wound. For some reason, this upset me greatly. I imagined the metal teeth biting through the bandage and burrowing into my wound.

I tried to explain this to mother. I was weak and close to hysterical. I knew my thinking had to do with all those horror movies haunting my vivid imagination. And I knew those horror stories were not real. My imagination still got the better of me. I thought I could feel the metal teeth of the fastener gnawing through the layers of the bandage into my skin. It was like what happened in the earwig movie! The teeth were going to bite clean through me like a vampire sucking blood! Or saw away at me like a bladed pendulum!

Mother shushed me and carefully unwound the bandage. I had begun to hiccup in my hysteria, which was my misfortune. I knew from past experience that my hiccups could last for several hours. Sometimes I had them nonstop for a couple of days. I tried to breathe deep from my belly and exhale slowly.

I knew I could not bend to drink water from the far side of a glass. That sometimes helped me, but paper bag breathing had never worked. Mother rewrapped the bandage around me. This time, the fastener was all the way over on my left side. I felt my mind trying to run away with crazy thoughts. I had to concentrate and work hard to make my imagination stop. Stop.

I caught mother's hand and cradled it against my cheek. Hiccupped thanks tripped out of my mouth with "I love you, Mommy." I knew the Ace bandage kept my insides in. That is what stayed with me—that the Ace bandage kept my insides in. I also thought of the hole in my chest as my curtain rod wound and remembered how it resembled a Vienna sausage. For years, I remembered the shape and feel of it: a little spongy, yet compact and smooth. The sausage similarity stayed with me for a long, long time.

Propped up on extra pillows, I lay in my bed in my little room at the back of the house. I looked at the crows circling lazily above the orchard trees. They were ready for their afternoon naps. I could tell by the sun that it was lunchtime now, and I was ready for a nap too. mother knew it. She lay me down and kissed my cheek. She said, "When you wake up, Ladybug, you can have whatever you want." While I slept, the sun warmed me in my bed, and mother washed me clean.

I awoke hours later and got to have my sweet-and-sour treat of grape Kool-Aid and sugar as I lay propped up in bed. I looked at the soft shadows swaying into my room from the happy world outside my window. The sky was a deepening blue. Soon it would be nighttime.

The sun had set on the horizon. It shot out streaks of pink, orange, and indigo. Closer to me, slender fingers of high, thin, white clouds stretched across the heavens. I was in heaven. I was in my bed in my little room at the back of the house, and I knew mother loved me.

I listened to the crows squawk as the cool mountain night sauntered down into the valley of the lush green rice paddies. I knew the crows fought for their beds in the fruit orchard trees. They fought for beds every night, in the back of the garden, way back where high stone walls formed a deep and shadowed corner. It was the best vantage point from which to see the whole compound. The dawning sun would find those crows perched atop the trees. The sun would touch them with warm golden fingers and brush their raven wings with copper highlights. Then the crows would squabble, squawk, and stretch their wings. They would fly away singing into the new day.

Yes, in the morning, Buddha's breath would kiss the gentle mountain valley with life and peace. I listened to the crows through my open windows. I loved them. They woke me in the morning and serenaded me at night. On this night, in my little bed, worn out from the events of the day, I noticed that although my windows were not well dressed yet, my curtain rod wound certainly was.

Blackie and I

I had a dog named Blackie. He was a Lhasa Apso from Tibet. He was cheerful and sweet and had shiny, long, black hair with white on his chest and belly. He loved to be brushed and would let me braid his hair and tie on ribbons and clip on barrettes.

Well, Blackie was not really my dog. He belonged to my father. My father always had a dog or two. Blackie was the nicest and friendliest of them all. He was small like me and didn't boss me or tell me what to do. I liked Blackie. I think he liked me too, even after the day I nearly made his tail fall off.

I was playing dress-up, by myself; my sisters and brothers were at school. I was not in school yet, but mother said I would be going there in another year. I guessed that was okay. I didn't think about it much but when I did, I was secretly afraid I would miss mother.

I knew it was a privilege to go to school. I knew most of the children where we lived never got to go to school. They had to work in the fields. Even children as little as I had jobs. It was the only way their families could grow enough to have food through the winter. Everything they ate, they had to grow.

I had seen the fields where children even younger than myself worked. They were rice paddies, and they were terraced down the hillsides into the Kathmandu Valley. My father traveled to those hills in his work. A couple of times I got to go with him. He drove in a Jeep. It was beetle-bug green and the seats were hard as boards. We had to take all of our food with us and water too.

We boiled our water at home to make sure no germs were in it, because even though you could not see them, germs made you sick. If germs made you very sick, sometimes enough germs together killed you. My father worked to build a teaching college where nurses and midwives would be trained. With more nurses, and medicine for the people, those germs that killed would not be able to do so anymore.

Whenever I scraped my elbows or knees I had to have mercurochrome put on them to stop any germs. It stung almost as much as a bee sting, only not for as long. The stinging just meant the mercurochrome was doing its job. Big girls didn't cry, so I had to take my medicine if I was going to be rough-and-tumble. That was another reason I liked Blackie. He was never rough. He was happy and smart, and I hoped he liked my company as much as I liked his.

On the morning of the day in question it rained, and I had to stay inside the house. Mother was making a sea-green chiffon gown for the Marine Ball that was coming up soon. I loved the fabric, and as she often did, mother gave me scraps to play with. I found a nice long piece to tie around my head. It trailed down my back onto the floor. Mother said, "Careful, Ladybug, don't make it so long that you trip on it."

I always listened to mother. She said it was important to listen so that I learned well and would be saved from the Hard Knocks School. It was a different school than the one I would be going to. The Hard Knocks School was a school nobody really aspired to attend, was what mother said. She was wise and she knew everything, so I listened to her.

I had to make the chiffon shorter, so I asked permission to use her heavy pinking sheers. Mother said it was respectful to ask to use things that didn't belong to you. She let me use the pinking sheers to cut the chiffon off where it reached my ankles. The pinking sheers made the edge all ^^^^^^^, and you used them only when a fabric tended to ravel. I knew because I had seen this to be true.

I looked over at Blackie. He had been sleeping on the floor by the window seat. He often stayed with mother when she sewed. He liked her company as much as I did. Blackie stretched and yawned. I saw his small white teeth. They were sharp, like the points on the pinking sheers, but not as even. I went over and tied the short piece of chiffon around his neck in a double bow.

I had just learned how to tie my shoelaces, and since then, Blackie had let me practice tying anything I could find on him. He followed me down the hallway to my little room, where he sometimes slept under the foot of my bed—not too often though, because Blackie snored. His snoring would wake me up, so he didn't usually get to stay all night under my bed.

Sometimes I brushed Blackie. He liked to be combed and brushed. I got to brush him more than I got to brush the horses. Babu Shamraya said I was too small to brush the horses; they might step on me even if they didn't mean to. So I brushed Blackie often. As much as I liked to brush him, I got tired of it before he did.

Blackie had a white belly and a lightning-white streak on his forehead. His shiny hair was long and soft. I made a tiny ponytail on top of his head. I found a fat, brown rubber band and made a ponytail of his tail too. Blackie didn't like that ponytail, and before I could take it out he yelped, squirmed free, and ran away.

As he ran in the direction of the back stairs, I scrambled up to get him. When I rushed out of my room, I heard mother calling me. I was to always go immediately when mother called. I changed directions and ran down the hallway to where she sat at her sewing machine. Before she could ask, I told her about Blackie. Her eyes turned sharp and she said, "Now, Ladybug, you know you have to find Blackie and get that rubber band off." I knew.

I also knew from his yelp that Blackie probably would not come to me. Babu Shamraya said animals were our charges, and that when you hurt an animal, it could no longer trust you. This was a matter of survival for the animal. Babu Shamraya knew everything about animals. I was worried that Blackie's tail might fall off before I could get to him. I also worried that he would never trust me again. I felt like crying, but I knew there was no time to fall into tears. Blackie needed me to be strong and find him soon.

I looked everywhere, even in my father's office where I was not allowed without express permission. I went in there that day because it was very important to find Blackie. I didn't like going there because my father had a tiger skin rug on the floor. The head of the tiger was on it!

I knew it was just a skin with a stuffed dead head, but I didn't like the way the tiger's big green eyes looked at me. His big head lay open-mouthed on the floor. He still had his whiskers, and his mouth bared sharp, pointed teeth that I thought might grab at me if I got too close.

I walked around the tiger rug to look under my father's desk. No Blackie. I looked at the tiger's teeth. I wondered if they might rip me to pieces when nobody was looking. I knew those teeth were dead in the tiger's big head even though they sat grinning on the floor.

Those teeth were just as dead in the tiger's head as the long strong claws were dead in his paws, but both were still very sharp and to my thinking could still do damage. Blackie was not in my father's office. I closed the door, happy to leave the big-headed, long-whiskered, green-eyed tiger rug behind me.

The problem was, we had a big house. Almost all of the doors were wide open. Blackie could be anywhere! I had already gone through the house once looking under all the beds. I looked everywhere I thought Blackie could hide. I went back upstairs to search again. I didn't think Blackie would be in my room, but I looked in there anyway.

When I got up off the floor after looking under my bed, mother was standing in the doorway. She had her ball gown on and she was a vision of loveliness. She told me it had been more than twenty minutes; I was to find Babu Shamraya and ask him to help me find Blackie. I ran to find Babu Shamraya. He was as hard to find as Blackie. It had stopped raining, so after I looked in the kitchen, I ran out to the courtyard and looked in the stables too. Without success.

I had to stop and send a prayer to God to help me find Blackie. I looked up, and the clouds rolled away. The Himalayan blue sky took over and the sun grew brighter with each word of my whispered plea. Still, I didn't find Babu Shamraya or Blackie. I knew every inch of our compound, even every inch of the places that were out of bounds for me. I looked everywhere, but I didn't find Blackie.

I decided to walk around the house, all the way around, starting from the kitchen. Cook had not seen Babu Shamraya or Blackie. I told him what I had done, and he shook his head and gently said, "Do not you worry, little Ladysbug, the Blackie will be unhurt, you will see." Cook always tried to make me feel better. I loved him for it. Still, I dared not feel cheered when Blackie was in great danger. Tears of worry sprang into my eyes. I was so afraid about Blackie's tail. I nodded to Cook and quickly resumed my search.

I walked across the side patio and looked into each of the stone box planters. No Blackie, no Babu Shamraya. I walked through mother's flower garden and along the side of the house all the way to the front gate. It was closed, but the side gate was open. Blackie had run away! I would too if someone hurt me badly, I thought. I rushed to the side gate, and before I got to the opening, Babu Shamraya came through it with Blackie in his arms. I told Babu Shamraya what I had done. He said that Blackie was unhurt and for me to come hold him and talk to him softly. I was to take him inside. Blackie came with me willingly. I could not tell if he was angry.

Needless to say, I was very glad that Babu Shamraya had found Blackie and saved his beautiful tail. I promised Blackie I would not tie anything around his tail ever again. He licked my face. I brought him inside, and Cook gave me fresh water for him. Blackie drank it up. I petted him and said I was sorry, and he licked my hand. I think he forgave me.

At lunchtime, Blackie sat under the table at my feet. We were not supposed to feed any of the dogs from the table, but I gave Blackie food off my plate. He ate it. Later in the day, after I had taken my nap and played in my room at the back of the house, mother said I could walk four houses away to visit her friend's daughter Janine. Sometimes Janine would come to my house. Our mothers would walk us to the road and stand watching until we reached the other's house.

I asked mother if I could take Blackie with me. She told me it was fine, but I had to promise, cross-my-heart promise, not to let Blackie's leash out of my hand. Even if Janine wanted to hold the leash, I was not permitted to let her. I promised, and mother watched as Blackie and I walked down the road to Janine's house. Janine and her mother stood along the road waiting. We all waved. I turned and mother blew me a kiss. I caught it and put it in my pocket, but not before I blew a kiss back.

At Janine's house, we played with Blackie. I think he was fully recovered from the morning of dress-up. After a while, Janine's mother called us in for a snack; she said to bring Blackie in with us. She had water for him. We went inside and I wondered why the cellar door was open. I had just learned that a cellar is like a basement. I remember wondering how alike these two things could be with such different names.

I knew that people with different names could be alike, so I guessed it made sense. But I hardly had time for this to go through my mind. I still wondered why the cellar door was open. Then Blackie pulled hard on the leash. I remembered that I was not to let go! So Blackie and I flew down the cellar steps.

Blackie ran down the steps on his fast little legs. I crashed down the steps on my face behind him. I didn't let go of the leash. I smelled that concrete smell. It was wet and cool and gritty. I was completely flattened. Janine called her mother, and I saw a shadow-shape blot the rectangle of light pouring in from the open door at the top of the steps. I lay still on the concrete; I held the leash tightly in my hand.

Out of the corner of my eye I saw movement and felt a tug. It was Blackie—he was all right! I was so glad he was not hurt. I could not move yet, but I didn't think I was hurt either. Janine's mother rushed down the steps. Blackie pattered over and snuffled into my shoulder. When I turned my head he licked my face with his little pink tongue.

Before I could think "Oh, you love me!—I love you too, Blackie, my friend, my dress-up pal, my furry bundle of good cheer," Blackie turned away. His leash pulled out of my hand and Blackie ran past Janine's mother. He raced up the cold hard concrete steps as fast as he could. I heard his claws clatter all the way up and through the basement door. It was as though he was saying, "I may be your friend, I may let you dress me up in ribbons and bows, but you are not the boss of me."

I knew that. Was I not lying at the bottom of the basement steps? I rolled over slowly and pulled myself up off the floor. I thought Blackie must be home by now, probably napping under the dining room table. Janine's mother checked to make sure I was okay. She brushed me off and held my hand. I was okay. I was bruised, and my chin was scraped, but that was all. We started climbing back up the steps together. I realized that Blackie did forgive me for nearly breaking off his tail. My feelings were not hurt. Blackie had forgiven me and had even paid me back with interest.

Babu Shamraya Said

We had a python! I wanted to see it. Oh, it was not our python. The snake didn't belong to us. The python just moved into mother's vegetable garden one day. Babu Shamraya said it would be good if it ate the mice before they found their way into the kitchen or pantry. I knew if the snake ate the mice that went after mother's corn, it would help the corn grow by keeping those hungry pests away. I loved fresh corn from mother's garden. It was delicious—it tasted of sweet, high mountain sunshine and smelled like honeybee clover. I was not certain, but I thought the corn syrup we poured on mother's ambrosia waffles came from the sweet corn in her garden.

Babu Shamraya said the python was not poisonous. I do not know why, but he knew I knew that already. I knew that pythons squeezed their prey and crushed the bones to mush. Then they swallowed their victims whole. I also knew that some snakes, like cobras, were venomous-poisonous. We didn't have one of those yet. Babu Shamraya knew I was not afraid of snakes. Even so, he exacted my promise to come get him if I wanted to go into the vegetable garden.

I told him I wanted to see the python. He said it would stay in the shadows, probably off the ground so that it would have a good vantage point from which to see potential prey. There would be just one, as the python is a solitary hunting creature. Babu Shamraya knew how I loved to hold the garden snakes that we found in the squash beds. They were smooth as glass and sensed objects with their tongues. They tickled when they wound up your arm. I tried to imagine—would snakes look like lizards if they grew legs? Babu Shamraya told me the python was dangerous; I was to look out for it, I was not to go looking for it.

I understood. Babu Shamraya knew that. I spent so much time in the compound with him that he often called me "Babu Shamraya's shadow." If I was not in mother's flower garden or playing among the cornstalks in her vegetable garden, I was with Babu Shamraya. He showed me hatchlings and cocoons, wasp's nests and lizards. It was more fun being with Babu Shamraya than doing anything else.

We discovered that the python was growing. Near the end of our walk around the vegetable garden we found the skin he shed rustling in the high grass, sighing on the soft, valley breeze. It was a beautiful, bubbly, delicately textured sheath, caught in the spiky grass at the bottom of the stone steps leading up to the orchard. The shed skin was thin and crackled like rice paper. It was pale yellow, like the water when it first came out of the pump outside near the stables. The piece we found was longer than I was tall and bigger around than my leg. Babu Shamraya said that we had only part of the skin, a part that had broken off. The python in our yard was a very big snake. I wanted to see it!

One of the laying hens was gone. The python had eaten it the night before. We would be short on eggs for a few days before we got another hen at the market. Babu Shamraya and I examined the ambush spot together. Some of the hen's feathers were blowing in the brush. They were fluffy flags of color, her last gift to us from the life she had lived. I wanted to collect them, but Babu Shamraya said we must leave them to mark her passing. Babu Shamraya said it was the cycle of life, come to completion for her. I had a question. If our laying hen came back as a python and met our garden python, would our hen python know that our garden python had eaten her when she was a hen-hen?

I asked Babu Shamraya if, when the hen was reincarnated, it would be fitting that she come back as a snake. Was that possible? Possible, yes, Babu Shamraya nodded. However, such seemingly fitting cosmic fates didn't often work the way our human wills wanted them to. That is what he told me. Babu Shamraya said, "We can never even calculate the probability of such a possibility. Why to try?"

LADYBUG

Babu Shamraya said I asked questions like an old philosopher man but how was that possible when I was just a little Ladybug? I told him I had heard the commotion the night before when the python got the hen. I told him I had wanted to go see what it was when it happened, but mother said no, it was animal business.

Mother said animals had their own way of doing things and it didn't concern us. More specifically, it didn't concern me. I understood. I told Babu Shamraya that the laying hen had squawked frantically and the crows in the orchard trees cawed like crazy. I told him how I could see the sky darken when they swarmed out of the trees and milled about in the air like angry black bees.

After the orchard crows swarmed, it got very, very quiet. The crickets even stopped singing! The crows didn't call or caw anymore when they flew back and settled into the orchard trees to sleep. Because they were scared, right? I had really wanted to go see! Mother said it was nature's business, not any of my business and I was not to go explore. Besides, it was past my bedtime, and had I remembered to brush my teeth?

Babu Shamraya said most snakes wanted nothing to do with people. Snakes ate to survive as did the simplest and most complex creatures. And each creature had its purpose in life just as we people did. Some of the snakes might have been people once and they were snakes now because their karma said they had to live life in another form. That was their part to play in the order of the never-ending cycle of existence which unfolded as the result of one's individual actions. I asked him if karma made you go from a plant to a bug to a duck to a goat to a cow to a person. Babu Shamraya said karma didn't work in measured steps such as that, it was not a system of punishments and rewards. Actions in this life determined a person's future life and how they might be reborn. Karma, I should understand, was still very much a mystery.

I understood. I said to Babu Shamraya that the karma cycle was practice, right? It had to be practice since people's present karma made them go to whatever form their previous life's karma made for them to pass into. I told him it was like living the words of the hymn mother sang: "...from glory to glory He's changing me, changing me, changing me." I said that if glory to glory was like karma to karma, then whatever we were before gave us practice for what we would become later. He nodded solemnly and said I worked my Ladybug brain as hard as a strong ox pulled a heavy load.

I asked Babu Shamraya why, if Buddha was God, and God was Jehovah, and Jehovah was Allah too, did people fight about religion? He asked what I thought. I told him I thought all these had to be the same in some important ways. I said since they all made the galaxies and the heavens for planets and stars, they had to be the same. Our own sun and moon, and the oceans, rivers, mountains, and valleys of the earth were their creation.

I said maybe the reason countries fought wars against each other was that way back in Babylonian days, when suddenly nobody understood anyone else, that was the karma of the entire universe. So we all had to live over and over and over before we all could understand and accept one another again. Just as with the python and the laying hen. Babu Shamraya again nodded solemnly and said I had big, deep thoughts in my little Ladybug head.

Babu Shamraya and I had many discussions like this. We walked though the compound together checking on the chickens and the horses, making sure the bees didn't build their hives too close to the house. And we talked. We checked on what flower blossoms were spent and which rosebuds would soon bloom.

Sometimes when he slaughtered a chicken for dinner, I sat with him and helped pluck out the feathers. You had to pluck them fast and firm while the chicken was fresh dead. If you waited too long, it was a whole different story. This was simply part of our general routine in those carefree days before I had to go along with the other kids to school.

I told Babu Shamraya I felt strongly that I had been a squirrel in my previous life because, as we both knew, there was very little I liked better than digging in the dirt. He laughed for a long time. I laughed too. I told him I wanted to believe that one day maybe I would be a bird!

As much as I loved playing in the vegetable garden and crawling in the dirt through the tall rows of corn looking for bugs to harvest for the chickens, flying was most certainly better than crawling on the ground. Most of the creatures I knew so far crawled or walked like me. I said if I flew, I could fly up high and play in the snow-capped mountains that guarded our beautiful valley paradise. Or fly to the moon to see if it really was made of cheese!

Babu Shamraya said cheese or no cheese, I must promise to get him if I wanted to go near the vegetable garden. It was very important. See, Babu Shamraya knew how I loved to weave in and out between the tall rows of green, growing corn. He knew how I loved to gather sunflower seeds for my bird, Myna. Babu Shamraya said the python didn't know me, so he might try and hurt me.

The python was a reptile; therefore, he thought like a reptile. It was impossible for the python to think like a person. So he saw me as food just as he saw the hen he had eaten the night before as food. It was his character. The python didn't know I was his friend and that I would do him no harm. That is why I was to get Babu Shamraya if I went near the vegetable garden.

I understood. I knew the bees would sting when they thought they were threatened. The bees didn't ask if you meant them harm; they could not because they didn't speak our language. I knew the rooster protected his territory. He didn't care if I just wanted to play with the baby chicks. He was a guard of the coop, and his job was to keep every chicken safe. I knew our horse, Cousin, liked to bite. Biting was mean, and although Cousin knew we never hurt him, he just didn't like people. That was his character.

Babu Shamraya meant that the snake did snake things just as the bees did bee things, just as the rooster did rooster things, and Cousin, well, he was just mean. You could give him a salt lick or an apple and he would still try and bite you as thanks. Nobody really knew why. I thought maybe it was because he had been a tough Himalayan mountain horse before he came to live with us.

Maybe it was that same toughness that kept him alive on the rough and treacherous rocky trails. Maybe he wanted to go back there and since we didn't let him, he was mean. I knew how hard it was for me to stop sucking my thumb. That is how I knew that Cousin could not change his karma very easily and neither could the python. Neither could I.

Babu Shamraya said that although we knew the snake had eaten the hen, since it was new to our company we didn't know its hunger pattern. It might go a couple of weeks or even a whole month without eating again. Or it might not. We knew that our python was a very big snake. Babu Shamraya said he was not sure if the hen was a bowl of rice or a pot of mutton to the python. And, as I well knew, one meal was more filling than the other.

Therefore, we didn't know when our snake would be ready to eat again. It had snake habits and would be very aggressive when it got hungry. Being a snake, it didn't know or care about our habits. Babu Shamraya reminded me that I was to remember to be very careful outside. I was to get him if I wanted to go into or near the vegetable garden.

I understood. I stayed away from the vegetable garden for days and days. Our compound was gigantic; I had plenty of room to run free. The python wanted the cover of the scraggly trees along the barracks wall of the compound and the coolness of the tall underbrush of the vegetable garden. If I stayed away, I was in no danger. I stayed away from the vegetable garden for a couple of months.

Mother or Ayah Lemah or Babu Shamraya or Cook always had their eyes on me. The snake had to cross the rooster's territory, and Babu Shamraya said we would surely know it if that ever happened. I wondered how the python got to the hen under the rooster's beak. How did the rooster miss him that first time? I was careful. I stayed away from the vegetable garden. Eventually, I forgot about the python.

Our twice-yearly freight shipment from the United States had arrived! When the freight shipments came, it was almost as exciting as a birthday or Christmas. Mother ordered stuff from the Sears and Roebuck or JC Penney catalogues, and six months later the huge wooden crate bound with metal stays arrived. That crate was as big as the guard house where Cousin was sometimes stabled. It would sit in the driveway circle for days before all the loot got unpacked.

And, even though Christmas was far away, I knew there were probably gifts that came in the crate too. The huge wooden packing crate and the big cardboard boxes that were inside became a fort after school for my brothers and the neighborhood kids. In the morning and after lunch they were my bakery and tea house. I played with my aluminum pots and pans, made tasty mud pies, and drank Tang out of my teacups. Sometimes I took my afternoon nap in the soft, high valley sunshine.

I loved to wake up in the full color of the flower garden. It was how I imagined being inside a rainbow might be. I did not always want to go inside the house when mother came outside to get me. She made it easier by the quiet way she said, "Ladybug, Ladybug, wake up, my sweet little Ladybug." She knew I didn't like my given name and I sometimes cried when she called me by it. I do not know why I didn't like it, but mother called me Sweet Pea and Sugarplum and Honeybunch because she was kind. Of all the names, I liked Ladybug the best. I think she did too.

When I opened my eyes, from my naps in the sun, there she would be looking down with the sunlight bright around her. Her eyes twinkled and her mouth was shaped in a smile just for me. I always told her she looked like an afternoon angel. And when I told her I loved her with all my heart she always said, "I love you more."

Long after the excitement of the arrival of our freight shipment had worn off, mother called me to her. She said she had a surprise for me. I remembered that one time it was two packages of white cotton underpants when I had been hoping for a carrying case for Barbie. I thought surprises were supposed to be fun and exciting...

This time, with that recollection in mind, I dragged my feet to where mother waited. And it was the best surprise! She gave me a pair of crystal-clear princess shoes, and it was not even my birthday! The princess shoes had high heels like mother's fancy dress shoes. They were perfect, with fluffy, pink pom-poms. Of course, I played dress-up for the rest of the day.

LADYBUG

I was thrilled with my beautiful new shoes. I said, "Thank you, thank you!" I threw my arms around mother. I gave her a big kiss too. I went to show the baby chicks; they were my only friends besides mother, Ayah Lemah, Cook, Babu Shamraya, and Blackie. Mother said to be careful if I was going outside; it had rained that morning and the ground was wet. She said the heels on my new shoes were pointed and would sink right down into the soft dirt. She said to stay on the patio and the walkway where Cook could see me through the kitchen windows; the bread was almost ready and I could have a piece when I came back.

I loved mother's fresh-made bread! It was best just plain, still warm from the oven. I liked the end piece best, but any slice was heavenly. It was heavenly beautiful outside! The early morning rain had washed the air so that it sang a song happy, sweet, and clear. The flowers were so loud with color I heard them talking! The clouds rolled by way up in the sky, and the day smelled like deep, rich, mountain valley earth. It could not have been more perfect. I clomped along, clack-clack, clack-clack. Babu Shamraya was working in the orchard behind our house, above the vegetable garden. I called to him; I knew he didn't hear me.

Babu Shamraya was singing while he cut the tall grass between the orchard trees with his sickle. I wanted to show him my new shoes. I tiptoed on the soft ground so my heels would not sink down into it. I slowly made my way to the stone steps of the orchard. I heard the rhythmic swoop-swoop of the sickle shearing all the tall grass that was the perfect place for a python to hide. Rebel and Cousin would eat some of the fresh sweet grass for dinner, but not too much of it. Too much would give them gas. I hesitated; I knew I was not to come to the vegetable garden without telling Babu Shamraya. I was standing alongside it. Was that the same thing? I thought I was safe in the gentle valley sun.

I stood there undecided, in my princess shoes, at the base of the stone steps. I wondered if I should go back inside or try and get Babu Shamraya's attention. I didn't have time to do either. I heard the heavy slam of the kitchen door. It caught my attention because we were not supposed to slam doors. I was surprised to see Cook running fast in my direction. He had the big chopping butcher knife in his hand. I could not believe my eyes. He was shouting in Nepali. Although I didn't understand the words, I caught their urgency. Babu Shamraya shot a rat-tat-tat answer back to Cook from behind me.

BUMP.

A great heaviness fell upon my shoulders. It was the python! I might have jumped with a start, but the weight of it prevented that. I felt a tightening across my back. And my feet in my beautiful new princess slippers were nailed down into the soft dirt of the earth. Babu Shamraya's voice boomed in my ears and made my heart skip a beat.

"Do not move!"

I had never heard that voice before. It roared out and pinned me to the spot. I was paralyzed. Babu Shamraya's voice scared me even more than seeing Cook run at me with the big chopping butcher knife in his hand. I felt a sharp arrow of air slice by one side of my head and down to the ground. In a flash the air rushed down, slammed into the dirt, and bounced itself back up to shudder all around me. The force of it was so strong that the bottom of my dress swayed.

I didn't understand—the day was clear and calm, not windy. I heard a thick, heavy, wet sound and an abrupt stop like when Cook chopped heads of cabbage in half on the big wooden cutting board.

CHOMP!

There was a flash of bright sun hitting metal. It glinted and sliced down on my other side.

CHOMP!

The great and sudden weight bumped at me. It bumped and rolled down my back. I felt it hit against my legs. It came to rest hard against the heels of my feet. I was anchored firmly into the ground. I was trapped there in my brand-new, fluffy, pink pom-pom shoes.

I turned slightly toward that last swift movement and froze. There was Babu Shamraya's wicked sharp sickle. It rested, point down, deep in the soft, rich, brown earth. The wood handle stood upright, adorned with ruby dots. They pulsed and bobbled, rich and lustrous there on the wooden handle that pointed like an accusatory finger at the high valley sky. Blood shot out everywhere! It was a cheerful, happy, cherry Kool-Aid red.

That same blood was splattered in my hair and on my face and arms. The red sprayed all over me. It was a fine, misty shower down the side of my dress. It soaked my feet and wilted the fluffy, pink pom-poms on my new princess shoes. The fluff was flattened by the weight of wet blood. The pom-poms were ruined.

Cook shouted. He was not waving the butcher knife as he had at first, but he was still running. I understood. I knew now why he had come outside with it. As he got closer, it looked as though he was bobbing up and down. Only, it was not Cook who was bobbing, it was I. My head shook and so too did the rest of me. Behind him, I saw mother and Ayah Lemah running in our direction. Mother's face was stone hard, her eyes as sharp as sewing scissors. I had never seen them like that before.

The expression on mother's face frightened me witless. I started to cry. I heard Cook say he would take care of it. Babu

Shamraya scooped me up in his arms; I heard a quick snap and felt the heels of my shoes break off. I cried even harder. We reached mother on the pathway. Her eyes were softer; she touched my face. Ayah Lemah rushed ahead and held the doors open. As Babu Shamraya carried me into the house, Cook called out, "Do not you cry, little Ladysbug."

Ayah Lemah ran up the back stairs ahead of us. Mother stayed close by as Babu Shamraya took me straight to the big bathroom where the water ran splashing into the tub. He set me down and mother said, "Thank you, Shamraya, blessings to you." Ayah Lemah came in soon after with my pajamas. I didn't understand. It was time for lunch—I didn't want to go to bed! My new shoes were broken! I cried and cried while mother washed me and Ayah Lemah cooed over me.

I cried while my hair was dried and oiled and braided. I cried in my bed with mother beside me in my own little room at the back of the house. I cried to the point of getting hiccups. I could not eat the slice of warm fresh-baked bread Ayah Lemah brought up from the kitchen—with butter and cinnamon sugar on it just for me. Mother soothed me with her loving sweetness and kissed away my anguish. I tumbled into an exhausted sleep.

Babu Shamraya said I was a good strong girl. It was the next day and we made our regular morning round through the compound. He said it was important to do as you are told and that I did what I was told, even when I was in grave danger. It may have saved my life, he said. The python had wanted to eat me; he didn't know I was anything other than food. I felt bad because I had gone near the vegetable garden without Babu Shamraya to take me there. I knew I was not to have done so. I wondered how he could be so generous with his praise of my obedience.

I told him I knew that if I had not come near the vegetable garden, the snake would not have thought I was his food. I told Babu Shamraya I was sorry he had to kill the snake. Babu Shamraya said it was the snake's time to join in the never-ending cycle of life. He said not to worry my Ladybug head, the python would now be reborn, perhaps in another form. I told Babu Shamraya I had just wanted to show him my new princess shoes but now they were broken. Babu Shamraya said I was just as much a princess with or without those shoes. What mattered most was that Ladybug was healthy, alive and, most happily, unbroken.

That is what Babu Shamraya said.

Rooster King's Kiss

We had an injury in the yard. The older kids had run out of pine nut missiles to throw at each other and took to throwing rocks. They started out with pebbles and quickly progressed to larger projectiles. Rocks really hurt, you know. Mother put a stop to the rock throwing immediately. She said we should all have sense enough to know better. We got a stern lecture on throwing things like that and how it was dangerous and could put out someone's eye. I knew that. I had not been throwing rocks or anything else. My feelings were hurt that mother thought I would throw rocks.

The other kids didn't seem to take her scolding so hard. They huddled to discuss different playtime activities. As usual, I was excluded. This was nothing new. With the rock throwing curtailed, the big kids decided to play freeze tag. They didn't want me around because they said I was too slow, too small, and basically just in the way. I just watched, wishing I could join in. Somehow the game spilled over into the vicinity of the chicken yard and quickly degenerated into a run from the rooster.

Our rooster didn't have a name. I just called him the mean ol' rooster or Rooster King. He was a healthy hunk of a bird and very protective of his haggle of hens. I deliberately avoided him because he liked to chase me, and since he and I were about the same height, my head and face were especially vulnerable to his puncturing pecks.

I already knew his beak was a hurtful weapon. He pecked me in the back of my arms sometimes, or if I was really unlucky, on my neck or face. His perfunctory pecks made triangulated puncture wounds and stayed sore for several days. And of course there was always the danger of infection. If Babu Shamraya was not around when I wanted to visit the new baby chicks, I stayed clear of enemy territory.

Occasionally, the mean ol' rooster would boldly strut off his regular run and march into mother's flower garden. He chased me away from my teatime activities and pecked around in my pots at his leisure. We were never friends, he and I. We had never paused for a "how do you do." I tried to stay far away from Rooster King's bloodying beak. His sudden appearances ran me off in seconds. And I ran as fast as I could with my arms flailing, screaming all the way.

The older kids thought it was fun to out dodge Rooster King. Of course they were faster, taller, and tougher than I. With the curtailing of the rock throwing and the engagement of that mean rooster in a bloody game of peck-tag, our yard became a scene of carnage. Rooster King was enraged by the enemy's intrusion into his territory. He stood his ground and fought to quell their advance.

Rooster King's willingness to do battle so delighted the older kids that they egged him on and enticed him to chase them far out of his normal jurisdiction of the hen yard. The kids' tactic was to encircle Rooster King and then, all together, advance on him. Rooster King would spin around in a dervishlike frenzy, wings flapping, and suddenly spring forward and zero in on a particular child to chase. He usually got one too. Everyone loved it.

I watched this game of clucks and badgerers from the height and protection of the side patio near the kitchen door. I thought if the winds of fortune changed, I could effectively flee from the fracas. My plan of escape failed me. One of the rooster's targets ran onto the patio and vaulted over the opposite side. All the big kids ran laughing to the other end of the yard.

This left me in full view of the raging rooster. I was caught with no way of escape from the angry bird. When he saw he was denied his original prey, the mean ol' rooster advanced on me with *peckful* purpose. His beady little eyes held nothing but injurious intent. I suddenly had an unscheduled private audience with the King. He rushed at me with wings spread wide.

The afternoon sun blinked, and time slowed to the pace of a slug's slow and slimy slide. I noticed the rich colors in the Rooster King's feathers. They were beautiful—purple, green, orange, and a tuft of brown with hints of red on the top of his head just behind his comb. I stood petrified in the corner. I was caught between the edge of the patio and the door to the kitchen. Rooster King advanced steadily. His claws clacked on the patio stones. I was trapped. I had no way to escape.

Rooster King rushed me! I was pinned and corralled by his flapping wings. And then I suffered the injuriousness of his vicious beak. I shuddered with fear as he pecked me on my arms and head. My shock was silent—my voice had fled. My arms were bloody and there were empty patches on my scalp. Luckily for me, Babu Shamraya appeared to save me from further injury. He gathered me up in his arms and whisked me away to safety.

The mean ol' rooster had not thrown rocks, but he managed to almost put out my eye with his angry attention. Each time I look in the mirror I see the scar above my right eye. It is the indelible mark of the Rooster King's kiss. My fondest remembrance? The last time I saw the Rooster King was on my plate at a Friday night dinner. He was a southern-fried drumstick.

The Painter Dorian Gray

I met Dorian Gray. Or, to be more precise, I met a man who I thought was just like the fictitious Dorian Gray.

It happened shortly after I saw a movie all about him. I didn't want to see the movie. It was a horror movie I had to see or else. I had to see it because it was one of those mandatory outings with my siblings, and the rule was that if I didn't want to go, none of us went. It was a got-no-choice outing. The or else part was something I never wanted to experience. I went to the movie. That was how I knew who Dorian Gray was, and why I recognized him when I met him. I didn't read *The Picture of Dorian Gray* by Oscar Wilde until I was much, much older. Even then, the fictitious Dorian Gray frightened me.

The real-life Dorian Gray whom I met as a child frightened me too. This Dorian Gray was an artist, a painter, alive and ornery in Kathmandu, Nepal. He had been there for quite some time. He was also a veteran, having fought in the same big war as my father. Sometimes he came to our house after my bedtime and smoked cigars with my father in father's office on the first floor. I heard their voices as deep murmurs rumbling in the quiet night. Their cigar smoke wound up into the night air and found its way into my little room on the second floor at the back of the house. Cigar smoke was so stinky I always I tried to make sleep come quickly so I would not know I smelled it.

LADYBUG

The Dorian Gray I met got a wooden leg from the big war and earned a Purple Heart. I was afraid of his wooden leg, but I do not know why. His brown hair was unruly and scraggly, and he wore it pirate long. He also had a thick stubbly beard and cold, hard, if-looks-could-kill, gray eyes.

I was to be his first official little girl portrait in Kathmandu. I was to sit for him once or twice each week for one whole hour. I didn't want to go! My parents said I had to. mother said father felt it was important to extend to the painter a "professional courtesy." I wondered why I had to be the one to sit for the portrait. My father should do it, was what I thought.

My parents had portraits of my two older brothers. The painter Dorian Gray was going to paint mine. On the day of my first sitting, mother came with me. The man posed me and told me not to move. I had to sit still for an hour while he did sketches. On the second sitting, I was there at his house in that same room with him and his scraggly pirate hair, stubbly beard, and cold, hard eyes. We were alone together for a whole hour. It seemed much longer than an hour to me, but I didn't have a watch or know how to read one yet. Mother came to walk me home.

I told mother it seemed much longer than an hour, and she said it had really only been one hour. Mother said I would walk by myself the next time and the painter Dorian Gray would tell me when it was time for me to go home—I would come straight home, right? Mother didn't call him Painter Dorian Gray, I do not know what his real title was. He used an army name like Sergeant Major or Colonel General; I didn't know army names. They all sounded the same to me.

Major General Sergeant Colonel Painter Dorian Gray smelled of unfiltered Camel cigarettes. He smoked cigarette after cigarette, sometimes lighting the fresh one out of the pack from the almost-finished one in his mouth. The thick slate-colored smoke swirled around him, made him waver, made my eyes water. I coughed from the smoke too, and he didn't like that. I think he thought I coughed on purpose.

I could not help it. The cigarette smoke was cloying and stinky, like his fingers when he came over and moved my head by pushing or pulling on my chin. His fingertips were like rough splinters on my face. They left the smell of burnt tobacco behind. I imagined that an invisible residue ate away at my skin wherever he touched me, because I could feel his splintery touch for a long time after.

The painter Dorian Gray lived by himself in the very last house on the very last street behind our compound. I didn't want to go near his street because the big kids said it was haunted. I didn't know how a whole street could be haunted. I do know that some of the big kids egged his house one Halloween night. The next day they all had to go over and clean it up. Those same big kids said Dorian Gray ate children. Since I spent quite a bit of time with him one year, I will confirm that I never saw him eat any children.

The Dorian Gray I knew ate sardines out of the tin with Saltine crackers. He soaked the crackers in the oil on top of the sardines in the can. When they were soft enough, he mashed the crackers down into the sardines. After mashing the soaked crackers into the sardines, he scooped the mush out and ate it off the blade of his Swiss army knife. After eating the mashed sardines and crackers, he wiped his Swiss army knife clean on the hem of his pants, on the wooden-leg side. He wore khaki shorts all the times I saw him, and he kept his Swiss army knife in his buttoned back left pocket.

Mother loved sardine and brown mustard sandwiches on thick slices of bread with the crusts cut off. Sometimes she included her garden-fresh beefsteak tomatoes. I loved a sardine sandwich with mother's juicy tomatoes too. That was back when I could still eat tomatoes. I became allergic to them even though they were my favorite fruit. Now if I eat them I might die. When I could still eat tomatoes, sardines mashed with mayonnaise and a couple drops of Tabasco on crackers was really good. It was crumbly and messy, but delicious all the same. I ate the tomato like an apple.

I also liked a sardine sandwich, composed of mother's home-baked buttermilk bread with mayonnaise and fresh-ground green peppercorns. That was superb even without the tomatoes. I didn't even mind crunching all those tiny sardine bones.

Oh, the painter Dorian Gray. He drank warm beer right out of the bottle along with his sardines and crackers. He ate while he painted and sometimes stopped to sharpen the blade of his Swiss army knife on a whetstone. He never offered me anything to eat or drink while I sat for him. He burped too, and never once said, "Excuse me."

I dreaded going to Painter Dorian Gray's, but my parents wanted to buy the portrait of me when he was finished. I understood that I was obligated. Mother used that word. It meant I had to go; it was my responsibility. Besides, how could he finish my portrait if I didn't go? I had to leave home in plenty of time to get to Painter Dorian Gray's house. Mother watched from the wall at our compound as I walked the dusty streets, trying not to drag my feet on the way to another hour of Painter Dorian Gray's torture by portraiture.

The best and the only good thing about my sittings was the dress I got to wear. Mother had made it. It was China silk bought from the traveling salesman on the Palace Road. The dress had a full skirt, and she trimmed it with white lace and made a ruffled petticoat for me to wear underneath. I also wore my lace-trimmed, white dress socks and my black patent leather shoes. Mother tied a soft blue silk ribbon in my hair, making a floppy bow. It was the color of the Kathmandu sky in early morning springtime—soft, tender, snow-capped mountain blue, shiny as a glacier lake.

Sometimes the other kids would tease me when they saw me walking over in my Sunday best. They repeated their taunts that Painter Dorian Gray ate children and was really a troll. It was hard not to hear what those kids said. I went from bright summer sunshine to dim dark smelliness when I went for my sittings. I wondered if dim dark smelliness was the normal condition for a troll house. I knew I was obligated to sit in that dingy, oil paint-stained room in my beautiful dress. I had to sit without moving for a very long time. I was afraid that if I thought about what the kids said, I might be more afraid than I already was. I had to put their words out of my mind so I could keep my fears at bay.

Usually when I arrived, it would take Painter Dorian Gray a very long time to answer the door. Sometimes the door was open and he stood there in the dark maw of the entrance, chewing on a cigarette, waiting impatiently for me. One day I knocked and knocked and knocked. I knocked some more, waited, and knocked again. He didn't come to answer the door. I started back down the front walk. I was puzzled but very glad to be starting back home. I got as far as the sidewalk before he thundered from behind me—"Get back here. You're late!"

I was confused because I was not late. I had been on time; he just had not answered the door on time. I turned back, but he was not waiting at the threshold. My spirits plunged, my poor heart sank. I walked to the gaping doorway of the house. The big entry hall was in shadow as always. The front door was open at my back. I stood in the doorway, the light hardly reaching past me into the foyer. The light from outside got swallowed up into bottomless dusk. It just evaporated. I could make out part of the banister. It angled up and out of sight as it curved around to the second floor. Dust motes danced in the slice of light that lingered near the doorway. As my eyes adjusted to the dimness, I saw movement in the corner, to the side, near the bottom of the steps.

The movement I saw was the painter Dorian Gray. He sat on a step, second to last from the bottom, with his back against the steps. His eyes were closed and he leaned with his head turned, forehead pressed against the wall. His shaggy hair fell in a ragged curtain. It hid his face. He held a small glass vial in one hand. It had a bright aluminum cap with an eraser-red center. I had seen vials like that before. It looked like a container for medicine. He sat there on the steps with one shirtsleeve rolled up. There was a thick rubber strap around that arm, just above his elbow.

The painter Dorian Gray held a silver syringe in his other hand. It had a long needle. He stuck the needle into the eraser-red center of the small vial and drew some of its contents into the syringe. He set the vial down beside him on the step, held the syringe needle up, and flicked a finger against it. Then he pushed the plunger of the syringe until liquid squeezed out of the tip of the needle. While I watched, he plunged the needle into the arm with the rolled-up sleeve. He stuck the long needle into the vein on the inside of the elbow. That is how I knew he was very sick.

I knew, from my visits to the teaching hospital with my father, that syringes were used to put powerful medicine directly into the body. The syringe was faster than a pill. Very sick people had to have medicine given to them in this way. The painter Gray was very sick. I was sad for him, but I didn't like him any better. But I think I understood his bad manners better. Being sick made him mad and angry. I understood. Sometimes anger spurted out as ugliness, if you didn't know how to meditate it away as the yogis taught. Babu Shamraya told me that. I wondered if Painter Dorian Gray had ever meditated.

As I looked at him on the step with his head back now, eyes closed, face not in a snarl, I thought meditating was grown-up business. I was just a kid. I would ask mother bout it when I got back home. When Painter Dorian Gray didn't move, I wondered if the medicine took a very long time to work. I knew some medicines were stronger than others and thus worked faster. I also knew you didn't have to be hospital sick to get shots with a syringe.

I got my vaccinations with a syringe when I had not been sick at all. The vaccination gave me a fever and even made me a little sick. Still, mother said it was better to be a little sick than to be very sick and die from the disease the vaccination was made to prevent. I understood. I understood that Painter Dorian Gray was a little sick, but not so sick he had to be in the hospital. He never looked well. I stood there and waited. Finally, he sighed a deep and heavy sigh. Then he opened his eyes and looked at me. His eyes were still the same cold, hard gray. He squinted and then barked at me—"Close the door! Get into the studio!" He was a Grinch-type person. I thought that even though he was sick, he was still mannerless and mean. And I knew that, sick or not, I liked him no better.

The painter Dorian Gray captured the spirit of my image on canvas. Through the slow-dancing dust motes moving in the smoky air that rested between us in that room smelling of sardines and cigarettes, he fashioned my portrait from tubes of color, bad temper, talent, and a dozen different brushes. I think I felt myself change as he took away a part of me and immortalized it. I am not sure I wanted to have part of me missing or lasting forever. And then, one day, Painter Dorian Gray said he was almost finished painting me. I asked to see my portrait. The answer he growled, loud and ugly, was "no!" I do not know why he had to shout at me. I still had to sit a little longer—several more times. Nothing really changed about my visits as the painting neared completion.

I still sat on a rickety cot in the semidarkness of a lonely house with an anguished artist who chain smoked and burped unashamedly. The mountain valley light streamed into the room through a slit in the dark fabric of the heavy curtain in one window. I thought of the light as my beacon, shining just for me, lighting my way of escape as a lighthouse on a rocky coastline guides ships to safety. I wanted to touch my tika for reassurance, but I knew better than to move. The cot was still positioned on the floor, so light from the slit in the curtain at that one window touched just one corner of it. The painter Dorian Gray never did let me see my portrait progress as he painted me in his studio.

Over those many months, those many lost hours while I sat for posterity, I concentrated on that single sliver of light beaming through the stingy slit in the curtain. All the other windows in the room were shuttered from the outside and hung with heavy dark drapery on the inside. Sometimes I would almost fall asleep while sitting there. I didn't plan to fall asleep, and I tried not to fall asleep, but sometimes I almost did. At those times, Painter Dorian Gray would bark at me: "Stay awake!" "Sit up!" "Be still!" "No crying!"

In order to sit still, I tried to imagine being a bird, flying high above the valley. It didn't always work. Painter Dorian Gray shouted, barked, and jabbed his paint brushes at me anyway. "Be still!" "Don't move!" "Keep your head up!" "No tears!" "Fold your hands!" His voice was low and rough like the sound of a growling dog. It rumbled out of him like thunder, mean thunder. It frightened me. I sat as still as I could and made my mind float away into the high summer mountains I could see outside my bedroom window. I tried to be quiet and calm inside my skin so he would not snarl at me. I tried to be quiet and calm inside my skin because I knew he was very sick.

When my portrait was finally completely finished, I got to see it when Painter Dorian Gray showed it to my parents. At that time, he had what mother called an "unveiling." There was a cloth over the canvas, and he pulled it away with a flourish. I have to say the portrait looked like me, like the me I saw when I looked in the mirror. It was big like me, too. My head in the portrait was as big as my head in real life. There was even the faint scar over my right eye from the rooster's kiss.

When my parents asked to buy the portrait, the price was so high I think they got upset. I think that before he started, Painter Dorian Gray told them one price but then after he finished told them a different price. For several weeks after that, there were talks between my father and the painter Dorian Gray. One day, my father came home and closed himself in his office without speaking to mother or me. He stayed in there until dinnertime. Now there was what mother called "bad blood" between my father and the painter Dorian Gray. I saw Painter Dorian Gray hardly at all after that.

When I finally did read *The Picture of Dorian Gray*, there was much in it that reminded me of my time with the painter Dorian Gray. One thing was the fear and loathing I felt sitting for the portrait. I understood that that was the feeling I had hovering over and around me during my time with the man I had met so long ago. I wondered if he might have had a canvas in one of the other rooms in his house that took on all his bad qualities, as with the fictitious Dorian Gray. I thought all of his meanness might store rather nicely in his wooden leg. It was hollow, after all.

Whereas the fictitious Dorian Gray stored all of his imperfections, obsessions, and obscenities on a canvas, the painter Dorian Gray wore all of those things on his person, in his expression, in his manner, and in his voice. I could also believe that the painter Dorian Gray might have stored all of his best qualities in the hollow of his wooden leg. I wanted to believe something like that. Well, really, I needed to believe something like that. I needed to believe it to explain his exceptional ugliness in general and his ugliness toward me in particular. I knew that I had to sit there for my portrait because my parents said so, but even then, I think I also understood that a favor was being done. A favor was being done for him, and he was anything but happy about it.

I also needed to believe some kind of explanation because otherwise I would have been too frightened. My own imagination and the taunts from the big kids were enough to keep me in a constant state of wariness. Still, I had to go to the shuttered, stale-smelling, dimly lighted house in my best shoes and beautiful dress to sit for a painting. Without the explanation that I invented for this man's behavior, I would have been too frightened to sit still and remain silent while the tortured artist painted.

Other than that, the painter I met was not like the fictitious Dorian Gray. I do not think I ever knew the painter Dorian Gray's real name. I am sorry my parents didn't buy the portrait he painted of me. I cannot imagine why anyone else would want to buy it. Why would they want a portrait of a girl they didn't know? Every once in a while mother said she wondered where that portrait ended up. It was exquisite, she said. I was sad that she didn't have it. She once said that the painter Dorian Gray had truly caught me on canvas. Actually, I was secretly glad not to have that image of me in perfection around as a reminder of what I might have to live up to.

I do not know where that portrait of me might be. I think if I ever saw it again I would try to buy it. I would buy it so I could see myself the way I was back then when I was perfectly exquisite. Perfect in the exquisite, white, China silk and lace dress mother made for me. Perfect where I blossomed in paradise, thrived in peace, and bathed in sunshine and harmony. I would buy the portrait so I could see how I was before the world took pieces out of me, chewed them up, and spit them out. I could see myself and all the possibilities that existed back then, despite the time I lost with the painter Dorian Gray.

Wart Equals Witch

Pain was nothing new to me. I do not think I sought pain out, not purposely. Nevertheless, I was no stranger to pain. Besides, pain always seemed to find me. Unfortunately, when it did, it usually stayed a while. Because I was the youngest of five, I learned early on not to cry in public or I would be ridiculed and excluded from group activities. Sometimes a group activity was something I didn't want to do, but I didn't dare decline. Declining was not encouraged because if I did not want to participate it was an instant pox on any activity my siblings had in mind. If we did not do something together, we did not get to do it at all.

Group activities often meant going to the Mission to see a film. If the chance to go to the movies came up and all of us kids didn't want to see it, none of us could go. Yes, it was an all-or-nothing deal. As one can imagine, this generated quite a bit of pressure if someone didn't want to go. I felt I had to always accept. Thus, at a very early age I was bombarded with images in films that were inappropriate for me in my tender years. Or, more accurately, those images were inappropriate for me and my wild imagination.

The big kids sat eagerly awaiting the opening titles. They had their popcorn and were ready for the movie to begin. The adults would be next door with their cocktails. Some of them were ready to play bridge. It seemed as though most of the movies we got were horror films. I worried that the Wolfman or a vampire or Frankenstein would find me. I knew they were supposed to be imaginary beings. That did nothing to stop my wild imagination from going crazy.

One movie my sisters had seen in the States was so scary in the telling of it that when the film came to Kathmandu and we went to see it, the ominous opening melody was enough to send me out of the theater. I spent the evening crying tears of fear and self-pity in the snack lounge. I shed those tears about a movie I never did see. It didn't matter that several people told me the movie was not very scary. My imagination made it horrific, and I had no desire to see the movie to prove myself wrong.

I like stories much better than movies. Most of the stories read to me were by my favorite author, Dr. Seuss. Those were what I liked best. Sometimes I heard scary stories about witches, warlocks, vampires, gargoyles, and other mean creatures. I was not interested in scary things because I knew I had to sleep alone in my little room at the back of the house. I didn't like scary stories at all. And that brings me to the real story. The real story was my quest for truth. I looked for it as much as I could, given my crazy little self at that time. I thought I knew truth.

I knew that the chicken eggs I sometimes helped to collect would not hatch unless they had been fertilized by the rooster. That is why we had him. And I knew that those eggs still would not hatch unless the hens sat on them to keep them warm so the baby chicks would grow inside. I knew that the python that killed the chickens in the yard just wanted to eat. It was not his fault. He was a snake, and of course he had to eat like any living creature. I knew the crows in the orchard ate the ripe fruit before we could pick it and liked to eat the chicken eggs too. Yes, I knew many truths.

I knew the honeybees in the orchard would not bother me if I didn't bother them and I knew not to play with an animal (not even our pets) while they were eating. I knew that the rooster in our yard would peck me to pieces if I didn't carefully avoid him. I knew that the mud in the yard was best primed for my mud cakes after a drenching high valley rain. I knew that mother's fresh-baked bread was better than store bought and that her kisses were without rival. And I knew that disinfecting a cut or scratch was very important because germs could grow quickly and make you sick enough to die!

It is this last part that I found most interesting. Not exactly the germs part, but the disinfecting part. I found it interesting that disinfecting was such an important measure to take to prevent germs. I knew about alcohol, calamine, and mercurochrome. I was subject to one application or the other of any or all of these medicinals several times a week. Because I was such a tomboy, my cuts and scratches were ever present and I knew the disinfectants rather well. I counted them among my acquaintances; they were not exactly friends. They were tough, and they kept me from my own personal disasters with disease, so I respected them. I understood their importance to my general welfare and I believed their stinging fires of purification demanded my dry-eyed endurance.

One day, after mother finished reading L. Frank Baum's *The Wonderful Wizard of Oz* to me, I was very unsettled. For some reason, I was obsessed with the idea of warts. I know that there was much more to the story than warts, but my little brain could not leave the wart factor alone. I had many wart-related questions. My obsession about warts consumed me.

What did warts do? Why were they a wart and not a mole? Why did only bad witches have warts? If you had warts, were you a witch? Would warts make you become a witch? I decided I had to take proper steps to make sure no witch marks could claim me. I had a wart on my left knee. It was a knobby protrusion that I had picked off a few times. I knew that the wart was witchy because it always grew back!

The first time it grew back I was fascinated. The second time it grew back, I thought it very curious and briefly wondered why. No matter, I picked it away again. That was before mother had read the *Wizard of Oz* to me. The third time it grew back, I somehow believed it was the mark of a witch. That was after the reading of the *Wizard of Oz*. This is the truth about what I got out of weeks of bedtime reading. Others came away with Dorothy's triumphant return home and the power of positive change and how to face fear and not let it rule you.

I, however, filed those fundamental truths away. Instead, I wondered about the bad witch and her warts. How did she get bad? Was it because of the warts? I didn't want to be a witch. I felt I had to find every way to prevent myself from turning into one. I had to do everything in my power to prevent such a catastrophe—mainly because I believed that the wart on my knee would somehow transform me into a witch! It had grown back three times! I didn't want to become a witch. I worried that if I was a witch, I would have to live in a witch-world with other witches. I would never see mother again.

The thought of not seeing mother again is what kicked me into action. I got a pair of scissors. Not mother's sewing shears—I knew better than that. I also got a few cotton balls and the alcohol from the small bathroom next to my sisters' room. I brought my instruments to my little room at the back of the house where the sun sparkled brightly in the late-day sky.

I arranged everything in the order in which it would be used: scissors, cotton, alcohol, cotton, and an adhesive bandage. I sat on the floor with my back against the frame of my bed. I pulled my left knee up close so I could see that witchy wart right on top. I opened the bottle of alcohol and used a cotton ball to absorb a goodly amount. I cleaned the top of my knee and cleaned the blades of the scissors. Before I could change my mind, I cut the wart off.

The wart didn't come right off. It was not just a quick snip. The wart was too rubbery and tough for that. I had to cut at it and keep cutting at it three or four times. Even the blood hurt. It screamed down my leg. I bit my tongue. No time for babies; no crying either. I had to finish what I had started. I concentrated, snipped carefully, and finally got the wart cut off. I blotted the wound with a fresh new cotton ball and alcohol. It stung! No tears, no crying! I was not allowed to cry. I was doing this for my freedom from witchery. I had to be brave.

I pressed the cotton ball hard to the wound. When I pulled it off, there was an opaque oval hole in my skin, right where the wart had been. I put the adhesive bandage on and threw the soiled cotton balls into the wastebasket. As I limped down the hall to put the alcohol back in the bathroom and return the scissors to where I had found them, I felt good about my budding surgical skills. I congratulated myself on heading off any evil potential connected with the wart.

That night, at bath time, mother found out all about my foray into surgery. She said not to be cutting myself anywhere, for any reason. Did I understand? I understood. I told her there were witches in real life and I was just protecting myself so that I would not be mistaken for one. She would not hear of my wart-equals-witch explanation. She asked me where I got such a crazy idea. I explained about the book. She said I needed to use my head! The book was make-believe; we lived in the real world. Surely I had better sense than that? She said she knew I knew the difference and I had better remember it if I was going to be successful in life.

The wart on my knee grew back successfully. I showed it to mother as proof. She told me not to be silly and made me promise not to cut the wart off with scissors again. I hated to promise Mother anything because promises were not to be broken! If I promised her, then I absolutely could not break my promise. I would not. How could I? Well, I promised because I had to. I promised mother I would not use scissors to cut the wart off again.

The next time I cut the wart off my knee I used a razor blade. So far, it has not grown back.

Ride to the Roses

I learned to ride a horse before I knew how to read. We had two horses. Cousin was a brown and white long-haired mountain horse and stood at fourteen hands. Not kid hands, grown-up hands. Cousin was cantankerous as a mad cow and liked to bite. Our other horse, Rebel, was a palomino and stood at sixteen hands. He was a precision-trained, retired circus performer with a thick, cream mane and a long, luxurious tail. I loved them both but for different reasons. The first day I rode Rebel alone, Babu Shamraya put the saddle on him and I insisted that I do the rest. Ignoring Babu Shamraya's protests, I elected to finish the task by myself, but I could not cinch the saddle properly. I cinched it as best I could.

Rebel had the habit of puffing up when being cinched and, determined as I was, I had neither the strength nor the inclination to fight with him about it. Babu Shamraya stood by to lend me a hand, but I would not let him help. He took special exception to this when I mounted Rebel from the right by standing on the patio wall. I found my seat and reined Rebel around for a walk in the yard. Babu Shamraya kept telling me the saddle was not tight. I heard him, but it was on Rebel's back and that is all I cared to know.

The next thing I knew was the ground at my head. The saddle had twisted. I found myself hanging upside down, feet in stirrups, reins in hand. Gravity and the loosened cinch strap brought me the rest of the way down, slowly but gently onto my head. Clearly, the saddle needed adjusting. After Babu Shamraya cinched it properly, I set out again on Rebel's back. This time I was more appreciative of the finer points of tack.

Rebel was a beautiful horse, and I believe he was the envy of the neighborhood. Several of the families had horses. My sisters rode with their friends and played racing games on the national parade grounds where King Mahendra's guard did their maneuvers. This was also the place where his hunting party assembled for the tiger hunts he took my father on.

I rode with my sisters sometimes too, always riding double, never solo. I really wanted to ride solo. I knew I was lucky that my sisters even let me tag along, but I wanted to do more. I thought that if I could ride and control Rebel in our big yard, I could ride him to and on the parade grounds solo the next time we went. That is what I thought. That is what I hoped.

Our yard was the size of a football field. We lived across the street from the second prince in a house built for his sister. The second princess lent her brand-new house to mother for her service to the royal court. Mother had her Masters Degree in home economics. She taught the second princess, as well as her ladies of the court, nutrition and hygiene. This was as a service to the Kingdom of Nepal.

The King's guard barracks were on the other side of the southern wall, which was made of stone and ten feet high. To the southwest along that same wall was a little orchard, and to the right of that, a multipurpose courtyard with two small stalls and an entrance on the right into the servants' quarters. Part of the western wall housed mother's flower garden, where she planted pansies, petunias, geraniums, and marigolds.

Poppies grew along the northern wall, and that wall met the eastern wall at the front of the house. The eastern wall supported gigantic climbing rosebushes with razor-sharp thorns. This wall connected with the gatehouse, which was sometimes used as Cousin's stable. The wall continued for a short length on the other side where the big iron gate into the compound took over.

As I mentioned, Rebel was precision trained. He would race with a click of the tongue and stop short with a tap on the haunches. Or was it the other way around? I walked him back and forth and up and down. West to east and west again. No matter how I clicked, Rebel maintained his walking pace. A flick of the reins was as ineffective as my clicking tongue.

On what I had decided would be our final turn of the yard, I nudged Rebel in the haunches and he shot forward at a full gallop down the straightaway from west to east. We were racing, and the eastern wall was fast approaching. Rebel didn't alter his pace. I pulled and strained and pulled and pulled and still he didn't slow down. I was yelling by now in a fit of panic. It was those roses I feared, not falling or speed, but the flesh-ripping tenacity of their sharp, hooked thorns.

We flew across the yard like a falcon after prey. We flew! However exhilarating it was, I knew I had a problem. I had also had more than enough time to think of what would happen when we met the wall. In a last-ditch effort I clicked my tongue, and Rebel stopped. I pitched forward like Humpty Dumpty off his wall. I opened my eyes surprised that I hadn't fallen. My legs were wound around Rebel's neck, and I was holding on to his ears. The top of my head was caught tight in the thick wall of roses. Rebel stood perfectly still, breathing normally, patiently awaiting my next command.

The climbing roses crowned me with their pointy green buds and soft fragrant petals. They bestowed bits of twisted, tangled, rough hooked wood and tiny spiky furled green leaves anywhere they found purchase. I was scratched, pinned, and poked all over my neck and face. Furry brown honeybees buzzed around my head, mercifully ignoring me for the moment, busily collecting rose bounty for their hive. To move at all meant to lose some hair. My dilemma was how to lose my hair, for lost it was going to be. To fall meant to have it yanked out by the roots and risk a rash of bee stings for the trouble.

Falling could work. I never considered that I might break something. However, I chose the slow and arduous method of climbing back down Rebel's neck. Bit by bit I inched down and held on to his mane. My hair was inexorably pulled from its braids and broken off my head. This was of no consequence; it simply didn't matter. Bad hair was a small price to pay because, on this day, I had mastered riding Rebel alone.

Run, Ladybug, Run!

I remember the instant I understood I could read. It was a bright and lazy afternoon. It was in early summer, just after the awakening green freshness of spring, when everything smelled sweet and budding flowers perfumed the air. I was sitting cross-legged on my bedroom floor, and I could hear all the other kids at play through the open balcony doors. I had been watching them earlier; that was all they allowed me to do. I was too little—a baby, they said. I got in the way, and they wanted to run fast and play hard. I was used to this. I played alone a lot. It was nothing new.

It was also nothing new that I liked to sit on the floor of my bedroom. I felt closer to things there. Closer and more connected. I was tired. I uncrossed my legs and looked at my shoes. I smiled at my good fortune—they were brand-new! I thrilled at them on my feet with my white cotton socks. My Keds still smelled new! They were my very first pair of non-hand-me-down sneakers from the order catalogue.

Well, I had gotten a pair the year before, but there had been an error with the order. I got two left shoes. I wore them that first day anyway, but when mother noticed, she would have none of it. She made me take them off. She sent the two left shoes back. Now I had a brand-new pair. They were just like the ones my sisters wore. I loved my new navy blue Keds.

My legs tingled; they were prickly from sitting cross-legged on the floor. They were trying to fall asleep. I was sleepy. Not prickly-sleepy like my legs—warm and sunny mountain early-summer-green sleepy. The kind of sleepy in which you can close your eyes and still hear the birds chirp and the horses neigh and the hens cluck and the rooster crow and the kids play and it does not keep you awake.

I stretched out onto my stomach and opened the book mother had been reading to me. It was not like my other books that had bright-colored pictures. My favorite of those books was "The Cat in the Hat" and "Green Eggs and Ham" by Dr. Seuss.

I learned I didn't like his Grinch much. The Grinch was mean; he scared me. Even though he turned to be good, I remembered the harm he did before his heart got healed. I could not forget how mean he had been before that. I didn't like the Grinch. I had met people like him. Those people still had not turned good yet.

The book mother had been reading to me was called a "reader." It was the same book my oldest brother had read when he was younger, and that is what it was called. I opened the book as I lay on my bedroom floor. It had pictures, but they were not in color. This book had a single picture on each page, and below that, one line of print. That line of print was bigger than the print in my other books.

Since this was a schoolbook, I thought the print was bigger because the words were probably more important. They were school words, not funny words. Mother told me that after summer I would be going to school. She said I would ride to school on the bus with the big kids. I didn't say anything. I secretly thought I wouldn't like riding anywhere with the big kids.

I looked at the open page. It was not the first page of the story. The book just liked to flop open on that page. I do not know why. The picture on the page showed a girl who had on a short skirt and a short-sleeved shirt and shoes that looked like my saddle shoes, except that her shoes were all black. I guess they didn't really look like my saddle shoes, but they looked sturdy. My saddle shoes were sturdy. I heard the kids shout loudly and scrambled up to see why. The big kids were playing baseball in the yard. Sometimes they waved at me on the balcony, but mostly they didn't.

I could see that the bases were loaded, and before I looked at home plate I heard the crack of the ball on the bat. It was a good hit. I could tell because the ball went fast on the ground. Those kinds of balls were harder to catch. They went really far, and you had to have a good arm to throw that kind of ground ball in from the outfield to the pitcher. The right fielder missed it. The ball went far. Everyone was jumping and screaming. It was going to be a home run.

"Run, Bobby! Run!" They were too loud for me. They were loud like the flock of crows that fed in the garden in the early, early morning and woke you up before it was time to be awake. Those crows didn't care. They had their breakfast in the dew of dawn just before the high mountain sun smiled into the fertile green of Kathmandu Valley. My stomach grumbled. I went back into my room.

My stomach grumbled only when I was very hungry. There was a time when I had to tell mother everything I ate because she wanted to be sure I didn't get sick. As a much younger girl I had eaten a lot more. They said I had a tapeworm. It lived inside me and ate all the food I put in my mouth. None of the food I ate got to my body because the tapeworm ate everything first. Mother and father worried because I ate all the time and never got bigger. They took me to the doctor and got medicine. I took the medicine for a long time. Then, one day, I didn't have the tapeworm anymore.

I wondered when supper was. I could smell mother's fresh-baked bread. Sometimes she cut my favorite end piece and let me have it before dinner. It would be warm still. I got to have it with sprinkled sugar. With butter too—if the butter had been out of the refrigerator for a while and was soft enough to spread. Mother's bread, just plain, was already heavenly delicious. I didn't need sugar or butter. When I still had the tapeworm I got a fat slice of warm bread with sugar or jam or butter to put more meat on my bones because mother said I was wasting away.

I scrambled back down on the floor in front of the schoolbook and looked at the flopped-open page. I knew the girl's name was Jane. She was in school. I was going to school soon, and it was important that I know my letters and my numbers and how to read. I did know my numbers and my letters. I didn't know how to read. I had stories read to me at bedtime almost every night, and mother read to me sometimes when all my brothers and sisters were at school in the late mornings. I sat on her lap, and she had her coffee with evaporated milk from the can and three even teaspoons of sugar. Her skin was soft and she smelled soap fresh and newly ironed summer linen.

I rested my chin on my folded hands, lying on the floor in front of the book. I was sleepy. I was hungry too. I didn't know which I was more—sleepy or hungry. I still had to take naps sometimes. I liked naps. I took them almost every day. I wondered if I should go sit at the table before mother called me.

I think I was more hungry than sleepy. I looked at the words in the book on the page under the picture of Jane. My stomach was growling now. My eyes were closing, and the words were wavy on the page. Jane's legs were bent as though she was running. I blinked. Jane was running. I saw Jane! I saw that Jane was running.

In that single moment, an avalanche of understanding burst into my consciousness with all the force and certainty of a rock slide on the Tribhuvan Rajpath. I knew that road over the mountains into India. It was a long and zigzagged climb up, up, and up forever. At just this point, my brain ignited. I felt it warm up. It seemed to hum, the way it does when you sing in your head and nobody else can hear the song. My eyes popped wide. I could not tear them from the page.

My mind was smoldering the way the pit fires did when my father came home from hunting and brought a wild boar to roast. Those pit fires were white hot and dug deep into the earth. I felt an awareness that deep in my head. It was deeper and clearer than anything I had ever experienced before. I knew what the writing below the picture on the page said. I heard myself thinking it. I made the connection: "Run, Jane! Run!"

I got it! I leaned up on my elbows, I pulled the book closer. R-u-n. Run. I sat up and pulled the book onto my lap. I could hear the kids outside. They were still loud. They were still happy that Bobby had hit a home run. His team won the game. In the book, on the page with the picture of Jane in her black shoes, short skirt, and short-sleeved shirt, Jane was running. I saw Jane running. Saw = See! I turned the page: See Jane run.

On the next page, on the left side, there was a picture of a boy. He was running too. He was running, and so was Jane. Jane's picture was on the right side. The big-lettered words below the picture of the boy said: "See Dick run." I saw him! I saw that the boy was running. I knew his name was Dick; I didn't really read that, but remembered from when mother had read the book to me earlier. Jane was on the next page.

I turned the page again. Dick and Jane were together on the same side of the page. They were running! "See Dick, see Jane. See Dick run. See Jane run. Run, Dick. Run, Jane." I saw Dick run and I saw Jane run! As clearly as I had seen Bobby head for first base after he hit the ball out in the yard where the big kids played, I saw both Dick and Jane. In the book, Dick and Jane were running. I turned the page. There was a ball now. Dick had the ball. I traced the letters with my finger. I said them to myself out loud. I understood.

The words flew at me from the page. I kept reading. I traced the letters of a word with my finger and made the sound of each letter. If I sounded them all together, I could say a word I knew before I knew I knew it! I had to tell mother I could read! Just then, I heard mother call from downstairs. Supper was ready. I snatched up the book and jumped to my feet. I was so glad. It was time to eat and I could read!

> See me run.
> See me in my new shoes.
> See me run down the steps.
> See me run down the steps in my new shoes.
> Run, Ladybug, run!

The Splitting of the Hairs

I am not sure I should be telling this story. Oh, well. Anyway, I never knew a hair salon. I didn't have to. I had two older sisters and I watched them. As soon as I could manage a brush and comb, I did my own hair. That would have made me about five years old, I guess. It was a necessity, combing my own hair. Nobody else cared about my tender little scalp.

The most benign of hair brushings was torture. Hair

grooming bred scalp injury and pain that lasted half the day. Try as I did to fight against the humiliation, hair grooming ultimately deteriorated into fits of woebegone crying. Oh, sure, it always started out okay, but how many times do you want your hair pulled and scalp pinched and scratched for no good reason but tidiness?

I learned to braid my own hair around the same time I learned to read. It was never as good as with mother's skillful touch, but I could do it fine. With practice, I did it with ease. Three braids, that is all. One in the front on top slightly to the right, and one behind each ear on the side of a centered part in the back. The top braid was woven into either of the back ones and their ends were secured with barrettes. The two back braids with their barrettes were just long enough to do harm if I managed to shake my head vigorously. With the right shake, the barrettes could be weapons of pain and maiming because they were just long enough to hit my nose and eyes.

I do not think I really understood what a hair salon was, but I knew the barber. His name was Veejay (rhymes with Deejay) Singh (as in "sing a song").

He was originally from Ranaghat, India. The nearest towns were Santipur and Kalna. Mr. Singh had family in Kathmandu. He had moved to be with them a week before his birthday twenty years ago, he said. He had been a boy of ten. His father was a barber, and his father's father had been a barber too.

Mr. Singh came to our house about once a month and cut my brothers' and my father's hair. I sometimes watched from the doorway of the big front bathroom. They sat in straight-backed card table chairs with a towel draped around their fronts and another tucked in at their necks. The big window opposite the bathroom door spilled in bright light, but even so, the electric ceiling light was turned on.

Mr. Singh had a set routine. He cleaned all of his tools in alcohol and sharpened his razors on a long black strop, one end of which he attached to the bathroom door handle and one end of which he held. He pulled the strop tight and whisked the silvery barber blades back and forth until they were glistening with sharpness and could split hairs. That is how the barbering always started—with the splitting of the hairs. He would pluck a hair out of his own head and then, in a flourish, slice the shaft lengthwise to show us just how sharp the blades were. He gave each of my brothers a half a hair. I do not know about them, but I was very impressed.

Sometimes I had to leave my brothers to the clippers and stay near mother. On the day in question, dinner interrupted the barbering. We were having mother's melt-in-your-mouth homemade butter horns! My brothers jumped out of their seats and ran out of the room. Mr. Singh carefully arranged his tools and covered them with a clean white cotton towel. I went to wash my hands in the girls' bathroom. On my way to the dinner table, I thought I heard my brothers' voices. I went past the big front bathroom looking for them. I think they took the back stairway because I didn't pass them in the front.

I turned back around to go down the front stairs, and a shiny twinkle from the towel-covered tray across the sink in the big front bathroom caught my eye. I stood at the doorway and looked in. I saw the clippers peeking out from under the towel. I deliberated. Then I stepped into the room and walked over to the sink. My thick, pink, rubber-soled black and white saddle shoes were silent on the hard floor tiles. I looked, I listened. I lifted the towel to move it to cover the clippers completely and then stopped.

Shiny, smooth, and sharp. I was mesmerized, intrigued, and out of my league. I picked up the clippers, and they were surprisingly heavy. I almost dropped them onto the white tile floor. I caught them in time, but they clanged against the porcelain sink. I almost upset the whole tray. The clippers were in my hand.

I held them the way I remembered seeing the barber do. The curve of the handle was cool and quite comfortable. I squeezed them closed and marveled. I was fascinated by the crisscross action of the square-shaped cutter head. I looked closely and squeezed the clippers again. When I squeezed them, the checkerboard pattern with the tiny open holes closed up! When the clippers opened, the holes reappeared!

I wondered what they felt like clipping hair. I stood to the side of the sink looking in the mirror. With the clippers in my right hand, I put them against my right temple. Before I could change my mind I squeezed, and that quickly, a hunk of hair sprung off my head and dangled to my shoulder. I had a smooth and stinging perfectly bald square where hair had been a blink ago. I pulled at the fallen locks and looked at myself in the mirror. I felt my stomach drop to my knees. This was going to be noticed, this square bare spot on the right side of my head. I wanted to cry, but I knew it was my own fault. Even so, I was mortified.

Mortification aside, I thought it only fair to even the score. I took the clippers and did the same to the left side of my head. The bald squares at my temples stung. Tears pricked in my eyes. My eyes stung. Still, I would not let the tears fall. It was my own fault plain and simple. I put the clippers back on the tray and covered everything carefully. I made sure the towel was smooth and straight. I took one more look at the barbershop bathroom and walked down the hall to my little corner room at the back of the house. I stood in the middle of the room with my hair in my hands. I wondered what to do.

I found a pretty silk scarf. I wore it on my head. Of course everyone noticed. I had to take the scarf off because it was not proper attire for the dinner table. Mother asked what happened to my hair. I said I had pulled it out. My brothers spit out their food laughing. The truth was plain to see. I had two bald squares where hair used to be. Those spots stung for days. I ignored them as best I could. And I stuck to my story.

As mother used to say, "If you believe that, stand on your head."

I am sitting in a chair.

Myna, Won't You Sing?

I once had a bird. She was a gift from one of my father's colleagues, a registered nurse who taught at the nursing school he had helped establish in the Himalayan foothills. I was afraid of the bird at first because she was loud and jumpy. As the weeks wore on, I became more comfortable with Myna. Her dark eyes were quick and lively when she fixed her gaze on me if I came near. She hopped from perch to perch, fluttered her wings, puffed out her chest. Sometimes Myna threw out a word or two. I think she knew it would get my attention.

There came a time when I practiced with her each day to build her vocabulary. I had just learned the word "supercalifragilisticexpialidocious," and Myna seemed determined to stick with "super cowlick, super cowlick!" I thought she was commenting on Dennis the Menace's unruly hair. It seemed logical to me. I figured she had plenty of time to read. After all, the comics often lined the bottom of her cage.

I taught her to say "Myna wants a cracker." I thought it quite the original phrase. Myna was a happy bird. She sang each morning when her night cloak came off the cage. She ate rice regularly and crooked her head just so to study me with her bright black eyes. I got to watch Cook feed her if I was up very early. He cleaned her cage and gave her fresh clean water each morning before the rest of the house was awake. Sometimes, during the day, Myna's cage was hung in my little room and she watched over me as I played with my friends, Barbie and her sister Skipper.

Myna's feathers were a dark, dark blue with what looked like gold and green. Her feathers had a sheen to them that caught the light now and then to make her look as though she wore a star-kissed suit of shimmering blue midnight sky. She was beautiful. Myna hopped and chirped and chattered and sang.

We often had conversations about my siblings. Myna was a good listener. I wanted to let her out of her cage to fly around my room and perch where she liked. I was devastated to learn that her wings had been clipped. She could no longer fly. Still, we spent many happy times together, she in her cage and I in my little room at the back of the house.

As Myna's vocabulary grew, so did my curiosity about her avian habits. I took an interest in her diet. I pestered Cook with questions about Myna as he prepared her suet and rice. Her fluffy brown rice was kept in a small container on the counter in the kitchen. I watched Cook carefully as he measured it out and put it into her dish. He changed her water each day and filled her food containers, but never to the brim. That way they would not spill over when Myna put her beak in. Then he replaced the carpet of newspapers.

I watched carefully so I would remember. I knew I could care for Myna just as well as Cook did, even though I could not reach the cage when it was hung in my room or in the hallway on the first floor near the side patio door out of the draft. I was determined to tend to Myna as judiciously as did Cook.

The day came when, with the aid of the little wooden footstool from the kitchen pantry, I was tall enough to reach inside Myna's cage. My job was to change her water each day and replace the soiled newspaper at the bottom of her cage. I folded the paper with care so that it fit perfectly edge to edge. I performed these tasks meticulously under Cook's supervision.

Often, I was rewarded by Myna's "Thankyouverymuch." Sometimes she would serenade me with the nursery rhymes I had taught her. She occasionally used language too shocking for my tender young ears, but I never took much notice because I was not interested in anything other than the little tidbits she had learned from me.

Finally, I was allowed to feed Myna on my own. Cook carefully explained that she ate suet and rice and sometimes sunflower seeds. Mother grew sunflowers in her vegetable garden. The giant flowers stood at attention in a single row like the soldiers during inspection at the barracks on the other side of the orchard wall. Even with the stalks bent way over from the weight of the round heavy heads, the faces were too tall for me to reach on my own. If the crows and chickens had not picked the ground clean of them, I knew I could find lots of seeds at the feet of the tall happy sunflowers.

Those first weeks Cook set Myna's food aside for me on the kitchen counter, to the side, on a low shelf where I could reach it. One day, while preparing suet for Myna, Cook reached for the rice on the counter next to the refrigerator, and a tiny mouse ran from behind the container and down onto the floor. I was delighted and wanted to catch it for a pet. Cook disagreed. He said the mouse had to go outside. I argued with him, and mother came to see what the commotion was. She sent me out of the kitchen while she and Cook looked for the mouse. I was upset. I didn't understand why I could not have the little mouse to play with.

Hours passed and I played by myself in my little room. Mother called me to lunch, and when I got downstairs she said they had found the mouse and I could look at it, but I could not have it. I was very happy to see the mouse. Cook had him in a small woven basket. His long whiskers poked through. Mother said I could go outside with Cook to release him. We tried not to kill anything except for food, because life was precious and God made all the creatures for a purpose. You didn't kill them if you could move them elsewhere to live in peace. Mother said the mouse could find a home in the orchard, so she and Cook and I went outside.

As we walked through the vegetable garden, I asked Cook if the mouse would be okay in the weather outdoors. He said the outdoors was the mouse's house and he would be fine. We walked on the stone path across the irrigation ditch up the five stone steps and into the orchard. Cook let the mouse out at the very back where he would have more shelter and a better chance to find a place to make his nest. I never saw the mouse again. I was still a little sorry I was not allowed to keep him, but I was glad he had a new home.

Mother said the mouse in the kitchen could have left diseased droppings that might make us sick. She and Cook washed the kitchen from top to bottom and checked the pantry too to make sure there were no places for any other mice to live or hide. They inspected each box and bag to make sure none had been gnawed open. It took them just about all day.

Cook inspected the container of rice that the mouse had been hiding behind on the countertop. There was a jagged hole near one corner. The rice was probably contaminated, so Cook threw it out. It was very important to keep our food clean and safe from any kind of foreign contaminant so none of us would get sick. I understood. I knew about germs. They were invisible, but they could still make you very sick. Sometimes they could kill you.

Mother said not to worry about the mouse. He had to live a mouse life just as I lived a little girl life. I understood, but it didn't make me happy. I went to my little room and tried to cheer myself up by thinking happy thoughts. I remembered sitting on mother's lap a few days earlier at the dining room table. That is where she had her late morning coffee with three teaspoons of sugar and evaporated milk from the can.

I had asked mother why she called me Ladybug. I knew she knew I didn't like my name. I felt a little bad about not liking my name, especially since she had picked it out for me. But I didn't feel bad enough about not liking my name to start liking it because she had picked it out. Mother said that ladybugs, though tiny little things, were sturdy and tough. They were valuable and indispensable (that meant impossible to do without), for a healthy flower garden.

She said that without the ladybugs, the pretty flowers would be eaten up by pests, and that would be sad. Yes, I told her I also thought that would be sad. Mother said that I was her ladybug. I made her happy, and that kept pests away. I knew that this was very important for me to remember. I decided to always try and do my best so she would always be happy with me.

Thinking about that, I went back to the kitchen. It was all scrubbed clean. Mother was making bread for dinner. She dusted flour onto the counter, poured the dough out of the bowl onto the flour, kneaded it a few times, and put it back into the bowl to rise. I asked her if she would write down the letters to spell Ladybug for me. I didn't write yet, but I could trace and draw and color. Mother showed me in a dusting of flour. She wrote it big so I could see it well:

L-A-D-Y-B-U-G

I made a picture for mother, of flowers from her garden. My perspective was from the flower bed itself, where I loved to nap in the high mountain sun. I included ladybugs, and way far back in a corner, by the wall, I put the little mouse. I found mother and gave her my picture.

I told her I would be a good girl, a real ladybug. She said that I wrote well and that I could practice any time—she would get me paper. Mother traced her finger over my carefully written L-A-Y-D-B-U-G. She smiled and said it was beautiful, but not as beautiful as I was.

Our routine soon got back to normal, and each day I rushed to wake up so I could help with Myna. Cook always had the food ready for me. I carefully cleaned the containers and filled them—rice and suet in one container, sunflower seeds in the second, and clean, fresh water in the third. One day Cook asked me if I knew where the rice was kept—well, of course I did! I was thrilled.

Cook always laid everything out for me, and I was happy to do my job of caring for Myna all by myself. Feeding Myna and cleaning her cage, making sure her needs were met, was something I looked forward to every day. This was the responsibility I had been wishing for. I was so happy.

My morning routine was predictable. First thing, I removed the night cloak from Myna's cage and she hopped from one rung to the other, her little black eyes sparkling and alert, her wings a-flutter. She went through her repertoire. "Someone's at the door" sounded more like "Someone's hat is sore." Most of her phrases had a slight twist to them and I wondered if someone might be coaching her that way. But, no matter, she was my charge. I took good care of her.

My routine with Myna rarely varied. Each morning, after carefully hanging Myna's night cloak on the long hook on the wall next to the side patio door, I changed the paper. I put fresh paper in, folded exactly to fit the bottom of the cage. I carefully removed her two food dishes and her drinking dish. I carried them to the kitchen on a small tray. Cook and I would visit while I washed the food dishes. Then I filled Myna's dishes and put them back into her cage.

One morning everything was on the counter except for the rice. No matter. I knew where the rice was. We had a gigantic burlap gunnysack full of rice in the pantry. It sat on a cookie sheet on the floor. It was bigger than I was! Of course I knew where the rice was kept. I filled one of Myna's food dishes with a little suet from the lidded crock just the way Cook showed me.

Three careful dips of the teaspoon measure. I went to the pantry and took three big pinches from the giant gunnysack. Why had Cook asked if I knew where the rice was? I filled the other container with fresh clean water, but not to the brim. I then placed the containers on a tray to take to the alcove where Myna perched on the center bar of her cage. She began to eat at once.

Leaving Myna to her food, I played all day under the Kathmandu blue sky in the happy mountain valley sunshine. I came inside only to eat my lunch of peanut butter and mayonnaise with dill pickles on big fat slices of mother's homemade buttermilk bread. Delicious. Out again I went into the big wide world of our yard. I didn't think of Myna until after my bath and bedtime. I had to put her night cloak on and wish her sweet dreams. I ran cheerfully down the back steps and tiptoed to her cage. She was so very quiet that I was certain she was already sleeping. And she was, but not of her own free will.

In a flash of understanding that washed over me like the sudden connection made when I realized I could read, I knew instantly why Cook had asked if I knew where the rice was kept. I suddenly and regretfully remembered we had kept it in the refrigerator since the visiting mouse. Each morning Cook set it out for me. On the one day he didn't, I had, to my deep chagrin, mistakenly given Myna raw rice.

There in her cage, perched on the center bar, Myna had her beak open as if to sing. Her eyes, however, had lost their sparkle, and her song was now forever silent. Myna's bright and curious spirit had flown far and away. I was left behind, bereft and broken-hearted.

It Felt Like Okra

His name was Larry Abrams and he was my best friend. He was my closest neighbor and my best friend from the first day of school on. We started kindergarten together and continued on into the first grade. We rode the school bus together and both had older brothers. Our brothers, when left to watch over us, often ran away. After several incidents of such abandonment, our mothers decided it best to keep us wee folk closer to home. Larry and I became best friends out of proximity, necessity, and shared interests.

My personal world of exploration expanded exponentially. I was no longer made to stay put; that is, watch the older kids run around while I remained moored to one spot. I got to leave our compound over the ten-foot wall, cross a dead-end street, and go into Larry's yard all by myself to play.

And play we did, from sunup to sundown. We did not know that our mothers had their eagle eyes upon us. We spent days and days constructing intricate sandbox towns for matchbox cars. We smoothed our sandy streets with shortened straws put to use as steamrollers. Skyscrapers grew from dominoes, grass sprigs became hedges, broken twigs became bridges, and submerged saucers from my tea set became small bodies of water. We floated ants in the water atop life rafts of curly geranium leaves.

The matchbox cars belonged to Larry, but the engineering and construction were mostly mine. My skill at construction and engineering was born of my long hours spent with Barbie and Skipper, my two favorite playmates before Larry. I obtained my architectural and engineering experience while designing their multilevel, Himalayan valley house and its surrounding neighborhood on my bedroom floor.

Our mothers knew we would not stray because we depended on them for our snacks and meals. In the morning, after breakfast, we spent hours driving our cars up, down, and around our vast sandbox city. Sometimes, if it had rained the day before, we had to repair the city. Or a stray animal might have bedded down in it for the night. We were forever building and rebuilding to the very edges of the sandbox. Being the youngest children in our families left us few opportunities to control our environment, so the sandbox was our paradise. We were gods, and this was our universe.

Often, when we were not in school, Larry would have breakfast at my house; other days, I had breakfast at his. Sometimes it was both breakfast and lunch. Our city planning was absorbing and exacting work and, like the ants we had not yet transferred to leafy riverboats, we were always trying to move, repair, and build.

We never fought, Larry and I. Perhaps it was the nature of our play, which was cooperative and companionable. If we got thirsty, we crawled on our bellies to the edge of the well, put our lips to the water, and sucked it up in deep, cool mouthfuls. We never stopped to remember that the water in the tanks at home or in the ceramic pitchers on the kitchen counter was boiled for a reason.

As each day passed we scavenged for items to add to our sandbox city. Empty wooden thread spools made pylons for bamboo bridges. Bits of straw fortified riverbanks. Did you know that spent matchsticks made a really nice picket fence? Have you used sunflower seed shells for cobblestones? These were some of the discoveries we made as we fine-tuned our sprawling sandbox city.

One day, in a rare moment of heeding our hunger, Larry proposed that he ask his mother if we could have our afternoon snack early. I accompanied him as far as the foot of the outside stairs. There I got sidetracked by the sight of a shiny, fat slug. It was sliming slowly along the concrete walkway and I watched it creep along where the side of the house and the sidewalk met to form a ninety-degree angle. As I had a bamboo plank handy from a recent bridge repair, it seemed natural to poke the slug with it. Larry paused and watched for a second or two before he let the screen door slam shut as he proceeded upstairs—but not before cautioning me to stop.

Squatting beside my find, I poked first one end and then the other. The slug was like a wiener-shaped water balloon. I liked water balloons, but I didn't like slugs. Larry soon returned and said his mother would call us when our snack was ready. We could play in the sandbox until then.

"Come on!" Larry called to me to help him secure the pinecone tower we had tied together with young and supple dandelion stalks. He told me to leave the slug alone and, as long as I was over by the driveway, to get some pebbles to line the sides of the main boulevard. "Come on, Melanie!"

I paid him no mind. He called me by my name and I didn't like my name, so I didn't answer. I had no time for any sandbox. I was not interested in collecting any pebbles either. I was too busy poking the slug. When I pushed this way, the lateral stripes expanded, and when I poked that way his tail end became a bubble. This way. That way. That way—PHOP!

I inhaled with surprise, and the slug was no longer on the pavement at the base of the house next to the wall. It was no longer there because it was lodged in the back of my throat right where my tongue meets my tonsils. I recoiled and gagged in horror and coughed and wailed and whirled a desperate dance of disgust and revulsion. I ran to the well at the back of the yard as fast as I could.

Once there, I hit the deck and scuttled on my belly to the edge of the well like a beetle bug scurrying over sand. At the rim of the well I planted my lips on the surface of the water and sucked it up like a parched leech on a blood worm. It didn't matter.

No amount of water would wash away the slime. No amount of coughing could regurgitate the crime. For no better reason than cruel curiosity I had poked a plump and slimy slug into oblivion. I shocked myself with my single-hearted cruelty. Larry fell over laughing, holding his sides: "I told you so! I told you so! I told you so!"

It felt like okra going down.

Kicking Cousin

I wanted a horse to ride! Rebel, our palomino, needed to be shod. The blacksmith was coming the next day. I asked mother if I could ride Cousin, our long-haired mountain horse. She said if Babu Shamraya said it was all right, then yes, I could ride him. I understood.

Truth is, I liked Rebel for his beauty and grace but I loved Cousin for his firm seat and brawn. Although his gait was surefooted and solid, he himself was dependably cantankerous, and just a little bit mean. It was because of his disposition that mother relied on Babu Shamraya's expertise with the horses. He knew best as to when they were suitable for me to ride.

Cousin liked to bite. He liked to chomp and dig his feet in to get his way. After my triumph of mastering Rebel, I found Cousin's temper tantrums only mildly irritating. I liked his broad back and surefooted gait. Cousin liked the sugar cubes I slipped to him as treats. He also liked to be groomed and had a beautiful, thick, long, brown tail. His mane was shaggy, and I loved to tether him by the kitchen door and stand on the patio wall to braid it. He tolerated me.

Babu Shamraya said, "No, not today, Cousin had a bad night." I didn't like that answer, however, I was bound by whatever Babu Shamraya said, so now neither horse was available to ride. I understood that Cousin had had a bad night, but it was early afternoon. Was he not recovered by now? I knew that when Cousin had had a bad night he was not suitable to ride the next day and that tomorrow would be better. Still, I was hoping.

I followed Babu Shamraya around the compound as he continued on his daily rounds, willing him to let me ride Cousin. It didn't work. Babu Shamraya just smiled and indulged my attempts to help here and there with the many tasks that managing a micro-farm entails. I was content to tag along and did so quite often.

We made our rounds. We fed the chickens, harvested several ears of corn for dinner, picked green beans, pulled onions, slaughtered a plump brown hen, plucked out her pretty feathers, and washed her spattered blood from the courtyard floor and walls. We put fresh hay in the stalls, gave fresh green carrot tops to the goat, and bought coriander and rock salt from the door-to-door vendor man. Then we collected wormy fruit from the orchard floor and put it in the compost pile. All the while I still kept hoping I might ride Cousin.

Babu Shamraya finally sent me to the main house. I knew he had serious work to do and I knew I would be in the way. Being dismissed didn't hurt my feelings. Babu Shamraya was just too busy to keep an eye on me. Without relinquishing my hope of getting in a ride before supper and bath time, I went inside. Mother was sewing in the upstairs loft. She always said, "How's my Ladybug?" She had a hug and a kiss for me. Mother was wearing her Chanel No. 5 perfume, and her embrace was warm and safe and kind.

I sat there in the loft with mother, and she asked me questions about my adventures. I filled her in on the happenings of the day. Her sewing loft overlooked the gated front entrance to our compound. If I stood on the window seat I could see the gatehouse presently being used as Cousin's stable.

I stood on the window seat and saw that Babu Shamraya was at the gatehouse door. He had a bucket of water and a bag of oats for Cousin's dinner. I immediately jumped down to go and help. I ran down the wide marble stairs as fast as my navy blue Ked-clad feet could take me. I rushed out the front door to the sound of mother's warning for me to be careful.

As quick as I had been, I was still too late to help with Cousin's feeding. Babu Shamraya was closing the door as I approached. He shook his head no when I asked if I could give Cousin a carrot or two. He told me Cousin needed to be alone because he was agitated. Sensing that I found this to be a very unsatisfactory explanation, Babu Shamraya knelt down and looked me in the eye. He said, "Do not open the door."

Crestfallen, I turned to walk across the front courtyard and go inside the house. Mother watched from the window above and blew me a kiss. I caught it and put it in my pocket for later. Babu Shamraya headed around the side of the house to the stables at the back of the compound. Although I knew not to play with an animal when it was eating, I thought to myself that a little peek at Cousin surely could not hurt.

I could hear, but I could not see. Soft talking came from above. I didn't yet feel the gravel of the driveway beneath me or the cool kiss of the summer valley breeze. It was dark where I lay, but I could see thin ribbons of light and sharp bright shooting stars! Slowly I began to notice that my stomach hurt and that the pressure on my chest made it hard to breathe. There was a sour taste in my mouth and a burning in my throat. I could hear the Indian Ocean roaring in my ears and I tasted the salt.

When they finally decided to open, my eyes stung with tears in reaction to the bright light of the sweet valley sun. Through a blur, I saw mother and Babu Shamraya. They spoke in hushed tones above me. I tried to speak. A bullfrog's croak was what had become of my voice.

I learned that Cousin had taken great exception to my visit. I remembered opening the door to his gatehouse stable, and I remembered the warm smell of oats and fresh hay. I also remembered my great surprise at the tremendous force propelling me backward, up and out. I landed face up with a solid thunk onto the mica-flecked gravel of the driveway. It was the Kick of Cousin. He had knocked me out and silly in a fit of pique at being disturbed while feeding.

The greater pain, however, was the hurt of having been so summarily rejected—and even more importantly, the pain of shame. I had disobeyed. In an instant I had lost mother's and Babu Shamraya's trust in me to do what I was told, to obey, without question, for my own good and for my own safety. Cousin never apologized. We would never expect him to. Although mother said Cousin was a law unto himself, I knew that getting kicked like that was my own fault. Me? I guess one could say I got some sense knocked into me by my kick from Cousin.

LADYBUG

Ladybug's Kathmandu education:

- Love sustains us
- "Eat dirt," isn't just a phrase
- Caterpillars "bite"
- People can be Grinches
- Run, don't walk
- Karma is complex
- Some Cousins kick

U. S. A.

Shiny and new.

Out of Order

We were going to America! I didn't know what to expect. Although I had been born there, I never lived in my home country. My sisters remembered mostly good things, so I was looking forward to those good things too. After we arrived, in the U.S., what impressed me more than the Statue of Liberty and the Washington Monument were the big stores. Grocery stores, especially.

I fell in love with American grocery stores and I simply loved the supermarkets. I had never seen anything like them until we came home to the United States of America and lived in Kensington, Maryland. That year held many firsts for me. One of them was learning, from a stranger, that mother was an honest-to-goodness lady. I knew that she was beautiful and I knew she was kind and smart. I already thought Mother was a lady, but this was the first time that a total stranger saw and said it out loud for everyone to hear.

We went Saturday shopping to the big center in Silver Spring, Maryland. Some people called it "Silver Springs." There may once have been more than one spring; that I didn't know. The road atlas labeled it "Silver Spring," without the "s." While we lived there, I never saw a spring or any silver. It didn't really matter, though. I knew that many places had names the origins of which nobody knew.

I liked Saturday shopping the best. It was usually just mother and I. (That's what I liked best about it.) I was the youngest, and it was too much to ask my siblings to watch after me. They were busy with their friends and I was too little to tag along. It was okay; it had always been that way. I was used to it.

I was fascinated by the super big grocery store we went to. It was not like the markets I was familiar with. In Nepal, you went from vendor to vendor and bargained to get the best price for the item you wished to purchase. Here, the price was marked on each and every item. And you could buy food in the same place as toys or even clothes! Everything was all under one great big fluorescent-lighted ceiling that went on for rows and rows and rows.

I liked to go up and down each and every aisle, which is what mother and I did. She would check the meat to make sure that the fat had been trimmed properly and inspect the apples for soft spots or bruises. We got milk in boxes called "cartons," but it was not powered milk—it was liquid milk. I remembered powdered milk. It was thin and yellow and didn't taste as good as the carton milk. I really liked the new kind of boxed milk.

Naturally, our cart would get fuller and fuller as we shopped. When we were done, we stood in line for the cashier. Mother wrote in a small book on a piece of paper that she tore out and gave to the cashier. I remembered in Nepal that we used pretty paper money and coins called "rupees." Some of the coins had holes in them. At this big grocery store, we bought the whole heaping basket of food with that one little piece of paper. Then we went home and put all of the groceries away.

Since I was just a kid, sometimes I had to use the toilet. This was a problem because in the super big grocery store in Silver Spring, where all the main roads met to go north, south, east, or west, you had to get a key for the toilet from the manager's office. I do not know why we bothered, because the bathrooms were almost always "out of order." This was bad. I was just a kid and could not wait for very long. When this happened, mother left our shopping cart in the store to take me to the barbershop across the street.

Mother always asked the grocery store manager if she could leave our overloaded cart for ten or fifteen minutes—we would be right back. He would make a quick nod, which we thought meant yes. Then again, I do not remember that he ever actually said yes. When we returned to the grocery store from the barbershop across the street, where they let us use the restroom, our shopping cart would be gone.

It happened like that three times. Mother always asked the manager where our cart was. He said it was an "unfortunate misunderstanding." Mother looked him right in his face and said, "Yes, unfortunately, you did misunderstand." The manager's face flushed a bright, hurting, pom-pom pink right up to his short, starchy straight hair that stood at attention on his head. His cheeks were chipmunk puffy, and I thought his face might pop like an overblown balloon.

There was a fourth time. I went to the manager's office. He stood outside the door. I asked him if I might please have the key to the restroom, and he said the restroom was out of order. I had looked at the restroom door on my way up to the manager's office, and there had been no sign on the door. I told the manager this.

He looked at me. He folded his arms across his chest and just looked at me. Then he said he had not put a sign on the door yet because it had just become the case, just now, that the restroom was out of order. The cashier closest to us made a big pop with bubblegum. I glanced over and she was looking at the manager and shaking her head. I walked through the store to find mother.

As we had done three times before, we parked the cart. Mother spoke to the manager, telling him we would leave the cart and be back very shortly. We were not finished shopping; she wanted him not to misunderstand. She said you always had to give a person the benefit of the doubt. We walked past the row of cashiers to leave the store.

Just as we got to the doors, mother saw that I had a pack of chewing gum in my hand. She told me to go back and put it in our cart. I had to hurry; my bladder was close to popping. I walked as quickly as I could past the row of cashiers, and when I got to our cart, the cashier closest to the manager's office was speaking to the manager in a loud voice. The people in her line were all looking at her and the manager. The bag boy stood at the end of the row with an open brown bag.

The cashier said: "Stop it, Percy, you just stop it. Now you know that woman has always acted like a true lady. She's never given you cause to act so ugly. Every time that lady tells you she'll be back, this is what you do. Every time. I'll bet she hasn't even got out of the store, and here you are unloading her cart. You're lucky that lady hasn't reported you to the front office."

I stood and watched, with the package of gum in my hand. I realized there was no doubt at all. There had never, ever, been any kind of misunderstanding. Here was the manager of the grocery store emptying our cart when mother had told him we would be back. I didn't understand why he would do such a thing.

It made me think of the other times I had gone to ask for the key to use the store facilities and the manager had told me they were out of order. That is what he always told me, even the time I had followed a woman who was returning the key to the office. She handed the key to him, he took it, and when I asked for it, he told me the bathroom was out of order.

The woman who had handed him the key had only said thank you. I didn't know how that meant that the bathroom was out of order. I had not understood how the manager and the cashiers and the bag boys and the butchers and the bakery people could go all day and not use the toilet. Now I did.

I remembered back to the first time I had ever used the public toilet in the store. I had gone to the manager's office, and the cashier closest to the office told me to hurry to the restroom because a lady had already borrowed the key and I could get it from her. I waited by the restroom door. When the lady came out, she held the door open for me and said she would take the key back. Before I could go inside, the manager walked up and told me to stop. I did, and he went inside. He had an empty brown grocery bag with him. He snapped it open with one hand, walked into the room, and closed the door behind him.

While he was in there, another lady arrived and stood in line next to me. When the manager came out of the bathroom, he was carrying the brown grocery bag and it was bulging. I didn't see with what. As he passed by, I held the door open and then went inside. I then realized he had taken all the toilet paper and hand towels out.

Why would he do that? No matter, I used tissues from the nifty travel packet in my pocket. After I washed my hands, I used my Mary Poppins handkerchief to dry them. I opened the door to go out, and the manager was standing in the hallway. He wore a tight, mean little smile, and his eyes were bright with expectation.

I gave the lady who was waiting to use the toilet my nifty tissue travel packet. She said, "Oh, thank you, young lady, that's so kind of you. You'd think this store would keep such necessities in the restroom. You are a true dear."

Just before she went through the door, she stopped. She called out to the manager, waving the packet of tissues. "You're the manager, aren't you?" she said, "Why is there no tissue or paper towels in here?" Mr. Percy didn't answer. He turned and quickly walked away.

Now, here mother and I were again, needing to leave the grocery store with the out-of-order restroom, and I stood with the pack of gum in my hand. What should I do with it? It didn't seem to make sense to put it in the cart, since the manager was tossing all of our groceries into the various sorting bins for discarded merchandise. His back was to me, but the cashier lady saw me when he said, "We don't need no damn nigra money or nigras in the store. I'm the manager and I'll empty this cart if I want to."

The people in line all looked at me. I don't know why. Mr. Percy turned around and saw me. The top of his head was wet with sweat, and his eyes got wide with surprise before he could help it. I recognized him as one of those Grinches who never turned good-hearted. As I watched, his face got blotchy pink and turned a deep dark shade of blood-orange red. He looked at the customers in line.

The cashier leaned back, watching him with her arms folded. She blew big pink bubblegum bubbles. Everybody looked at Mr. Percy and then everybody looked at me. Ping, they looked at Mr. Percy. Pong, they looked at me. I held up the pack of chewing gum and asked, "Should I put this in my mother's shopping cart, or in these bins?"

Mr. Percy snorted like a bulldog and started to walk toward me. He shoved the bag boy aside. I stepped back, and the cashier was suddenly at attention. I heard a chorus of gasps at the same time I felt mother's hand on my shoulder. She pulled me to her. Mr. Percy stopped in his tracks, shook his head, and turned on his heels. He stomped off in the other direction. Everybody started talking at once. We put most of the things he had taken out of our cart back in.

The cashier said, "Ma'am, I apologize on behalf of the store. That man has got a problem. I think he's gone and blown a gasket. Now y'all don't mind if I take this honest-to-goodness lady and her little girl and ring them on up ahead of you?"

Mother said, "Thank you, that is very kind of you all, we will take our place at the end of the line."

Then Sherry, the cashier, pointed to the front: "Well then, this here is the back of the line so you just pull you cart right over." Before we could, the bag boy did. Sherry rang us up out of order.

Rickover Road

I got wheels! My first, very own, brand-new two-wheeler bike. It was back when my family lived for a short time in the U.S.A., in the state of Maryland, in a town called Kensington. We lived in a house at the top of a wide, winding street named Rickover Road.

My new bicycle had a golden frame, white fenders, silver handlebars, white-fluted hard rubber handles, and a ding-da-ding-ding bell! But that was just for starters. It also had a really comfortably cushioned gold and white wedge of a seat, a silver rack over the fender in back, and a light brown wicker basket with darker brown leather straps in front. That bike was bigger than I was! Mother said it was something for me to grow into.

What a day of celebration! All of the neighborhood kids... Well, not exactly. That year, I learned a new concept in Kensington, Maryland. We were the integrating black family. This was not very good news to some of the Rickover residents. Some of the kids and their parents thought skin color was contagious. They all quarantined themselves against us in their Rickover homes. I wondered if their minds brewed racism and it overflowed and coated them with ignorance.

Before our move to Kensington, I never knew people as colors. This idea was very hard for me to understand. I knew that some people were good and some people were bad. Most people I had ever met were more good than bad. I still thought people were people. People as colors was foreign to me. We did have a few neighbors who treated us kindly from the very first day. They knew we were just people like them. They didn't treat us like a bad germ or an ugly color.

I knew colors. My Sunday shoes were patent leather and shiny as polished onyx. Those shoes were black. My cousin on my father's side had eyes as blue as azurite and skin the color of cornstarch. He was called "black." I called him Uncle Joe. I had seen crows with lustrous black feathers darker than a moonless midnight sky. I knew that was black.

What I didn't understand was how so many things that I could see with my own eyes were not black, were called black. I wondered if anyone had read "The Emperor's New Clothes" by Hans Christian Andersen. I thought the self-quarantined Rickover residents needed to believe their own eyes. But I was just a kid; it didn't matter what I thought.

Most of the neighborhood kids gathered around my new bike to admire and touch it. These kids had bikes too. There were bikes with banana seats, handlebars trailing foot-long streamers, horns, tiger stripes, and daisy-flower paint jobs. The most favored activity was racing down the long lazy sloping smooth black tongue that was Rickover Road. That was what these kids did at every opportunity.

Skateboards, skates, and bikes took to the road that was just made for riding. Most of the parents in cars treated us kids with great care and caution. We hogged the road in play, and the parents were patient and indulgent. Sometimes, inching to a complete stop, they let us rush by screaming and laughing with thoroughly raucous glee. These were races nobody ever really won or lost.

From sunup to sundown, it seemed, we stayed and played on Rickover Road. From the crest of the hill to the bend by the hooting owl's oak tree, to the broad sweeping end of the road's ribbon of a black tongue, we crissed and crossed and ran out of steam. When rested and recovered, we rushed to do it all over again.

LADYBUG

Was it Christmas or a birthday? Just now, I do not recall. I do know my Raleigh was the bike of bikes, with whitewall tires and sparkling silver spokes. I practiced riding across the street and back again in front of our house at the top of the hill. The other kids did the usual whooshing down that dragon's back of a road. They then trudged back up to the top for a repeat. My new ride was bigger than I was. To sit on the seat meant that no pedals touched my feet, just my tip-tiptoes. I was content to push off and glide. I stopped with extra effort when my saddle shoes braked against the asphalt. It was rough stopping.

I liked this new bike, but it occurred to me that there had to be a better way to stop. The pedal brakes were missing, and even my little mind thought it was dumb not to have brakes on a bike. I thought my folks had put it together—maybe they forgot to install the brakes. My shoes weren't going to last at this rate. What would happen when I went really fast and needed to stop? Soon the other kids were revving up for a downhill race. I voiced my concern, and someone said to use the handle brakes. I got it. Perfect.

I didn't have time to reflect and feel silly, because now I could do anything. Handle brakes. They worked just fine. I practiced and learned quickly that left was slow on the back wheel and right was tight on the front. I learned quickly not to use the too-tight right brake alone or a bike flip would result. With the brakes engaged together very carefully, I could stop on a dime.

Brake, brake! Fast brake. Brakes lock—stop! We stopped, my bike and I. *Boyoy-yoing.* Whack into the weathered trunk of the wide and knobby old oak tree. We dropped, my bike and I. The bike fell hard to the left, with me on the seat, toe tips touching pedals, hands on the fluted white rubber grips. The hooting owl's song shot around my head like sharp and brittle

111

stars. It was good to know how well the brakes worked. The bike was a keeper. That night I used one of mother's shiny silver embroidery needles to meticulously carve my initials on my trusted Raleigh's frame.

The Real American Elementary School

We walked to school, my brother and I. He walked fast, I could not keep up with him. I usually ended up on the path by myself. Alone on the woodland path, I walked over a small bridge that crossed a trickle of a creek. I walked on along the path to the local school. I had never walked to school before. Walking would not have been remarkable except for the fact that I always found myself on the pathway all alone.

No matter how many children or parents there were walking with their children, headed to the shortcut through the forest to the school grounds, it seemed as though I always entered and exited that woodland path by myself. On this path, kids who played with me after school or on Saturdays pretended not know me.

I never thought to be scared on that path. The trees grew close together and branches grabbed at my hair, that was all. Sometimes the leaves were slippery under my shoes. Sometimes the wind made the leaves swirl and stick to my coat. At those times, I hurried up so I would be close enough to hear the people on the path ahead of me, or I slowed down a bit so I could hear those from behind. Maybe I was a little scared.

The school I attended was a real American elementary school. I had gone to Lincoln School in Kathmandu, Nepal, but I think it didn't count as real since it was not in America. My parents impressed upon me that this was a real American elementary school. I just wondered if I would have any friends there. I hoped so. I missed the ones I had left at the American elementary school in Nepal.

LADYBUG

There was talk of putting me back a grade because the principal didn't know if I could keep up with the other children. I was so proud to be in America, in an American school, that I didn't much listen. My ears tuned in when the principal said that he didn't believe my report cards from Kathmandu. How could I already know multiplication tables up to twelve and long division with three-digit numbers? I wondered why not, but I didn't say anything out loud. The principal told my parents that we could try third grade, but that if there was any trouble he would have to put me back to second.

The new American elementary school was odd. My new teacher was smiles and nods when the principal brought me to the classroom. While he watched, she told me to choose any seat I wanted. I sat in the middle of the third row. After I sat at the desk of my choice, she didn't look at me again, but I was careful to pay close attention to the teacher all day that first day.

The next day, the teacher, Mrs. Porter, moved me from the desk I had selected the day before. She moved me to the first row. Her desk was directly ahead. I do not know why, but she could not see me as I sat there. No matter how often I raised my hand, she didn't call on me. I didn't mind, really. The many other students could answer the questions too. After a while, I didn't raise my hand anymore.

Sometimes Mrs. Porter would come around from her desk and stop right next to mine. She asked me questions about what we studied the day before - I always knew the answers. Sometimes she would ask me one question, then another, and another and another. It was like a surprise test, but I was always prepared. Mrs. Porter didn't know how much I liked school or that I paid good attention in class or that I always did my homework. Sometimes I even did the extra-credit exercises, but she never graded them. That is, if she did, I never knew it because she didn't give any of them back to me.

One day I asked Mrs. Porter if I could have my extra-credit assignments back. She just stared at me. Her eyes were hard; her mouth was small, as though she had something sour in her cheeks. She didn't answer me, she just stared. I said, "Thanks anyway." Her face turned pink, like well-chewed Bazooka bubblegum.

Recess was mean. After a couple of weeks I realized that I was the recess for the other American kids. In some games the kids would make a circle around me and sing songs and not let me out. At first, I didn't know I was the joke. When I figured this out, I just stayed close to the schoolhouse doors near where we lined up after recess. It was closer to where the teachers were. The teachers never noticed me though; they kept their eyes on the other children. They stood apart, talking with each other, and smoked cigarette after cigarette until it was time to line up and go inside.

Sets of squares for hopscotch were painted on the blacktop near where the teachers stood. I played on them alone. Sometimes girls would come over—I would think they were coming to join me. They only wanted to play where I was. Without me. There were three separate games on the blacktop; the girls used only one, but they didn't want me there. They talked about me in front of my face.

Some of these girls were kids from my block. I had thought we were friends. We played together many times on Rickover Road. In front of our other classmates, these girls pretended not to know me. They acted like complete strangers. When they looked in my eyes their faces turned pink. In my head I called them *Bazooka* girls.

Other kids who were not in my class sometimes came over to where I was playing. They were never nice. Once they pulled me away to play one of their circle games, but by then I knew what those games were. I didn't want to go. I told them so. The teachers looked over with hard faces and let them drag me away. Some of the kids hit me. I looked for my brother, thinking maybe he could help, but he was in a different grade. We didn't have recess at the same time.

The mean kids called me dirty, I didn't know why. When I looked at the hands pulling at me and pushing at me, I could see caked dirt under the fingernails. I looked at my hands and could see that under my fingernails was white. My clothes where these kids touched them got smudged with dirt. I guessed that meant they made me dirty. Yes, they made me dirty. The teachers looked on. They stood smoking their cigarettes with stone-hard faces. Their brightly painted nails glittered at me in the distance.

One day a boy in my class came by the hopscotch. He asked me why I was playing alone. He said I could come with him and play over by the monkey bars. I thought, now here is a friend! The monkey bars were on the far side of the blacktop. When we got there the boy ran off laughing, and I was left with kids who didn't like me. They tried to lift up my dress and called me a monkey. One of the girls pinched me. Another stole a barrette off my hair. When mother asked about it, I told her I had lost it. I was careful to play only by myself after that.

I had never met people like these American kids before. My friends at the American elementary school in Nepal didn't act ugly and mean the way the real American elementary school kids did. Everyone said how things were bigger and better in the United States. Not everything that I learned about was better. I knew that how the kids behaved was wrong. I was surprised that they didn't know it. I decided that it was best to keep to myself and stay away from them no matter who in my class might try to get me to play. I was all alone at the real American elementary school.

Mrs. Wyler's Smile

Her name was Mrs. Wyler. She liked to smile. She lived on our street, past the curve at the bottom of the hill. She had three kids who went to my school. I didn't know her very well, but I think she didn't like me. At school, I sat in my classroom in the first row next to her daughter, Polly. Mrs. Wyler was a watchful mother. I think she wanted to make sure we kids played nicely together. She always watched from her kitchen window when the other neighborhood kids and I played in the road or on the sidewalk close to her house. Polly played in her own yard and was not allowed to join us. I think she wanted to.

One day we played kickball in the yard next to Polly's house. The kids let me play because the ball was mine. I could run fast and kick hard, but they didn't know that right away because I didn't get to kick until last. The game was tied and everybody on my team groaned when I stepped up to kick the ball for my turn. I didn't mind. I knew I could bring everybody home with the bases loaded, but they didn't.

I kicked the ball and it went fast and far. My team won, so the kids on my team liked me well enough that day. When the other team brought the ball back, it was close to dinnertime and we all began to head to our homes. Polly stood in her yard, and as I passed, she asked if she could play with my ball.

We stood facing each other. She stood on the grass in her yard, and I stood on the sidewalk. I had not made up my mind when Mrs. Wyler rushed out of her house. She bustled over to where Polly and I stood. It looked as though she had not had time to get dressed yet that day. She was still wearing her bathrobe and slippers. Her hair was in pink sponge rollers like the ones my sisters had.

Mrs. Wyler asked me what I wanted. Polly said she wanted to play with the ball. Before I could speak, Mrs. Wyler told me that it was important to share and that of course Polly could play with the ball. She took my ball from me with an ugly smile. She gave my red rubber kickball to Polly. Mrs. Wyler then told me to go on home and walked away. The hem on her bathrobe was out in the back, and a thread trailed all the way down to the ground.

I stayed, but I didn't say anything. Polly held the kickball, as though she didn't know what to do with it. When Mrs. Wyler got to her front door, she turned. She saw that I was still standing on the sidewalk. She made a loud noise like a horse's snort and charged toward us like a bull. She came back to where Polly and I stood and demanded to know why I was still there. She smiled.

Mrs. Wyler's lips were red, like the rubber of my kickball. Her teeth were big and straight. They were not very white. Her eyes were hard. They were a robin's egg blue, and the corners were yellow and puffy. I looked at her warily; I was afraid she was a Grinch person. Mrs. Wyler's eyes glittered like jagged bits of broken glass and looked to me to be as dangerous.

I said that Polly could play with my ball tomorrow, but I would take it home with me tonight. Polly handed the ball back to me. I took it and said, "Thank you, Polly."

Mrs. Wyler sucked in her breath and said, "You give my Polly that ball!" She smiled a Grinch smile, and the words came out through her teeth like steam from a whistling kettle. Her face was splotched with red. She dug in one of her pockets and excavated a bent cigarette.

I started to walk away, and Mrs. Wyler stepped off her grass to block me on the sidewalk. She said, "Have you forgotten how to share, little girl?" I stepped back. I looked up at her. She was big like a water buffalo and her fingernail polish was chipped at the very edges. It was a bright happy pink like fresh Bazooka bubble gum. Her bathrobe was not completely closed. Under it, she wore a see-through nightgown. It was blue, like her eyes, with a thick white ruffle down the front.

Mrs. Wyler lit her crooked cigarette with a shiny silver lighter and blew smoke directly into my face. The smoke made my eyes burn. I was allergic to cigarette smoke. I felt my throat get small. I didn't know what to do. I knew I didn't want to leave without my ball.

Just then, one of the kids from the other kickball team walked up to us. He lived two houses down from me and across the street. Bruce said he would like to be on my team the next day if I would let them use my ball again. I looked at Mrs. Wyler. There was no smile, not even a fake Grinch smile. She threw her cigarette near my feet and took Polly's arm. She marched Polly across the lawn to the front door of their house.

Mrs. Wyler pushed Polly inside the house. She stood on her front step with her hands on her hips. She glared at me. If her glare could have shot flames, I would have been on fire. Mrs. Wyler's beautiful, blue, robin's egg eyes were stone-cold flat with hatefulness. Polly was in the doorway behind her so I waved good-bye. Mrs. Wyler whirled her back to me and slammed the door shut.

Suddenly, it was much cooler. I shivered as I turned to go home. Bruce stood on the sidewalk, he was waiting for me. We walked up the hill together. He said I was a good kickball player. He smiled, and then he laughed. He said I had taken his whole team by surprise with that home run. His eyes were sparkling brown and warm, filled with good cheer. His mouth crinkled in the corners. I looked at Bruce and thought he should teach Mrs. Wyler how to smile.

LADYBUG

Ladybug's American discoveries:

- Grinches thrive
- People in the U.S.A. are colors
- Out of order isn't always
- Ugly is as ugly does
- Brakes are essential
- Share does not mean share alike
- Proceed with caution is good advice

MELANIE L. MARSHALL

UPPER VOLTA
(BURKINA FASO)

Uncompromisingly glorious. Truth in all her stunning beauty.

MELANIE L. MARSHALL

LADYBUG

Ungawa!

We moved to Africa! We went to live in the West African country of Upper Volta, now known as Burkina Faso. Nobody asked me, but I had mixed feelings about going—excitement, certainly, but mostly anxiety and fear. Fear and anxiety all tied up and lumped together to make my insides tumble. Anxiety and fear squeezing on my poor heart was what I felt at any given time. I didn't know anything about any place in Africa other than what I had learned from Tarzan movies.

I could see Tarzan calling for the elephants at the water hole—the water hole near the grass-hut village where little children got snagged and eaten by the crocodiles and alligators that lurked in the muddy piranha-infested water! And sometimes, sometimes, the grass fence around the settlement didn't keep the hungry lions and tigers out. Lions and tigers! The lions and tigers roared on the dusty dirt-brown paths looking to pounce on two-legged prey. Nobody could have told me otherwise. I could not articulate my dread.

A blast of heat slammed the breath out of my lungs. It shot in through the doorway of the airplane and beat at me with slapping hits and stinging punches. I struggled with the seat belt to deplane. It was a hard heat, solid steam. It was dense and mean enough to singe my hair; cruel enough to poach my eyes. I stood, near blinded, at the top of the roll-away stairs. With blurred vision, I saw a wide swath of undulating black licorice.

The licorice spread out in an unbroken dark wave. It was a molten river of rolling tar. No, it was the tarmac. The tarmac stretched out in every direction as far as my little self could see. Far and away, wavering shapes of people and animals stretched out like dancing fingers of smoke. Then, inexplicably, they vaporized into oblivion where the tarmac met the horizon.

I saw bright dots of rainbow colors and swirling dust before it dissolved and shimmered out of sight. Or perhaps I saw nothing. Whatever I did or didn't see, I know my eyes hurt. The stinging bite of heat was as bitter as a wasp's kiss, searing and raw. That heat ripped through my tender heart and stomped on my timid soul without any introduction or apology.

The ground melted into me, and each breath became a chemical burn. The fiery air grilled my lungs and cooked my blood. I think I felt my brain simmer; I thought it might pop right there in my head. It was so hot that I burned my feet because I stopped too long on the melted tarmac.

That black lava sucked my shoes off. I think my socks caught fire! My brand-new penny loafers got glued to the ground. Their rubber soles melted into mush beneath my burning feet. I struggled to keep up; each step was a walk-on-hot-coals experience. Those ahead showed no sign of slowing down in this, our first encounter with the scorching fire of Ouagadougou.

We sweltered in the shade of the airport terminal and unidentifiable odors assailed us from all sides. Here was the perfume of many people, livestock, carts, cloth, and kindling. Here was air so hot we should have been ashes. Here was slow-baked dust, born brown, burned red, turned orange, bleached yellow, and saturated with moisture. Here was mystery and intrigue, the incomprehensible language of Babylon. *Bienvenue*, said the sign at the airport. Welcome.

In our gigantic World Atlas, Ouagadougou sat in the center of Upper Volta. There was no Lower Volta, just Upper and Ouagadougou was the capital city. I tried to be appreciative as I struggled to breathe the dragon-fire air. My brain tried to register the fact that we were in Africa. I could also see with my own eyes that we were in the heart of an exotic, smoldering, pungent, and starkly beautiful land. I knew I appreciated that. I appreciated beauty and I wondered if it was possible that I stood on the very pulse of Volta. I knew even then that it was a place I would never forget.

After a few days in Ouagadougou we traveled from there, by car, in our sky-blue Ford country sedan, to Bobo Dioulasso. Bobo was a city in the southwest corner of the country. Burkina bordered several different countries: Mali to the north; Ghana, and Togo to the south; Niger to the east; Côte d'Ivoire to the south west, and Benin to the south east. Bobo Dioulasso was a city full of contrasts, full of life, full of surprises.

Back in Kensington, Maryland, when I had looked up Upper Volta in the World Book Encyclopedia, and in the World Atlas, I learned the country was one of the poorest in the world, the climate was tropical and there was a rainy season and a dry one. There were several lakes and three rivers that crossed the country. It was fun to say the names of the lakes, I made a chant of my favorites: Yomboli-Tingrela-Dem-Oursi-Bam!

I liked the names of the rivers too: le Nazinon, le Nakamb and le Mouhoun. They sounded mysterious and important. Translated, the names were ordinary: the Red Volta, the White Volta and the Black Volta. The Atlas didn't show the few trees or the color of the land. The reality stunned me. Neither reference book showed the miles and miles of flat brush country that baked in the stinging heat. The earth was ochre, the trees scarce and exquisitely beautiful because of their scarcity.

There were wide, tree-lined avenues in Bobo. They were witness to the country's French colonial past. A few lavish villas tucked behind high privacy walls were a testament to that same history. The water, when you could find it, sat in deep, pools or fell in bruising torrents from the white-hot sky. It lashed the earth from dark, heavy, thunderclouds or poured across the cracked and buckling ground in a great rush only to disappear in a second without even a trail of steam. In the rainy season, the floods came quickly and destroyed anything in their path indiscriminately.

It was as oppressively hot in Bobo as it had been those first few days in Ouagadougou. Even so, it was not hot enough to stem or deter my curiosity, despite my great discomfort. Also, I learned I would be leaving for boarding school soon, so I thought I could cheerfully bear a few burning months in Bobo.

I explored the town as much as I could. It was, after all, a fantastic place. Bobo was full of interesting sights and people who were both kind and generous. My first expedition on my own was an outing to meet our neighbors. The boy next door attended the French school. He introduced his sister to me. Kalima was two years older than I. She didn't attend school. Most girls didn't. That didn't stop Kalima from being one of the smartest and most beautiful girls I had ever met.

I loved our neighbors. I loved visiting with them. I watched how Kalima skinned a goat and scraped and stretched the skin so that it lay flat without even the hint of a curl. She could weave long, thin grasses together so that the warp and the weft were tight enough to repel water. I threw myself into all of Kalima's activities that I could. I sensed that this was important.

I knew it was important to learn from Kalima, I believed it was important for me to live as consciously in the present as she did. It seemed the most natural thing to do. I also wanted to prove to myself that I really was in Africa and that those lions and tigers and bears of my imagination, of my fears, would not eat me up.

I never saw tigers or bears, but I encountered bugs of all dimensions and improbable characteristics. The stick bug was my favorite. It looked just like a stick. If you wanted to find one, you would be disappointed, but when you least expected it, a twig would move! That was the stick bug. As a family, we met my father's colleagues and staff. They were beautiful people, and their kindness made living in a big frying pan of a place much easier. We even went to meet NoNo the gorilla in the Bobo Zoo. Nobody really knew how old he was. They knew only that he had been there forever and didn't like bananas.

If Your Mommy Says So

John Wayne came to visit! It was early summer, just before the rains. My brothers and sisters were home from boarding school, and a John Wayne Western dubbed into French was playing at the town cinema. I wanted to go with my siblings to the movie, but they, preferring to be free of a tag-a-long baby sister, told me to ask my father. If it was all right with him, they said, they would agree. I asked my father. He said, "Ask your mommy; if she says you may go, it is fine with me." I knew mother would agree. Elated, I ran through the house toward the kitchen where she was organizing the pantry.

We had just received our twice-yearly shipment of supplies, which included canned goods, clothes, and sewing notions for mother. The wooden crates banded with metal stays lined the entire hallway right up to the kitchen door. In my haste, anticipation, and excitement, I misjudged the angle of protrusion of one of the containers. I ran full force into the corner of one of the sturdy wooden crates.

I remember the shock of impact. I remember the pain. It was a deep, clean cut, clear down to the bone below my right knee in the shape of a perfect triangle. The white of the bone was exposed, and I watched in detached fascination as tiny pinpricks of blood bubbled and swelled. Each separate blot blossomed, burst, and slowly spread. It touched its mates and coalesced into a single blob of a glistening red. Then the blood spurted from that deep, throbbing gash as from a fountain. My brain noted this and catalogued the phenomenon as curious.

The initial shock of pain was soon a distant memory. At the moment, I felt immense irritation at the inconvenience of my injury. I knew that dressing the wound would delay our departure for the movies. With this in mind, I hobbled as quickly as I could all the way down the narrow hallway. I left a vibrant red and viscous trail in my wake from the point of impact with the box all the way into the brightly lit kitchen.

Holding my mangled leg up for mother to see and asking her permission to go to the movie at the same time didn't produce the result I expected. The deep cut gushed blood. My father came to investigate the noise he had heard in the hallway. He heard me ask mother if I could go to the movies and instantly vetoed my request.

Mother administered first aid to the offended knee, and father poured a medicinal shot of Cointreau. Mother coaxed it down my throat. It burned all the way down and then smoldered in my belly. I didn't cry, I was still hopeful. To cry would mean missing the movie. I just had to see John Wayne, it wasn't every day that a star like him came to town. I could not walk, so I missed the movie anyway. Then I cried.

My tears, which came after the tincture of iodine, after the shot of Cointreau, and after the mosquito netting was tucked in around my bed to shield me from the fever-spreading stinging pests, were for the lost opportunity. I would have hopped to the movies on one leg if they could have seen their way to letting me out of the house that night.

In my liquor-induced dreams I reasoned, quite soundly I thought, that my brothers and sisters should take turns carrying me to the cinema. After all, it was not even a kilometer away. There were four of them and there was only one of me. Mathematically, it worked out. The crate scar is still there—a silent reminder to take things more slowly, to watch where I am going. And perhaps, to be more careful if I really wish to get there.

You Gotta Speak Their Language

Heat ruled with ferocity in Bobo. There was not much to do for entertainment in the height of the Bobo Dioulasso summer. Daring dust devils roamed the streets along with belligerent incendiary breezes. The crickets didn't sing, and even the most persistent flesh-stinging blue flies found shelter from the scorching rays of the volcanic Voltan sun.

My brother and I were just two crazy-bored kids with play on our minds and the imagination to work at making up fun. I had heard it said that only mad dogs and Englishmen go out in the noonday sun. We were by no means Englishmen, but we met a couple of mad dogs one day.

It was siesta time, and all was quiet until my brother and I burst onto the marble walkway on the terrace level of the main building where we lived. We had our metal-wheeled roller skates on. I do not recall whose idea it was; I do know the noise we made was louder than the roar of monsoon rains on corrugated tin rooftops and we were having scads of fun.

Our marble rink was wide and smooth, with deep-set rectangular slabs of roller-skating luxury. The marble could be dangerously slippery, but we were careful to learn the nuances of turning like pros and the importance of coordinated stepping to miss the deep crevices between the slabs. It was paramount to remaining upright and unbloodied.

Playing with my brother was always a contest of wills—will he chase me, will I fall, will I hit that pillar? And, in this case, will I out skate him? This was the same brother who, with his friends, would dub me "IT" in games of hide-and-seek and then leave the neighborhood. Oh, I would find him eventually—later, hours later, sitting with his friends at their kitchen table eating a snack as though nothing was amiss. He often proposed rules of a game and then changed them without ever telling me.

Well, this was yet another country and another day and I let bygones be bygones. With time and experience, I didn't fall for the mid-game rule changes anymore; but whenever there was the possibility of being run over, run into, or just plain run down, it still paid to keep well away from him.

We had the latest in roller skates; the kind that slipped onto your shoes and were tightened with a square-ended key. I wore my skates with black and white saddle shoes, and they fit snuggly—so much so, that at times it was difficult to get them off. I wore my skate key on a yellow satin ribbon around my neck. The ribbon was long enough that I could pull it over my head but not long enough to get tangled and strangle me in a freak accident. See—I actually thought about such things.

Rolling from end to end of our marble-paved rink we made huge amounts of noise. We raced like Olympians in the burly-thick heat of the siesta-time sun. We rasped along the marble, metal to stone, mean with speed, disappearing from one another's sight between the twenty-foot-high columns at either end of the enormous cool marble terrace. I never lingered too long between the columns because there my brother sometimes took the opportunity to pounce on me roaring like I imagined NoNo, the mountain gorilla who resided at the Bobo city zoo down the street and around the corner from our compound might.

I learned that the fastest way to get through the tall and treacherous colonnade forest and avoid a fraternal attack was to hook an arm around the waist of one of the wide, fluted columns and let momentum swing me in whichever direction kept me farthest from my brother. In this way, I could propel myself to the other side and roll halfway across the wide white surface before he could catch me. I also learned that the more I jumped, or the more agitation I showed, the longer my brother would bother me. So my strategy was to be calm, stay calm, and never, ever jump. This strategy served me well, and I was congratulating myself on yet another perfect pass. Or so I thought.

Upon reaching the other side and safety, I was surprised to hear labored breathing behind me. Slowly I turned, bit by bit, careful not to roll too fast. I reminded myself: be calm, do not jump, and he will leave me alone. But instead of my brother, there stood before me a big, mangy cur of a black dog, snorting like an angry bull, wildly shaking his head as though he had a blue fly in his ear. On his left stood his twin.

These hounds had full, round jowls the size of frying pans and mouths that dripped like broken faucets. They snuffled like truffle pigs to the beat of my startled heart. They were clearly not of the friendly persuasion. They stood on point, chests broad and dense with muscle, tails straight like flagpoles, and produced a deep gruff rumbling sound like roiling, boiling, hot water in a kettle just before the whistle blows. This was danger personified, and I was in trouble.

Squosh-squersh-roosh! My brother careened around the column, startling both me and the beasts. He stopped short, and the dogs jumped sideways, bellowing like elephants on the rampage. They shook their heads and sprayed our feet with globs of spit, white as fresh-whipped meringue. With teeth bared, the beasts crouched low and began to circle us. The hair on their backs stuck out like cactus spines. The hair on the back of my neck did too.

Fight or flight? Flight it was, because my brother took off and I followed. Down the wide flat steps to the sound of scrambling paws. We were not going to make it. I felt the warm spray of spit on my calves, and in an instant the hem of my dress was seized in the jaws of death. I was stopped short.

Just as suddenly I found myself spinning in place, pirouetting like a prima ballerina as the lead dog flew by with a hunk of my yellow and white seersucker sundress streaming out behind him like a banner in a victory parade. Both dogs passed in a wave of tension and skidded to a halt between me and my brother. All for one and one for all. The fight gurgled up inside me—someone was going down!

As caution flew completely to the wind, my brother stopped abruptly, turned, and skated back. He sped forward with crashing metal steps, and I did too. The dogs backed into each other. I do not think they meant to, because they bucked like horses and snapped at each other. My hair stood on end. They looked first at me, then at my brother, as we rushed toward them on our shrieking metal skates, both of us screaming with genuine fear and false bravado.

I made tight fists of my hands—fingers tucked, thumbs alongside, boxer style—the way my older brother had shown me. The little voice in my head told me that my fist strategy was no match for fangs, but I could not afford to listen. The Cerberean mutts stood their ground their hair bristled like a prehistoric dinosaur's ridges. They showed their fangs with mouths a-froth and jowl-jaws a-snap-snap-snapping.

The distance between us evaporated in the scary high noon heat. My brother let out a roaring bellow fierce enough to fend off a werewolf. The hounds snapped to attention, and we saw madness in their rheumy eyes. I do not know if I had time to think what would happen when we met in a single space. Turns out I didn't have to.

Suddenly, and to our great surprise, the two flea-bitten, mud-and hair-matted fiends turned from us as gracefully as synchronized swimmers in an Esther Williams water extravaganza and sped away across the compound. In a stampede of thunder and a shower of dust, they hurled themselves through the jagged gap in the iron gate and scampered from our sight. I heard their nails rip at the orange-brown dirt of the roadway. I imagined they ran with tails tucked between their legs. I guess you had to speak their language, which was interesting, because we had never learned rabid.

All summer I got acclimated. Or I thought I did. Just when I got to thinking this was not so bad, new mysteries presented themselves. I got to explore them and to find out how amazing they were. As the carefree days of summer fun wound down, I stood for fittings while mother made me new clothes. I got to sew name tags into everything that was going with me, even my socks. Soon it was time to pack.

But I didn't get to pack. My brothers and sisters did. They packed up their clothes and shoes and books for boarding school. I didn't. I learned I would not be going with them.

After an entire summer of buildup and encouragement about going away? After an entire summer of new sights and sounds and tentative friendships? After an entire summer of experiencing the wonders of the Bobo Dioulasso market? After an entire summer of clean fresh air, delicious new foods, and teasing from my siblings? How did I feel about remaining in Bobo?

I was not crushed about remaining behind. I stayed in Bobo. I went to the French school. I was the new kid in school. Everyone knew about me before I even got there. At least I had a friend on my very first day. Kalima's brother, Nadim, went there too.

American Girl

Once again, I was the new kid in school. The first day of school came too quickly, and I was afraid. I didn't know the language, I didn't know the children; I didn't want to go! I went. I was a kid, what choice did I have? I went and I quickly became the teacher's pet.

Oddly enough, I did know a few words of French. I knew the French national anthem. I had learned it in Nepal. When my teacher, Mme. Priochet, found out that that was the little bit of French I knew, she insisted I sing it in front of the entire class.

So, that first day of school, I sang "La Marseillaise" flawlessly in French with proper intonation, perfect accent, and all verses intact. No one had heard it done before! In a single day I achieved instant celebrity. All I had wished for was anonymity. I was the new kid again and, now too, the teacher's pet. This was an enviable position and one I think I got without earning.

I was the American girl who could sing "La Marseillaise." Anonymity was not going to happen. That fact rather unsettled me on the first day of school. The few other French words I knew were "oui," "madame," "mademoiselle," "monsieur," and the most important, "merci." That is all.

Those few words were enough to start off with because my classmates were extremely kind to me. They thought my being an American was great and they treated me well. It counted for much in those days. Even better, I was a black American, most certainly kin to the great boxer, Muhammad Ali! They reasoned that all black Americans were, of course, related. Did I know him?

At that time, I didn't even know who Muhammad Ali was. Mother told me he had changed his name from Cassius Clay to Muhammad Ali when he changed his religion. With his new religion, he chose a new name. I didn't know who Cassius

Clay was either. As the weeks went by, all I knew was that I was the only person in the school who didn't know how to speak French!

I also knew that I was falling further and further behind in my homework because I didn't understand it. I was very unsettled and upset. I knew that, too. Mother said that before too long I would be speaking French. She said I would speak, read, and write it. Mother said to have faith and not to worry. She was confident that I would get it before too much longer. She told me to be patient.

I tried to be patient, it was very hard. Every day I went to school and sat in the very first row, in the middle, right in front of the teacher's desk. I tried not to worry that all I heard were strange sounds I knew were the words of a language I still didn't understand. I had the most trouble in the afternoon after lunch when it was wilting hot inside and flies buzzed lazily around the inkwells on our desks. Sometimes a fly would fall into the tiny bowl and drown in indigo ink. I didn't feel sorry for the drowned flies, I felt sorry for myself where I sat at the front of the class, listening to sounds all around me, with no real comprehension. It got harder and harder with each passing day.

One of my father's colleagues had a daughter who went to the French school. I was in her class. Her name was Justine. Justine and I played together often after school and on the weekends. Sometimes she stayed over at my house or I stayed over at hers. We often got to visit the Bobo Zoo. On this day we went to there and met the new attendant for the primates. He couldn't believe NoNo didn't like bananas, all monkeys did. Justine told him all monkeys might like bananas, but NoNo was a gorilla and he did not. How could he be caring for NoNo and not know that?

Justine knew so much about animals because she had a small zoo of pets at her house. I always thought it was more fun for me to go there than for her to come to my house. At Justine's at night, birds sang us to sleep. Justine said they were nightingales. One day we had to learn a song for school. We were to memorize the song and then, in our penmanship exercises, we transcribed it.

The song we had to learn was about a nightingale. For the first time, as the new kid in school, I was finally beginning to hear the French in my head and translate it into English so I could understand. I was surprised that I could understand the words. Justine and I sang the song over and over and over again. I practiced writing it, and when we had to transcribe it in class I was able to do so flawlessly. Mme. Priochet held up my notebook as a good example of excellent penmanship. That was the beginning of my big change in Bobo and the clinching of my title as "Teacher's Pet."

Learning the song about the nightingale was a big boost to my deflated ego too. I was happy to finally be able to understand. Mother said she stopped worrying about me when she heard me and Justine arguing. In French. She realized long before I did that I understood and spoke French. The way I noticed is that one day the words just came out of my mouth and I didn't even think of them in English first. From then on, life in Bobo was much easier.

At school, they called me "l'américaine," and it was the only name I answered to. It was my identity; I wore it with pride. When parents came to visit, I was always introduced as the best friend, "the American girl I told you about, maman." That is who I was, the American girl.

My new title stuck. It was a very strange thing because it followed me everywhere I went and I could not shake it if I had tried. In the U. S., I wasn't American enough; in Burkina, it was all I was allowed to be. I tried not to let my new friends down , I tried hard to be their American. It was a new kind of dance and difficult for me to step into the rhythm.

There was a routine of sorts even for us small folk. We lived in a world apart, a world of discipline, pranks, and negotiations. We ate bread with chocolate and got bloody noses at recess. However, nothing was worse than being caught acting up by Mme. Priochet. Nothing, that is, except getting caught twice in the same day.

Discipline demanded punishment. Punishment was severe. It was metal to flesh in the form of a rectangular ruler to the buttocks of the repentant perpetrator. In the front of the class with pants down, if you please. That was the worst. But just as painful, or perhaps even more so, was the trusted ruler to bent knuckles and then graded penmanship exercises to follow.

Seeing these carriages of justice in the classroom prompted me to become the model student and, because I was so thoroughly shocked into submission, it never occurred to me to be anything but exemplary in my behavior. Except one time. But in this case my behavior was well warranted, I was told by the classmates who witnessed it.

I broke Nadim Mulani's nose. He had been preying on me since the first day of school. He had been doing so for several weeks. On this day, silvery bright, high with humidity, when the playground gravel melted our rubber-soled shoes and the wooden benches branded the backs of our legs like lamb chops on the grill, he crossed the line. Nadim took it into his head that he should wrestle me to the ground. He got my dress dirty.

Mother had just made me that dress. It had matching shorts. The fabric was a checkered pattern of yellow and white. My new dress got dirty and torn on the first day I wore it. There was a big hole at the corner of the right side pocket. How was I going to explain that to mother? I hit Nadim in the face with my green plaid pencil box. I broke his nose. He then called me his wife, as no woman but such a good fighter could be the mother of his children. We never did marry.

Heat bumps, sunburn, drenching humidity, and biting flies were the story of my life back then. My days were mostly happy, though, and filled with fun. Life was very different than in Kathmandu and Kensington. I still explored and went on adventures, but it was not the same. I was different too. I often wondered what else there could be to surprise me. I then learned there was a very good reason you had to shake out your shoes before putting them on. In my case it was a flying cockroach the size of Gibraltar. Before that, I had learned more than anyone would ever want to know about termites.

Azmadou's Dinner

The termites were coming! It was said that when the termites came, they swarmed en masse. It was said that when the termites came, the air got so thick you could not see your hand in front of your face. The termites got into everything and anything above and below ground. It was important to close all openings and seal all holes to prevent the termites from getting into places they didn't belong.

Termites? They meant grasshoppers, or locusts, right? No. They were talking about termites. They meant termites. I wondered if that was why there seemed to be so little wood around. I didn't dwell on the issue, though; I let it pass. I didn't give the termite invasion season another thought since I believed I would be off at boarding school when it happened.

I had a much more urgent worry than termites. I was preoccupied with trying to smother my rising separation anxiety. I spent much of my energy struggling with the sad thought of leaving mother. I was trying my best not to be a baby about it. But I cried in secret because I was afraid. Termite news updates, if they ever were broadcast, never penetrated my scattered senses. So, when I didn't leave for boarding school after all, and the termites came as expected, they cruised right on in under my rickety radar.

When the termites came, I was riding in the car with my father's driver, Azmadou. Azmadou took me to and from school each day whenever my father was not on a field trip. We were headed back home from a Wednesday half day of school. My new school, the French school on the outskirts of town, had half days on Wednesdays and Saturdays. I found this very odd, but as such things were out of my control, I tried not to worry about them.

On this day, as usual, I sat in the car with all the windows rolled down as far as they would go. I wilted in the steaming heat and wallowed in woebegone misery. The climate took so much getting used to. Since before school had started, I had had itching, chafed legs and a stinging rash of heat bumps. I knew mother would have a cool baking soda bath ready for me when I got home.

I looked forward to my baking soda bath. I dreamed of my bath as I slouched in the heat, slowly melting on the back seat of the Land Rover. It offended me that I was stewing in my own personal pool of sweat. I felt wretched. I think my head was lolling from side to side, and I may even have been drooling. Even so, through my dejected torpor, I heard the words as Azmadou quietly said, "Roll up the windows, Mélanie Demi." "Demi" was short for "Demoiselle" as in a little Miss, Mademoiselle. Azmadou said I was still just a half a Miss, not a whole Miss, so I was not yet a full Mademoiselle.

As I sat on the hard hot car seat, I heard the words Azmadou was saying. I heard them, but as I was not completely tuned in, their import eluded me. I did begin to notice being distracted out of my brooding dejection by a distinctly perceptible shift in the atmosphere. This shift was oddly electric and it caught at my attention.

Since I was still trying to get used to the dripping humidity of Burkina, I had a fleeting thought that maybe this was yet another weird atmospheric anomaly—like when hailstones the size of baseballs that could knock your head in fell from the gods and then melted in seconds in a whiff of steam. I had another thought, equally fleeting, that maybe I should pay closer attention to this current strange shift.

I already knew that the air was thick and heavy and boiling hot. I already felt how it broiled my lungs when I sucked it in. And I already knew there was no getting away from sucking in big deep gulps of the thick and boiling air. I shifted in my seat to look over Azmadou's shoulder out the windscreen. There was a darkening of the sky in the distance.

It looked like churning gray thunderclouds that seemed to swell and roil way up the road ahead of us. Again Azmadou said, "Roll up the windows, Mélanie Demi." I caught the look in his eyes in the rearview mirror. There was no trace of the twinkle I was used to seeing in them. Alarm bells clanged in my sluggish, steaming brain. I rolled up the two back windows as fast as I could. Before I could scoot back to my seat, a tremendous humming, drumming rush of sound bounced off the Land Rover and made my teeth tremble.

Up ahead, the dark, glinting, pulsing cloud was shooting straight at us! I felt a sinking twinge, almost like goose bumps in the belly where the I imagined the bumps burst one by one from fright like miniature volcanic eruptions. I reminded myself that I didn't need to fear anything, Azmadou was with me.

This thought played through my head as I watched in eye-blinking disbelief as the tightly curled hairs on my arms stood straight up. Just then, Azmadou made a big U-turn in the middle of the road and pulled over to the shoulder. He grabbed the woven mats from the floor of the front seats and jumped out of the car. I saw him open the hood and put the woven mats inside. I figured a dust storm was coming, I knew they could be dangerous. It was important to cover the grill and as much under the hood as possible to minimize any harmful impact.

There was no such thing as a tow truck out where we lived. If your car broke down, a group of people pushed or a team of oxen pulled it to the nearest garage. If you were very lucky, maybe another car could give you a lift or a tow. Dust storms killed car engines. It was usually a quick death for a machine but a horribly slow one for people and animals. Getting caught in a dust storm was serious business.

I turned around and looked out the back. My attention focused on the rolling black wave racing toward us. Flashes of light bounced all over inside of it. As a body, the wave seemed to dip low and to skitter on the ground. It was not lightning, and there was no thunder. This was unlike any dust storm I had seen so far. I didn't know what to make of it. An eerie sound swished and swelled around us. It sounded nothing like the harmattan, the hot, dry season winds that blew in from the Sahara. Slam! Azmadou was back inside, saying "The termites are here." A big fat bug with gossamer wings came into the car with him. It clung to the collar of his brilliant white shirt.

Then there was a sudden gritty roar as hundreds of pebbles rocked against the windows and rained upon the car. But they were not pebbles—bugs were raining on us! There were thousands of bugs just like the one on Azmadou's shirt. It was as big as a chicken egg, with shimmering prismatic wings. Azmadou followed my line of sight, saw the bug on his collar, plucked it off, and popped it into his mouth with a grin. "Termites," he said as he crunched, "good protein."

I was simultaneously intrigued and disgusted. Then the sunlight winked out. A dense shadow of darkness pinched it out the way wet fingers do a burning candlewick. With sharp cracking sounds like ice breaking in cold water, the car began to creak and complain.

Termites! Millions! They were everywhere. They bombarded us like hailstones. I told Azmadou I was afraid the windows might break. He said not to worry. The termites would pass by quickly; they didn't like the taste of metal or glass. I crouched down onto the floor between the front and back seats. The Land Rover shook and shimmied, and the termites droned over us like a team of crop-dusting planes.

The termites pinged and ponged, thumped and bumped against the car. The motion of the car was like that on a roller-coaster ride. Well, I had never been on a roller-coaster, so I didn't know this for certain—I was just imagining. I watched with clinical interest as a termite squeezed up through the floorboards and flew around inside. Azmadou caught it, offered it to me, and promptly ate it when I declined. I heard him chewing as he sat in the driver's seat. I shuddered when he said that one tasted particularly roasty.

The flock of termites was gone, and so was the puddle of sweat on the seat where I had been sitting. I felt queasy from the weird bouncing of the car and, as much as I wanted to, I was not able to stop thinking about smoky-tasting termites. The air vibrated with a rough humming noise like the sound a refrigerator makes when it kicks on in the middle of the night.

It was dark as night and my heart was kicking in my chest like a big refrigerator. The rear guard of the termites roared over us and the sound then faded slowly off in the distance. Azmadou turned the car around, and we drove home crunching along a plush carpet of fallen termites. They covered the road like dust and popped and smushed under the hard rubber tires. The air smelled curiously metallic and damp.

The termites were bad news and good news. They got into everything, everywhere. Or tried to. They clogged drains, jammed windows, stopped doors, and made a mess out of any kind of engine. They were drawn to the warmth and often got roasted. After the termites had been through, the cleanup took longer than their visit. That was the bad news. Azmadou said that the termites were an important food source for protein. That was the good news. Azmadou said fresh was best and for the next few days simply snatched termites out of the air and ate them up.

The termites got harvested like any other crop. They were a prized delicacy, and much effort went into gathering them up. Containers were set out everywhere to catch them— on the roadsides, and every few paces all over town. Buckets, pans, and bowls were set out to catch as many termites as possible. In our own compound we had shallow troughs of salted water on which the termites would alight and then drown.

Azmadou said that the water wet their wings so they could not fly away and that the addition of salt to the water helped begin the preservation process prior to their being smoked, dried, baked, boiled, or roasted. Azmadou's favorite way to eat them was raw. His method of snatching them out of the air worked only for the first few days. He explained that one could hardly keep the termites in a coop like chickens. I agreed. Who had ever heard of such a thing?

I never knowingly ate a termite. I tried, under Azmadou's patient tutelage and supervision. I caught one out of the air the way he did and popped it into my mouth. It fluttered around inside, and I felt its legs walking on my tongue. I had to spit it out and do a crazy *heebeegeebee* dance. Azmadou said I had wasted a perfectly good snack. I was not brought up to waste food, so I didn't try to eat any more raw termites after that.

A couple of times, termites plopped out of the bathroom sink faucet when I turned the water on. They were drowned and bloated, too fat to go down the drain. I hated to have to pick them out but I did because it was necessary. Before my critter fears made me more timid than I would have liked, I sometimes ate pepper-roasted red ants and grasshoppers dry roasted like peanuts. Or chocolate-covered grasshoppers.

The ants were crunchy and rolled around on your tongue. The grasshoppers were more chewy than crunchy, but they were good too. Although I could appreciate the current termite crop as being nicely shaped, plump, and plentiful, for some reason eating termites didn't readily appeal to me. And even though I was not as hands-on curious as I had been before, I was still fascinated by them.

One day, under mother's supervision, I fried fresh-caught termites in butter for my father's lunch. They didn't take long to cook; you had to keep basting them, and the flame could not be too high or the butter would burn. I was careful to turn them over in the hot butter. They were nicely browned, like perfectly toasted peanuts. I scooped them out of the pan, put them into a small dish, and served them to father. He said they looked delicious, thank you, and sprinkled salt and pepper on them. I could not watch him eat, though. I had to run away screaming in order to preserve my sanity.

After that first day of the termite invasion, we still had to drive with the woven mats in the grill of the Land Rover. Each evening, I helped Azmadou pick out all the termites that had gotten caught inside the car and under the hood. Usually the ones close to the engine were roasted crispy. Azmadou tossed them into his mouth like popcorn. They smelled pretty good, earthy and warm like the orange Bobo dirt. I thought I might eat a couple. I said I thought I might.

Finally, after several weeks, when we were sure the termites were gone for good, Azmadou took the mats out from under the hood. Fortunately for Azmadou, and unfortunately for the termites, enough got caught under the hood for dinner. I held a big white enameled bowl, and Azmadou plucked out the termites that had gotten trapped. As each bug was added to the bowl, at Azmadou's direction I shook a bit of salt on them. The salt prevented them from flying, it curled their wings on contact.

When Azmadou was satisfied that the engine area was free and clear, we went to the coal fire we had built earlier. This was our evening ritual. The fire had gotten white hot while we were harvesting the trapped termites. Sitting at the fire, we skewered the crawling termites, one by one—out of the bowl and onto the ends of sharpened sticks. *Popf.* I do not know why I was not squeamish about the skewerings. My fright or fascination about bugs in those days was fleeting and impossible to anticipate. One day I felt like my old curious and adventurous self, and the next day even a little brown ant gave me the creeps or made me feel queasy.

The chickens pecked up the last of the termite stragglers. They waddled around the yard and sometimes fought over an unlucky victim. Peck! Another termite gone from the hard dry earth. Azmadou and I sat on low wooden seats with our long skewers over the searing coals. We turned the bugs slowly as the setting sun spread an orange-yellow glow on the far horizon. Mother waved at us from the second-floor balcony. We saluted her with our termite kabobs. Then, that quickly, the sun was gone.

As twilight kissed the coming night hello, Azmadou and I roasted the last of our trapped-under-the-hood termites. Their shimmery gossamer wings burned off in quick fits of flame. Their bodies swelled to twice their normal size. The juices were boiling! We turned our termite kabobs slowly and evenly over the heat like marshmallows. The plump bodies oozed and browned beautifully on our sticks. They smelled delicious, like fresh-roasted chicory. My mouth watered. I could hardly wait to eat a few.

Moisture dripped onto the coals. Flames sparked and the fire hissed. The termites browned to delectable perfection. Sizzle, sizzle. POP! Azmadou said to eat as many as I wanted. I told him thank you and blew on my neatly packed kabob. I worked my first termite off the skewer, licking my fingers to cool them down. I inspected my burnished, legless nugget—it was shaped like a peanut in the shell. I brought it to my lips and smiled with anticipation.

Just that quickly, as tasty as my termite looked, as good as it smelled, I was suddenly seized by the foolish dictates of my temperamental tummy. It stopped me from eating my appetizer. After all my patience and hot work, I could not eat the perfectly roasted, beautifully cooked critter. Even though it grumbled for a taste, my stomach betrayed me. I was very disappointed.

I gave all of my carefully tended, gorgeously toasted termites to Azmadou. He smiled. His eyes were happy; his bright teeth sparkled, and his crisp white shirt glowed in the comfortable dark. Azmadou's dinner was done.

Small Dark Places

Some bugs bite, some bugs sting, some bugs fly, some bugs sing. One of the first things I learned living in an uncomfortably warm climate, with very little shade, is that bugs love dark places. Be they large or small, bugs and their dark hideaways are made for each other. Along with this awareness was the more important fact that I had begun to outgrow my curiosity about crawlers and creepers.

Perhaps I had begun to outgrow my curiosity about all members of the insect universe. I now did my best to avoid bugs. I had actually developed an aversion to them. I was no longer an eager student of my once-favorite subject, *horriphology*. Simply put, I was afraid of bugs. This shocked me; I had liked them so much at one time. Now, each day, I carefully and systematically set about checking my shoes, slippers, and even sandals before putting them on.

On this particular day, I eagerly inspected my navy blue sneakers, which I had washed the night before. They had not been dry enough to wear to school that morning, so in the afternoon I tested them and was delighted to find that they were clean as new and ready to wear. I loved those shoes. Not much was better than Keds for a kid to kick around in.

Although eager to put the Keds on, I carefully checked each shoe as I had been taught: pull out the tongue, shake vigorously, tap the heel on the floor, turn upside down, tap, tap, and tap again. I did this twice for each shoe. It was well worth the effort. I had seen the kinds of hideous creepers that loved to lurk in dark places. I thought it best not to have to meet them there. At last I could put on my clean navy blue Keds. I did. I knew immediately that there was something in the right shoe. How could there be? I had been so careful! I pulled the shoe off without unfastening the laces.

I pulled on it so hard that it flew out of my hand and up to the ceiling, hitting the light bulb. I saw the shoe fly up and up, and by way of some fantastic feat of mitosis-osmosis-trichinosis it gave birth to the biggest bug I never wanted to see. Speechless with surprise and still riding on the wave of my good fortune in having my sneakers to wear, I realized quickly I had rejoiced too soon. This audacious bug was too stunned to fly. Instead, the gigantic Gibraltar bug fell smack onto my head.

I registered the weight of it instantly. I felt its spiky, scrambly, snaggy, leggy feet catch in my hair. They scraped my scalp. A split second later I shrieked and jumped and shook all over. It was still there. I twisted and shimmied my way to whiplash, unable to compel my hands to touch it, to brush it off my head. Oh, please. I could not bear to touch it. I m-m-mumbled, and gibberish gushed from my mouth as I hop-hop-hopped in a hell dance on my one shod foot.

The hopping eventually dislodged the bug of bugs and it tried to fly, but since I was still hop-hop-hopping, my up hop hit it. Down it fell onto my upturned face. The bug careened over my nose to my chin and slipped along my throat. It rocketed into the front of my shirt. The roach's crispy, crackly legs skittered against my naked skin! How could this get worse? I will explain how.

My shirt was tucked firmly into my skirt. The Godzilla bug was trapped at the waistline. I felt it crawling on my skin. It was scratching on me with every one of those spiky, creepy, dirty roach legs. I yanked my shirt free as fast as my fumbling fingers let me. I did this while I hopped, shook, and gibber-shrieked around the room.

Finally, I dislodged the bug. It dropped to the floor, and its armor-plated body clanged on the tile like a hailstone barrage against glass. In a frenzy of disgust and aversion I whacked it. I smacked it. I squashed that bug gooey with my treacherous right shoe until it was a mess on the floor.

The bug was a mess and so was I. Bug guts lay all around. They were a bubbly tapioca white and about that same consistency. The bug guts clumped on the sides of the tortoise shell brown of the giant bug's carcass. I stared at it. I was spellbound, or maybe I was in shock. The slowly waving legs sliced through the tapioca guts the way a wheel cuts through water at a gristmill.

I tried to catch my keening breath. Ironically, I was not in the habit of killing bugs. My first reaction had always been to examine. The second was to capture for observation, and the last was to release the thing into an area other than where I happened to be. This skirmish with the Goliath roach was quite the turning point for me as far as benign encounters with the crawling kind are concerned.

Shaken, and a little more than hysterical, I ran from the room of dead-roach delight. There was nowhere for me to go without shoes. I had to be practical. After several deep breaths, I talked myself into returning to the scene of the shrieks and the smashing. By this time I had the hiccups. Then, as sometimes happens even now, my hiccups lasted for several hours. Tears of trepidation welled up in my eyes. I didn't want to go back, but I knew I had to dispose of the b-b-b-bug.

I went back to the spot where we had last met. The bug was gone. Bits and pieces of it remained in the spot of the mad whacking. Globs of guts bubbled on the tile. Jointed legs and chips of brown decorated the glistening white tile floor. There was no trail to an escape route that I could find. The bug was gone. That simple fact was more frightening than a nightmare and more spectacular than magic. The bashed and battered Gibraltar bug was out of this world. *Unbugeevable.*

Four Goats, a Rooster, and Five Hens

Have you ever touched cow eyes? I mean dead cow eyes hanging from a hook? Just the eyes hanging from a hook all by themselves? I have. And, I found that dead or alive, cow eyes are really very pretty. Those were the kinds of things you'd find laid out for your perusal at the amazing Bobo Dioulasso Market.

There were no neat loaves of sliced bread, no boxes of crackers, cartons of milk, rows and rows of paper goods or small, white-papered cuts of meat in perfect packages. I found out many things I never knew before and I found the bulk of them in the Bobo Market!

As much as I loved American grocery stores, I was completely fascinated with the Bobo Market. Where the American grocery stores dazzled my brain with the sheer volume of selections, the Bobo Market ignited my imagination by the sheer volume of possibilities! Why were goat's beards sold along with woven sandals? Were they used to make sandals? Well, maybe the right question was why sell goat's beards? And, what could you do with ox eyelids or river fish tails?

If you wanted meat, you went over to where the butchers' stalls were. There were whole sides of meat hanging for your leisurely inspection. Want beef? Would that be with hide on or hide off? Chop it up yourself and freeze it in your own white, waxed butcher paper or buy just some parts and have to get more in a fortnight. Depending on what cuts you wanted, it was often cheaper to buy the whole cow. That is what we did.

What about fresh chickens? Did you want the butcher to wring their necks and pluck them for you, or will you do it yourself? Along with the colors and people came the warring smells of spices, dust, soap, manure, sweat and blood. Old blood and fresh blood? Either was for sale. Did you bring your own container, or will you buy one? That was the fascination of the Bobo Market.

I think too, the real charm of the Bobo Market for me was that its beating pulse and rainbow colors reminded me of Kathmandu. I missed home; that was what Nepal was to me. No matter where I had been, or what new wonders I had seen, no matter that I had memorized my U.S. address in Washington, D.C. before I could read, I remembered the Himalayas in the sunshine, capped with spring snow.

In remembering, I smelled my mother's garden flowers and I saw the honey bees at work. I even heard the crows squabbling in the orchard, and I saw the new baby chicks in their fluffy yellow coats roam among the sunflowers. In the middle of another country, with no scheduled return, I thought of Nepal as my home because, even in the fantastic, mind-boggling, vibrant, mesmerizing and glorious Bobo Market, that was where my heart was born. Nepal was where, in my dreams, I still lived.

All this to say, I once was bartered for in the common market. No, not stocks and bonds. It was among beef flesh, ox tails, turnips and cinnamon sticks. I was bartered for in the Bobo Dioulasso Market. On the day of the bartering, we went there to buy soap.

We actually had lots of soap. We had clothes washing soap, dish washing soap and flake soap for delicates. We had bar soap too. We had an entire case of bar soap. That was one hundred and fifty individually wrapped rectangular bars of soap. The soap we had in abundance gave me a terrible rash. I was already suffering from heat bumps, so with the combined soap rash and heat bump rash I was in a miserable state.

Soap at the Bobo Market was made fresh in a big black cauldron. Really. You made your purchase and it was prepared while you shopped or while you watched. You could buy soap in heavy rectangles shaped like blocks stone, or get slices thick as a brick and just about as heavy. If you wanted soap with scent, there were herbs from which to make a selection. Soap in the pot was sold by the half, which came to four of the brick-sized blocks. You had better really like the scent you selected because you were going to get a whole lot of it. The soap we finally selected smelled like dusty sunshine. The Soap Lady said it should last a little girl like me three and a half years.

After buying the soap, I followed mother as she browsed and bargained. I was just beginning to sew my own clothes and mother said I could go ahead and wait for her in the fabric section. She knew how I really loved the Mali cottons and the Ghana prints. Before too long, a man caught my eye, or more accurately, I his. He followed me! In his long, flowing white robes and with his tall, studded walking stick, the man followed me. I didn't like the way the man looked at me.

With each turn I made in the Market, he was there. I began to work my way back across the Market to where my mother was bargaining for onions and potatoes. Through the baskets and grain, skirting the hanging butchery, tethered livestock, beads and jewelry, at the end of spice row. He was there. I finally got over to where my mother was. I told her a man was following me; she took my hand and together we found my father and told him too. A moment later the stalker approached.

Chief Kolufasi, was his name. He was in town on business. Among other things, he was shopping for a new wife and liked what he saw in me. A plump, healthy girl to make many fine sons, yes? He asked for a moment with my father, if he would be so kind? Then, the two of them entered into a serious discussion. Too serious, I thought. What was there to discuss? The answer was No. No, you Kolucreep, stay away from me.

My father and the Chief spoke for a very long time. The Chief said I was "une fille très jolie." I kept them both in sight while I hovered near the rainbow rows of cotton fabrics. The bolts were bright and cheerful, and their colors seemed to paint the air above them. The air wavered, luminous as gems in the searing hot sun. I didn't know why the discussion between my father and the Chief took so long.

Mother continued shopping, I kept her in sight as well. I looked around the Market at the many women and girls and wondered how many wives their husbands had. It made me nervous and jittery to think along those lines, but I found it impossible not to. I felt the telltale pinpricks of a heat bump rash spread along my arms as Chief Kolufasi's heavy-lidded eyes followed me wherever I roamed. It was rather unnerving.

Father said he would think about the Chief's offer. It hung as a threat over my head for quite some time. Little Miss Goody Two Shoes was on her very best behavior. Chief Kolufasi was a wealthy man. He already had two wives and four fine sons. Girls too, but he dismissed any further discussion of them as inconsequential with a wave of his hand. I wondered what that made me. I knew I was worth something because I was plump and healthy. The chief looked me over. I think he wanted to squeeze me like one might a prized laying hen.

His purchase offer was quite generous: forty bushels of wood, a meter high stack of colorful bolts of cotton fabric, twenty-odd baskets of spices and several crocks of precious oil! Not to mention livestock. Four goats, a rooster and five hens. And a milk cow as a bonus! Yes, he wanted me. This simple fact kept me in line for a long time thereafter. I tried to hide my fear with good behavior and never-ending activity.

Mother said they never considered the offer seriously. However, they had to treat the offer with all due respect as warranted a person of great status. Chief Kolufasi was a powerful and influential man and my father often traveled through his territory when he went on field trips into the bush. One of the mid-wives in the Public Health program was distant cousin to the Chief. Later on, I saw the Stalker Chief many times at the Market, no doubt shopping for more wives. The sight of him gave me hives. Where, I wondered, will he find his next wife? In among goat ears, grass mats, horsehair ropes, pumpkin seeds, or rams' heads?

"Remember, we could have sold you." That phrase was sometimes left hanging in the air to manipulate me into doing things I didn't want to do. This threat was used by my siblings who got no end of delight rehashing the details. Ha! They had not even been there and the story changed each time they told it. And, they often got the purchase price wrong—or changed it to suit their version of the story. Still, even with the creepy chief, the heat and all the bugs, there was a magical, fairytale quality to life in Burkina despite the lurking nightmares.

Surprisingly, the magic held. Even with burning days of heat so intense it seared my skin. Not to mention the ever-present sheen of sweat that acted like a magnifying lens and broiled, baked and sautéed my flesh to new depths of burnished color. There was magic. The clean, clear daylight was sweet and happy. There was magic in the quality of the air after a night of torrential rain. Even the humidity was magical, it had weight and substance and a personality as well. Sometimes it was brash, sometimes it was bashful and it was always dancing to the beat of the Volta, be it slow or frantic, rhythmic or disjointed.

Just when I thought I would combust, when I thought I could not stand it for another second, my lungs re-adjusted and I was fine. I could suck in the wet air like a fish breathing under water. I ran and played with no sluggishness even though the heavy air clung to me like a spider web. In those moments, it no longer hindered me, but gave me new energy and hydration as efficiently as an intravenous drip. It was a fabulous time of adventure and learning. Even so, I began to notice a change in myself. I noticed I had become more cautious, more hesitant, and more tentative.

As tentative as I had become, I recognized the fact that I was completely in love with the mystery and raw reality of this new frontier. This love included the land, its people and their customs. I wanted to know everything! I was on fire for the fuel of knowledge. As hot and humid as it was, it didn't bother me as much anymore. The cacophonous, insect-infested nights bothered me greatly, because sadly, I was losing my love of them. I knew it and I was sorry for it. However, I was not sorry enough to try and prevent it. Even so, even with my rising fears and growing insecurities, it was such a wondrous time of discovery. Something like discovering the wheel.

Burning Rubber

I discovered speed. It was a thrill! My discovery was in the shape, form, and function of a mobilette, a mini-motorcycle of sorts. When it ran out of gas, you could always pedal to your destination. Pretty neat. The mobilette was lightweight and practical too. It belonged to my father's driver, Azmadou, who was a kind and patient man. He wore sparkling clean, crisp white shirts and taught me the value of looking, listening, and learning by way of aerodynamics. Specifically, he taught me why it very much matters which way the wind blows if you have it in you to spit out a car window.

Azmadou did it all the time. Spit, that is. He could chew on a cinnamon stick and still spit with precision. He could hit a biting green fly in midair! I chewed on cinnamon sticks too sometimes. Among other things, it was good for the digestion, and it kept your teeth and mouth clean. I had to chew on my cinnamon sticks in spurts because they got too hot for me.

I do not know how Azmadou kept one in his mouth. He held the long sticks between his lips like a cigarette. Azmadou said the heat in my mouth from the cinnamon stick would help cool the rest of me down. He said it took time. He said that with practice and time, I too might chew on cinnamon sticks all day and spit at biting green flies. Mother said to forget about spitting; it was a nasty habit and I was not to do it.

I wanted to spit. I was ready to spit. I told Azmadou one day in the car on the way home from school for lunch. My mouth watered from the heat of my cinnamon stick. Chewing on it churned up lots of spit. Azmadou said he would tell me when it was the right time to spit, and not to spit unless he said so. I tried to spit out the car window anyway, and it came right back in my face. Azmadou saw it in the rearview mirror. He laughed so hard that we almost drove off the road. I didn't spit anymore after that. I made him promise not to tell mother.

Oh, the mobilette. In short, it was a wonder machine. I was allowed to ride it anywhere within the confines of the compound where we lived. That was great. The only drawback was my inability to maintain a given speed without going through a wall. This required more skill than speed, but I wanted the speed. At the time, I was the only siesta-break entertainment. I know that everyone thought I was crazy, but I was indulged regardless of my stupidity. I was Evel Knievel in the bush of Burkina. Daredevil girl-child on wheels of fire—in a dress, of course, with shorts underneath for propriety.

For weeks I rode at lunchtime at the height of the heat, in the heat of the day. It was thrilling! It never occurred to me that I might be disturbing anyone. Nobody said I was, and nobody asked me to stop. I looked forward to my rides all morning. During our daily penmanship exercises at the French school, I daydreamed about what my afternoon stunts would be.

So far, I had jumped over the span between the dirt lot and compacted gravel of the driveway with ease. I did the front-wheel-to-the-sky trick and, for my favorite exploit, chased the chickens in the yard. I was fast and they squawked, scrambling to get out of my way. They flapped their wings, and their feathers flew though the chickens themselves didn't. But I could fly!

I did fly. Until the day of the burn—the cyclist's burn—the kind every novice motorcycle rider has heard about. The kind of burn that leaves an awful brand on many a left calf. In my case it was flesh on the grill. It was so hot it debilitated and maimed—an efficient, two-in-one combination. Wonder machine or not, it was the cause of a crippling burn. I put on a brave front for my midday audience.

I drove around for the remainder of my allotted time. I was too stubborn to forgo my lunchtime deviltry. The chickens seemed to sense that they were no longer in danger. They sauntered around the yard and ignored my half-hearted low-speed advances. My injury stung. I parked the machine, kicked down the stand, and went inside to nurse my wound. La fille du directeur had to give up her stunts. L'inferno limped. I had to give up the mobilette. Scarred for life, I thought, but worth it for the thrill. The skin swelled and bubbled, then settled into a shape that mirrored the grill of the metal that had scorched me.

That charred spot blistered and oozed painfully. Then it scabbed and left a distinctly patterned mark on my calf, making it hard for me to forget my midday misadventure on Azmadou's mobilette. I felt the pain of the burn for a very long time. It was in an awkward spot too. No matter how careful I tried to be, somehow or another I nudged, scraped, or bumped it. It took a long time for the wound to heal. Now, these many years later, I can find no trace of a scar.

Scars might have been badges of courage for some, but in my case it would be fair to call them signs of stupidity. Call me Scar Girl. There was the curtain rod skewer scar, Rooster King's kiss scar, the witch prevention scar, the caniveaux elbow scars, and the just-below-the-right-knee, can-I-go-to-the-movie scar. That one hurts even now when I think of it. However, truth be told, the most significant scarring came on the day Jean Louis Grangé laughed at me. I have since forgiven him, but his was not the only slight. Mother laughed too. She was allowed that privilege. This next story is not, in any way, for the squeamish.

The Wrong Way

The Bobo sky was a hard, sharp blue. It glowed like a gemstone as far as the eye could see. The heavens were cloudless and serene—maybe ninety degrees Fahrenheit in the shade. It was an unusually cool and beautiful spring day. Madame Grangé, Jean Louis' mother, had just presented me with a ring. Jean Louis was my classmate at the French school. I sat between him and Justine. Mme. Grangé said the ring was "une petite quelque chose—a little something for when you are a young woman." She said, "Too big now, Mélanie, but you are sure to grow into it in time." As was my lot and my promise to my parents, I could accept no gift without their consent.

Jean Louis and I cycled the half mile or so to the compound to give mother the note Mme. Grangé had written and to show her the ring. I suppose the telephone could have been used, but it might have been nightfall before the call got through. Besides, we had our bicycles for transportation and the energy to pedal ourselves all the way to Timbuktu!

For safety's sake, Jean Louis carried the ring and the note in one of his pockets. The ring was too big for every finger on my hand except my thumb; and as I had no pockets, we figured his carrying it was safest. I raced along the side of the hard dirt road well ahead of him. At fairly regular intervals there were rectangular concrete mounds of which we rarely took notice. On this day, however, they were to mark my fate.

A mule-pulled cart piled high with dry brush and kindling wood approached from the opposite direction. Unbeknownst to me at the time, a car was fast gaining on us from behind. I knew immediately with the honking of the car horn, however, that the road was too narrow for the cart, the car, and me. If I didn't give way to the two vehicles, we all three were going to crash. It was too late to do much of anything. The three of us ran abreast of each other. I was faced with the choice of hitting one of the rectangular mounds head-on at breakneck speed or swerving onto the road in the path the car. I chose to hit the concrete mound on my side of the road.

The concrete mound was a marker for the caniveaux. The canivaux were deep, open trenches along the side of the road, one on each side. The canivaux were for the collection of unprocessed sewage. All of the concrete mounds were rectangular blocks embedded in the ground parallel to the side of the road. I hit the mound, and the impact sent me into the air. I shot forward and the bike came down hard, skidded in the dirt, and flipped suddenly to the side. I plunged into the caniveaux with a splash. The caniveaux was full. I fell in upside down, holding on to the handlebars of my bicycle in a grip of terror.

I surfaced and with my first try for a breath of air I caught a mouthful of nasty tea. I gulped it down in shock and horror. I had to let go of my bike. It disappeared, swallowed from sight by the thick stinking stew. I treaded in the sewage as best I could. I wanted to scream and vomit, but I understood perfectly that I didn't have the luxury of allowing myself to react that way. I had to use every bit of energy to keep my head above the disgusting, warm and bubbling brew. Then I'd have to get out of it.

There was a pull, a current if you will. It forced me and the disgusting contents of the ditch to the end where more fluid entered. The fluid entered from the open mouth of a corrugated pipe about a meter above the surface. I could not fight the fetid, infectious pull of the current. The draw of it was strong and binding. I was caught. Soon I was under the drainpipe, and raw sewage was bouncing down onto my head. It was not at all like bobbing for apples.

I was caught in a tenacious whirlpool of liquid and not-so-liquid, well—shit. That's what it was. Every shape and color. No matter how hard I swam to get away, I got pulled back under the drain opening. The stuff rained down on me in fits and starts—sometimes slushy, often chunky. And my bike, my beautiful three-speed gold and white Raleigh, was submerged in the slimy, disgusting sludge!

Finally, I managed to brace myself with my legs against the filthy, slippery opposite wall. I looked up and Jean Louis was kneeling at the edge of the ditch, peering down at me. When he saw that I was not in bits and pieces, the fear left his expression and he started to laugh. He laughed when I could have been killed!

A very kind man who was passing by on foot saw the whole thing and helped me out of the sewer. He actually jumped in and swam to where I was. Then he hauled me to one of the sides and pushed me up and out. The man carried me all the way home in his arms. I began to feel the sting of my cuts. Blood oozed from my scraped arms, raw elbows, and cut hands and legs. When we got home, Jean Louis knocked hard on the big wooden door. I heard the sound echo off the tiles inside. I prayed for mother to please hurry.

Mother answered the door, took one whiff, then rushed ahead of us to fill the tub with water—water and my very good friend iodine. Once she ascertained that the major damage was to my pride, she too laughed. She and Jean Louis sat in the bathroom visiting, laughing, and drinking fresh-brewed tea with boiled-water ice cubes. I sat in the tub among gallons upon gallons of water laced with iodine.

I stewed in the tub at the indignity of it all. I was peeved about the fact that mother and Jean Louis were having much more fun than I was. I didn't think too hard about where I had just been swimming or about how much of it I had swallowed. I got a painful reminder for weeks afterward from my elbows, though. They worried me like my ever-present mosquito bites, and stung like them too. I knew firsthand how the mosquitoes feasted when they had the chance.

Once I let a mosquito bite me on purpose. She got fat with my blood. Male mosquitoes didn't bite; they just mated and died. When that mosquito bit me, I swatted her, confident that I was her last meal. She got away. She lumbered into flight like an overloaded cargo plane. I never did that again. It may be my imagination, but I thought that mosquito bite took longer to heal than any other I had ever had. Like my elbows, it reminded me of my vulnerability. I am not sure when that part of me will completely heal.

The kind stranger accepted no compensation for his good deed in rescuing me. His name was Monsieur Matala. He would not come into the house that day; he accepted soap and towels from mother and washed at the spigot on the side of the house. M. Matala was originally from Mali. He was a traveling salesman. On the Canivaux Day he was my savior. M. Matala returned the following day to check on my progress, and we asked him to please stay for dinner. He did, and over the years he became a valued friend of the family. He stopped by to visit whenever he was in town.

The bike suffered no undue harm. I do not think it was even scratched. Azmadou cleaned it up for me and it sparkled shiny as new. I still have that bike. Well, the last time I saw it, it was in my parents' garage. Who knows? My father may have given it to charity by now. Or it might be tethered to a No

Parking sign for all I know. If I saw it, I could identify it, even if it was stripped or de-wheeled.

That Raleigh was the bike I got way back when we lived in Kensington, Maryland, U.S.A. in the year before we moved to Africa. That bike and I had survived the sudden meeting with the hooting owl's oak tree on Christmas Day. I would know it anywhere because I would find my initials on it, etched onto the frame with great pride on the day of our inaugural ride down Rickover Road. The initials likely still mark the Raleigh's gold and white frame.

Fire Burns on Water

For my birthday, I had no eyebrows. I lost them a few days before my birthday in the year we moved to Burkina. It was all because of the movie *The Unsinkable Molly Brown*. It was about a cruise ship that broke up and sank in the ocean and some woman on the boat. The woman didn't interest me. What fascinated me about the movie was the idea that water could be on fire.

Fire could actually burn in water. I could not believe it. I just could not believe it. I asked my mother about it because I knew she knew everything. I asked, "Mom, how can water be on fire?" She explained that in this particular case the ship's hull was breached by an iceberg and the oil that spilled into the water was on fire, so it was actually the oil on the water that was burning and not the water.

Right. Even though I believed that my mother knew everything, her explanation didn't satisfy my curiosity. I admit that I didn't quite latch on to her explanation of this particular phenomenon. I mean, you could not see the oil, just pockets of fire, and some people were burning like flares. There were some lifeboats, but they got lost in all the smoke. It was a horrible scene. I was fascinated, and well, again, how can water be on fire?

I knew that fire was as dangerous as it was necessary. I respected fire. I'd been burned by the fire of the Voltan sun. I knew the heat of it could be dangerous. Still, I was curious. There were some things I didn't grasp fully by reading the dictionary or the *World Book Encyclopedia*. Fire was one of them. I liked to cook over an open fire. I remembered tending the white-hot fire at Ayah Lemah's house in Kathmandu. I did that often with Kalima, my neighbor across the street. I often helped Azmadou when he cooked his dinner over an open fire. I thought I knew fire. I knew I liked it. I wanted to explore the impossible burning of water.

Being a curious investigator and a student in the practice of keen observation as well as the scientific method, I felt compelled to solve the puzzle. I had to prove it for myself. I would conduct an experiment. I would experiment and note the results of my experiment. I then did something dangerous and stupid. I got a can of oil, filled the bathroom sink with water, poured the oil on the water, and struck a match.

The next thing I remember is the smell of burning hair. It was mine. Of course it was mine! I was so shocked—it happened so quickly, that I didn't have an opportunity to fully observe the phenomenon. So I did it again. I learned that day how indeed water can be on fire. That question sufficiently answered, I would not ask it again.

When I looked in the mirror above the sink, I had no eyebrows. I had no eyebrows and no eyelashes, and the hair in my nostrils looked like tufts of ebony cotton. What had been hair only seconds before was now stubby blackened nubs of charcoal. I touched them and they crumbled. My forehead felt tight. I felt my eyebrows lift in surprise. But I had no eyebrows. I watched in complete fascination as they floated down my face as though they had all the time in the world. Ashes—puffy, black eyebrow ashes—dusted off my face.

The ashes sprinkled onto the surface of the water where the film of oil caught at them. My eyebrows settled on the water and floated a little and then, like gelatin dissolving in warm water, slowly disappeared. I watched them swirl, deconstruct, dissolve. I pulled the sink plug. The evidence of my experiment was gone in a gurgle of protest, down the drain to feed the Voltan sewers with the fruits of my stupidity.

By this time, mother was knocking loudly on the bathroom door. I drained the sink. I carefully washed it clean. The white porcelain winked at me; all traces of ashes no longer evident. The smell, however, remained. I opened the door and the eau de cheveux grillés swirled out in a cloud. It skirted around mother and me as it swiftly escaped the bathroom.

"What are you doing?" mother asked.

"Nothing," I replied.

"Where are your eyebrows?" she asked.

"What eyebrows?"

Kalima's Cooking

I found an idol and her name was Kalima. Kalima lived across the street from me. I could see the dense, dry, thatched roofs of her compound from my bedroom windows. I knew of her before I met her because I went to the local French school with her brother, Nadim. Kalima was two years my senior. She didn't go to school, she didn't wear shoes, and she didn't get to play. Kalima was beautiful, smart, funny, graceful, and an excellent cook. I still played with dolls; I was not allowed near the stove unsupervised, and the only thing I did very well was listen. I stumbled over the realization that I was still just a little kid. I knew I was a little kid, only it shocked me how little a kid I was—that is, compared to Kalima.

I pondered, I knew this was my time to be a kid. Mother said time went by very quickly; that was why it was important not to repeat mistakes. I understood that too. But where my time and Kalima's time intersected was brand-new territory. In this newly discovered time, I crashed into unequivocal reality. It was by accident, and I almost managed to backtrack and recover, but then I tripped over it and fell flat. I could not get up and I blamed it all on the unrelenting heat. The heat in Burkina was so wicked that you either wore a tough hide or you got whipped into hiding. I got whipped. I hid.

I hid the fact that I now understood that where Kathmandu was loving and gentle, sweet and nurturing, and Kensington was shiny and bright, new and more than a little mean, Burkina was raw, razor sharp, fiercely beautiful, and brutally honest. There were no shadows, and there was no place to hide from my stark new reality. Burkina was a place of swirling vibrancy where you either stepped into the drumming dance, or the beat of it bludgeoned you senseless.

I hid by filling each day, and every minute of each day, with activity. I dripped into one adventure after another the way water eases out of a stubbornly leaky faucet. I kept going for as long as I could during the day, then tumbled into my bed each night, too spent to dream. As much as I wanted to learn, there was a part of me that was frightened to know, now that I understood more about the harshness that life offered.

The bubble, that shield of padded protection around my young self, ignited, burned, and blew away in smoke. My courage deserted me in stages. I felt it slip on by. Sometimes I tried to catch it. This was an automatic reaction that never worked because I saw it vaporize and disappear so completely that it was far too late to say good-bye. All the energies of my bold adventurousness retreated too. I didn't know how to get it back either. I knew I wanted to learn more, but the fire of my imagination was not as invincible as it once had been. I think it was because I felt like I was on fire every day. Some days I burned more intensely than others.

I am not talking about fire like when my eyebrows went up in flames. Or fire from the lashing burns from white-hot car seats at mid-day. I am talking about a fire of awareness; a simmering, smoldering, unstoppable awakening of searing intensity. I am talking about the uncomfortable grasp of the reality of the concept of birds and bees, live and let live, kill or be killed. That kind of fire. I am talking about understanding I had fallen into the crucible. The crucible was Burkina.

In this new arena, I learned about perceptions. All my new friends marveled that the American girl had left America to live in their country. At that time, their utmost desire was to get to America. Their perceptions about my home country were quite different than mine. I didn't tell them that my first encounter with my compatriots had left me bruised and bloody. I didn't tell them my compatriots didn't believe I was American enough to live in my own country. I believed I was the luckiest of us to be where I was in beautiful Burkina. It didn't seem like a thought wise to share, so I kept my mouth shut. I looked and I listened.

I looked for Kalima after school because to me she had become the epitome of life and the living of it. I knew what epitome meant. I had started reading the unabridged dictionary that year. I listened for Kalima's laughter in the afternoons. I tripped across the street to be with her. I hoped she would let me help as she did her chores or when she prepared the evening meal for her family. I marveled at the fact that Kalima was only two years older than me and was expected to marry in another year. I was alternately intrigued and frightened by this fact of Kalima's reality.

LADYBUG

As frightened as I was, I knew it was more important to spend time with Kalima in this stark and naked truth than to continue to play with dolls as my fast-growing timidity desired. As often as I could, I spent my long hot afternoons with Kalima. She had a way of saying my name, "Mélanie." The way she said it, was happy Volta music. Sharp as the sunshine, fluid as the hot and dusty breeze. It was from her pronunciation of my name that I learned to like it. This was a milestone for me in those tumultuous days of discovery. When Kalima called me to her, to help stir the huge pot on the fire or taste her stew, "Mélanie, viens," was music to my ears.

The first time my brain caught that this mattered, the way Kalima said my name that is, I returned home and told mother I was sorry I had not liked my name before. I felt bad about it. I told her I liked it now, and I said thank you. I thanked her for choosing it for me. Mother said not one word. She put her hand to my cheek and kissed me. I ran off to bug Hassim, the evening cook, for pumpkinseeds to feed to the chickens.

I think I realized I was as fickle as those chickens. I had not reached fickle in the unabridged dictionary yet, but I knew what it meant. I knew fickle fit me. The chickens scurried around the yard the way I scurried around in life. I knew what their fate would be, but I had no clue as to my own. I just never forgot how Kalima's saying my name made me feel so much a part of her world even though I understood the many differences between us.

At home, I had a bathroom with a toilet, a sink, and a tub with a shower. Across the street, Kalima had no indoor plumbing and cooked outside. Even in the rain. Kalima was serene where I was a goofball. She was lean and strong where I was soft with baby fat and weak with my heart full of hidden tears. Kalima was a quiet smile where I was nervous giggles. She was wise and kind and accomplished and knew her destiny. I was confused and crazy and conflicted for not knowing mine.

Sometime since arriving, I am not certain when, deep inside me, I felt the dissolution of my clarity. The bright shining light I had always followed, the goal and the prize, were no longer in view. My focus was completely blurred. I knew I was changed for the worse, and my crazy little conflicted self cried over it. Now too, against my fervent wishes, I was a crybaby.

I cried from frustration and fear, apprehension, loneliness, and my own tangible singularity. But mostly I cried for shame, and I cried in secret. I was ashamed of my hopelessly tender and easily bruised heart. I wanted to be strong and to seek my own truths with the towering strength of conviction.

Instead, I became afraid of my favorite creeping-crawling things. I no longer fearlessly investigated nature's mysteries and shadows were no longer dark puzzles, but murky threats. I was terribly frustrated by my newfound hesitations. I found the timid and confused person I had become so unappealing and unacceptable. I didn't know what to do about her either.

One day, I crossed the street to Kalima's compound where I had not been for several days. There were new additions to the household. Her uncle had brought a bitch and her puppies from his farm. They all looked happy with their new surroundings. In a few more days, the puppies would be sold. It was important to have a good dog; they were good guards, reliable company, and great entertainment. I spent the bulk of that visit pounding roots into paste. I didn't know how Kalima did it. My arms wanted to fall off after less than ten minutes.

A couple of weeks later, there was only one puppy left. He was a roly-poly bundle of energy. He was so fat he waddled when he walked. I was delighted to hold him and pet him and rub his tummy. Kalima's aunts were over, and it was Hair Day. Hair Day happened twice each year. It was an important event.

The girls and women got their hair washed, dressed with oil and herbs, and then wrapped tight with strong black cotton thread. Sometimes it was a straightforward and amazingly simple looking style. Sometimes the hair was formed into astonishingly intricate geometric designs that made your head spin. Either way, Hair Day activities took many nimble finger-moving hours.

The women talked about their own families too. Aunt Fati told about how her husband's third wife's breast milk had dried up. It was just as well, since the baby was teething much earlier than normal. Aunt Mignon said that was too bad because now they would have to worry about passing problems. I caught most of what they said.

To include me in their conversation they spoke mostly in French, but their French was peppered with many words from their own language, Dioula. I know I missed quite a bit. In any case, I sat there with them in a marvelous state of companionship and camaraderie. I did not worry about any words I didn't understand.

The aunties wanted me to tell them all about my family. This was nothing new; they were very curious, and I was used to it. I had learned early on that there was a certain protocol to follow. As direct questions were believed to be extremely rude and intrusive, they were never asked.

And so the pattern went:

One might suppose my sisters and I did each other's hair? With that, I knew I was to give a detailed description of how we washed and groomed our hair. If there was any special dressing or styling involved, I was to relate it step by step.

Then: *One might suppose that my mother went to Ouagadougou to go to the French hair salon?* This was where I said that my mother washed her own hair and sometimes rolled it up on curlers. They had seen curlers in French magazines, curlers were pretty ridiculous. They laughed and laughed about them. So did I.

They supposed that I got my hair from my father because my mother's hair was fine as spun cotton and wavy like the ripples in a deep pool of water? I answered that all the children had more my father's hair than my mother's. Then the women talked of many such differences in their own families. Hours passed. This was always the best kind of visit for me. I liked the easy company and what I felt was their acceptance of me as just another person.

I helped wash and feed the babies. Then I helped clean and peel fat orange yams. I pulled the greens off of turnips and washed them the way Kalima showed me. Kalima was making stew. I already knew she was an excellent cook; I had tasted Kalima's cooking before. She didn't even measure, and everything she made that I had tasted was delicious. Stew!

An hour later, it bubbled in the big pot on the cooking fire. It smelled heavenly, and although it was not that late, I had been there just about the entire day. I prepared to say my good-byes and get back home. Aunt Fati said that I must not leave before I ate. Aunt Mignon asked what my mother would think of them if they sent me home unfed.

I stayed. I really didn't want to go home anyway. We sat in the shade, under a canopy of woven grass mats staked to the ground on four sturdy gnarled posts. There was much laughter and good company. Jolie finished her mother's hair and took over to complete her Aunt Mignon's. Aunt Fati's hair stood straight up a good eight inches above her head. The pattern was circular in three dimensions. Imagine twisting three Slinkies into three figure eights, then tucking them together at the top. That was Aunt Fati's hairstyle; it was fabulous! She let me touch it and I was surprised. It was as tight and unyielding as a wire clothes hanger where I expected it to be softer and malleable.

The stew was ready, I was to sit and eat. I sat. A bowl of fragrant, steaming stew was passed to me. As was proper, I said thanks with many blessings to the hands that prepared it, blessings on the house that sheltered those hands, and blessings on the household for their generosity. At home I ate meat every day. At Kalima's I knew they didn't. Meat was expensive, and it was first for the men of the family. Or for guests. I ate every last drop of the delicious stew.

I was offered more, and I really wanted more, it was so good. It would be too greedy of me to accept, I declined seconds with many thanks as was proper. I already knew that apart from my mother's, Kalima's cooking was the best I had ever had. Her stew was spicy hot with peppers, nutty sweet with stick cinnamon, and thick with chopped turnips and their greens. The boneless chunks of meat were succulent and tender.

Jolie's two babies toddled over and I noticed that the puppy was not scampering along with them. I asked Kalima where the little puppy was, and she asked me what I thought I had eaten. "Qu'as-tu mangé?" Although I was quite shocked, I knew I had to speak graciously and respectfully. I knew Aunt Fati and Aunt Mignon were listening as well as watching me carefully. This was not a time to offend! I told Kalima that her stew was the best, because that was true. I told her I was very honored by her family's generosity, and I told her, yes, as with all her cooking, I had enjoyed the stew. I said thank you, for the kind hospitality.

Thoroughly horrified, I made myself stay a while longer. I wanted to run home and cry. I stayed and played with Jolie's sweet little babies. They were laughing, roly-poly bundles of energy. Aunt Fati kept exclaiming they were beautiful babies,

"Pretty enough to eat!" I knew it was just an expression but I couldn't stop thinking about the puppy.

When I finally left, I thanked my hosts. I made no promises about when I might return. I kissed each auntie on both cheeks and remembered to send my good-byes to Papa Mulani, Nadim and Kalima's grandfather. He ate his stew away from the fire on the other side of the compound. As I looked both ways before crossing the dusty road to the entry gates to my own home, I fully understood that once again, life in Burkina had socked me smack into kaleidoscopic reality. Confusion crashed around inside me, and my crazy conflicted spirit was neatly julienned with the keen awareness that I had just eaten a precious little puppy.

I sat in the middle of my big four-poster bed and hugged my trusted brown teddy bear. I felt sick with sorrow, but I knew what was done, was done. I cried for the roly-poly puppy in my belly. That was the reality of it. That, I understood, was Burkina in all her ferocious truth and beauty. She wooed and intrigued you, and when you least expected it, she revealed the simple facts of life without pulling any punches. I called them "Truth Knock-Overs," or "TKOs." These TKOs were as skillful as any ever executed by Muhammad Ali.

Another TKO soon followed. My parents told me I would be going to boarding school in the fall. I hardly listened, I could not stand for it to be true. I believed I would have a last-minute reprieve like had happened the year before. And, that night, tucked tight under the mosquito netting in my big comfortable four-poster bed, I admitted to myself that the future frightened me. And I cried. I didn't want to grow up because nothing was certain, everything changed in a minute. One thing I knew for sure: whether I went to boarding school or stayed in my beloved Burkina, I would never again eat Kalima's cooking.

LADYBUG

Ladybug's Truth Knock Overs (TKOs):

- Heat stings
- Fire burns on water
- Food is good
- Bugs come in all sizes
- Mad dogs are mad dogs
- Bananas aren't for everyone
- Love is best

FRANCE for a Moment

La pluie tombait doucement.

LADYBUG

Numéro Sept, Avenue Rapp

I remember the scent of the rain. It found purchase on the hats, coats and umbrellas of the people coming and going through the main entry's beacon bright brass and glass doors attended solicitously by Hervé, the day doorman. He wore a river green tail-coat and pin-striped pants. He didn't wear a hat but he always had a smile for me. He smiled from his eyes. They were green. He called me Princess Soleil and opened the door for me with a bow.

Numéro Sept, Avenue Rapp, Hôtel Rapp – Paris, France. It was spring. I was nine years old and mother and I lived there while my father was on loan from the Agency for International Development to the World Health Organization. We had a suite. I slept on a roll-away cot that had a soft mattress with an extra warm blanket made of Shetland wool. I had a feather pillow. It was light as air and very soft. It made my face itch.

I think it rained every day. Misty rain; steady rain; cold, cool rain. It was a fresh smelling, green-things-growing rain in Paris that year. It was constant and beat out promise on the sidewalk from where I sat by myself near a drafty window in an overstuffed golden brocade wing chair with my hands folded neatly in my lap. I do not know what I thought about while sitting there. I know the time passed slowly at first and then, in a single breath, it was gone forever. Maybe that is what I thought about. I often sat alone, I was used to it.

I was to stay there until called. I knew better than to move. I stayed there. I sat and watched the slow pulse of a rain stream make runnels fall from the green and white awning. It hit the paved stones of the walkway below with a slap of a drop. That drop immediately disappeared into the cracks. Another soon followed in measured paces. It repeated the feat.

Splot. Then it too slid away. The invisible place took it. And, again.

I do not know how long I watched this slow dance of the drops. I wondered if this water went to the same place as time - when it went through the cracks, was it gone forever too? Then I thought that just because it went into the invisible place didn't mean it was gone really, just that I could no longer see it. I liked thinking that way better. There was always the possibility that I might get to see it again.

Mother left me under the watchful eye of Monsieur Binet. He was the concierge. He assured her I was in good hands. I was. They were kind to me, the administrators and staff of the Hôtel Rapp of Avenue Rapp. M. Binet had a daughter my age; she was in school, she didn't live in the city, maybe I would meet her, he sometimes said. I kept my eyes on mother. M. Binet stood beside me with his hand on my shoulder and we watched together as mother walked to the front door. Hervé was there. He opened the door at just the right moment and held the big umbrella over her as she stepped into a shiny black cab.

Mother wore her powder blue wool bouclé swing coat with the sapphire satin lining. She had on white gloves that day and L'Air du Temps perfume; she smelled heavenly. Mother wore a hat too, but I do not remember which one. I didn't cry, but I already missed her, even before she turned to blow me a kiss, I missed her. I caught her kiss and put it in my pocket for later. I kept her precious kisses for when I really needed them. I had many. I often really needed them.

Miriam pinched my cheek softly and took my hand in hers. She was the assistant to the housekeeper which, I was told, was different than the concierge. I didn't ask how because I didn't care. We fell into the morning routine. Tea for me in the side kitchen with the upstairs maids. No "café au lait" for "la petite pomme." I liked the way it smelled, "mais le goût," the taste of it, was not welcome to my palette. Just tea for me and "une demi-baguette et du beurre, merci bien. "

The upstairs maids giggled. Miriam said they were young and silly, not like me. I was so serious for "une petite mignonne." A little darling. The upstairs maids liked to touch my face and my hair. They said my skin was so soft, like a baby's; however, I was not a baby, was I? I wondered what they might think if I told them I was a crybaby, because I did cry in secret. I was not proud of it. It was another one of my own special TKOs. I now cried over the smallest things. It was getting harder to hide my tears, they just popped out of my eyes. I had no control over them.

The upstairs maids could not believe I combed and braided my hair each day all by myself. They pulled playfully on my braids; they didn't know how tender my scalp was and I didn't tell them. They said I was a good girl. Such good manners, so sweet and always a smile! I know I tried to be good, I also harbored sour lemon thoughts and I didn't always feel like smiling. Especially not on that first day, the first day of my tutoring with Monsieur Ramon de la Croix. I was to bring only one thing. I was to bring notebooks for each subject, and on my first day, I had no notebooks! Not even a "cahier de poche."

"Je n'avais aucun cahier pour ma première leçon avec Monsieur de la Croix. Je l'ai oublier dans le taxi. C'était hier dans la pluie, j'en suis sûre. " I didn't have a single notebook. It was my first tutoring session in the sun parlor, which had only seen rain since we had arrived five days before. I didn't mind the rain. Where I had been was heat and red dust, burning sun and biting flies. Mosquitoes too, abundantly odd looking bugs and roaches the size of rats. And the rain, when it came, was torrential for days and days. No breaks for a time, just slick wet streets and mucky red clay. Sticky mud that sucked at your shoes, fought you for them.

I sat by myself in the sun parlor of the Hôtel Rapp. I figured the last I saw of my "petits cahiers," was when I put the bag from the "librairie" on the seat of the taxi. So, for this first day of my lessons, "pas de cahiers." I was mortified. I would have cried, but why? Yes, I think I left them on the seat of the taxi from the day before. I had fallen asleep and I scrambled awake when we got to the hotel. I am pretty sure the bag stayed in the cab. Maybe it fell to the floor. I knew it was not with my school books because they were all accounted for. The notebooks were to match four for four: one for math, one for writing, one for homework and one for civics dictation. None now.

"Quand il est arrivé, M. de la Croix, (Monsieur Ramon) me présentait un petit livre de poche – c'était un vrai Moleskine." For me, said M. Ramon. He gave me one of his Moleskines; it would do quite well for now. They came ruled, plain or with grid lines. Great writers like Hemingway used them! We did my first lessons in a slender black Moleskine there in the sun parlor at Numéro Sept, Avenue Rapp, Hôtel Rapp during a record rainy spring in Paris. And, I liked the "petit cahier" better than my regular school notebooks. I could put it in my pocket, I could tuck my blue ink Bic pen in the elastic band and I had a permanent ribbon to mark my place so I would not get lost.

Life at the Hôtel Rapp accepted me with tender generosity. Mother and I would have breakfast, early. Fresh fruit and a croissant with milk for me and Mother had the same but no milk to drink. She had coffee instead, with real cream and sugar. Three level teaspoons. She let me stir it in. Each day, after our breakfast, my father called. He spoke mostly to mother. Sometimes he would tell me to keep up with my lessons so I would not fall behind. After his telephone call, mother and I would go over my homework together.

Then mother left me with M. Binet and he handed me over to Miriam, and I had tea with the upstairs maids. They all listened to me read my writing assignments and sometimes I recited the vocabulary words I had to learn. They made me use each word in a sentence. I had to use each word in sentences having to do with the Hôtel Rapp exclusively. Usually, the sentences were really funny like - "M. Binet a trouvé un parapluie dans le bidet. " Mr. Binet found an umbrella in the bidet. We all laughed and laughed during the sentencings.

After tea, M. Ramon arrived and I had my lessons for the rest of the morning. On Mondays and Wednesdays near the end of my lessons, mother joined us and listened while I recited my new vocabulary words. I had to use each word in a sentence about Paris, or France. It was not as fun as with the upstairs maids and Miriam. After my sentencings, mother and M. Ramon went over my work together while I was allowed to read a book as I sat in the golden chair by the window.

Lunch with mother, a little after noon, was my favorite part of each day. She always listened to my chatter like it really mattered. That made me feel like I had important things to say when, in truth, it was mostly complaints and petty drivel. Later in the afternoon, when the shops reopened, she and I went to see different sights and to the museums.

I had to pay attention because sometimes M. Ramon quizzed me on what I had seen. My assignments were to write essays about the different scenes and sights. M. Ramon corrected my French, and then I had to translate what I had written for my lesson into English for mother to review. That was the routine. On weekends, my father returned and we visited areas outside of Paris. I had to write about those places for M. Ramon too.

I guess I learned quite a bit while we were there. I didn't fall behind in my school work. When we returned to Burkina, I was a couple of chapters ahead of the rest of the class. I got to tell them about my trip. Mother and I made a scrapbook of color postcards, ticket stubs, museum programs and matchbook covers for the school. Some of the students had never been away from home. They were amazed.

The Eiffel Tower was a big hit. And the Tuileries: all those plants, all that color. I was just glad to see my friends and play with them again. I thought of Miriam and how she was so kind to me, and how M. Binet gave me a tiny Limoges, and of M. Ramon and how he laughed at me when I told him I really didn't like all those mirrors at Versailles, and how Hervé kissed my hand good-bye. I did remember, those first few days back in the heat, in the red-brown dust and in the thick hot air, how I missed the rain in Paris.

LADYBUG

Ladybug's Truth Knock Over (TKO):

- There is no place like home

SWITZERLAND

Precise and disciplined. Reliable, trustworthy, and clean.

The Warmest Welcome

I had to go to prison, and I was just a kid. I wondered, what had I done? My incarceration took place the year of my tenth birthday, I went to a faraway alpine facility. The name of it was boarding school. I really didn't want to go. As usual, I had no choice in the matter. Decisions concerning my welfare and education had nothing to do with what I wanted; they were orders I was to follow in the normal chain of command. That chain started with my father and then trickled on down. I was a kid, I did as I was told.

My older brother and older sister would be at the same school. That was a plus on the list of pros and cons and it was a very short list. To say I was surprised to be leaving Bobo Dioulasso would be inaccurate. I was stunned. Then, as the reality of it sank in, I was very sad and more than a little frightened to be leaving mother. I cried about it in secret, wishing it not to be true. Finally, I made myself numb. I had to; that way it didn't hurt so much.

The year before, my whole family had spent the entire summer prepping me for boarding school. It was to be the American School of Alexandria, Egypt. This school was the only one in North Africa that would take a student as young as I was. All of us kids would be there together. On the eve of our departure, with trunks packed and carry-on bags organized, we got a telegram from the school.

The school informed my parents that for lack of students and thus lack of revenue, they would not be opening that term. My brothers and sisters went off to Spain and Switzerland. I stayed home. I was so relieved! That was the year I learned to argue in French, ate bread and chocolate sandwiches, fell into an open sewer, finished reading Webster's unabridged dictionary, learned to ride a motor bike and fought like Muhammad Ali.

The following year, I was not so lucky. Boarding school in Switzerland loomed closer with each passing day. I didn't want to believe I would actually go. I secretly hoped for a last-minute stay like the one I had enjoyed the year before. I thrived in Bobo—how could I leave? I remembered that before we left the United States, I had read some descriptions of Africa as the dark continent. Dark? It was all bright and colorful under a sometimes blistering citrine sun. I had traveled with my parents to Ghana, Togo, Mali, Côte d'Ivoire, Senegal, and Nigeria. It was amazing wonders of flora and scented air under crystal-clear diamond skies. I marveled at the ancient land, the mountains, and the many people of stunning beauty and bottomless strength.

I shrugged off cloudy, inaccurate descriptions for a reality of sobering heat, wilting humidity, and awesome beauty. There were many marvels for the senses. Time marched on, but this was a place where time was a mere second in eternity. The gem that sparkled and most enticed me was a place that ruled time as effectively as it came to rule me. I loved Bobo Dioulasso—the stinging heat, the pungent smells, my schoolmates, my singular adventures, and my life in general as the American girl. I wanted to stay!

Unfortunately, that was not to be; off to St. Galen, Switzerland I did go. It was a frighteningly harsh awakening, that little Swiss village in the shadow of the Alps. I went to boarding school, where I got two roommates who seemed to be afraid of me. I guessed that was okay, because I was not too sure of them. Neither of them smiled when they met me. I know I didn't feel as though I had anything to smile about either.

My roommates were both two years older than me. Louisa, the more gregarious of the two, was German and spoke

Italian and French—so we could at least talk. Gerta was German and spoke only German. She refused to shake my hand and didn't even look at me. I wondered for a hot minute if that meant I didn't exist. If I was not acknowledged, if I was ignored, it meant I was not there. Right?

Gerta's reaction was harsh, but it was not new to me. I had encountered that same behavior before in the United States of America, at a real American elementary school, where my skin shade situation was an issue. After a brief moment of wondering about Gerta's reaction, I put it from me. I had to. I knew I could not pause too long over the whys or wherefores, because the answers they produced were sure to hurt. I had recently begun to notice that those particular kinds of wounds bruised deeply and took a very long time to heal. Gerta was another of those Grinch-type people.

As I was the last to arrive, I got the bed by the window with its matching closet and drawers. While unpacking I witnessed an intense drama between Gerta and Louisa. Although they spoke in German, I knew their conversation had to do with me. I was holding my frightened heart together with all my energy, so I tried not to notice. What I did notice was that the place was quite a change from the sweltering heat and humidity of West Africa.

The degree of cold was as foreign to me as the alpine climate was shockingly sterile. I had only light cotton dresses, knee socks, a navy blue sweater, and penny loafers. It was September in Switzerland. The Swiss walked about in shirtsleeves, but I put on two dresses and put on my only sweater over those. I didn't have a hat or a winter coat, and nobody seemed to notice. I didn't want to bring any attention to myself, so I kept my discomfort within.

I think that when you live with people, you learn things you would rather not know. I grew up knowing, believing, that

God saw everything I did. Knowing this, believing this, didn't prevent me from doing bad things. I am sorry to say it didn't prevent me from doing bad things, but I think maybe it kept me from doing worse things. Perhaps not by very much. I often prayed for the strength to be honest and true and then purposely, with complete awareness, was not. It was a see-saw of a problem for me, one I struggled with often. I spent many hours trying to work it out.

That is where Gerta comes in. She was my more reluctant roommate. I think she was afraid of me. I was not certain, but over time, I figured out it had to do with my skin shade situation. As I was powerless to change it, I decided to never react badly when she brought it up against me. I decided that if God made us all, and I believed that was so, there was a very good reason we were in so many different shades.

I agonized over Gerta's aversion to me, trying to discover the reason for it. It confused me and picked away at me like a woodpecker drilling holes in a tree trunk. I spent much time trying to mend my wounds. I lost too much time tending wounds I didn't want. Finally, I figured out that I might never understand. I figured out that I had many questions that would never be answered. I understood also that I might not know how to ask the correct question.

My question concerning Gerta was no longer why she despised me, but how I could be less of a target for her hating eyes and vitriolic tongue. When I had first arrived at school, Gerta's bed was next to mine. By the time I had unpacked, she had switched beds with Louisa. While Louisa sat on her new bed and wrote a letter home, Gerta sat on the edge of her new bed and glared at me for hours. It was very unsettling.

The first German phrases I learned were insults. I thank Gerta for that; she had many. She spat them at me whenever we were alone. Gerta literally recoiled with distaste when she came upon me unexpectedly. I memorized all of Gerta's insults as well as I could. After a few weeks, when Louisa was more comfortable speaking with me, I asked her to translate them for me.

The first time I asked Louisa to translate Gerta's phrases was the last time. Louisa's face grew still and solemn. She asked where I had learned such phrases. I told her it didn't matter, to please translate the German into French for me so I could understand. She did. I believe that for as long as I live, I will never understand. I had to bury Gerta's words away inside where I could not hear them anymore. I thought that trying to understand Louisa's translation was like trying to get an answer for one those questions I had for God that never got answered because it was not the right question.

After the translations, Louisa was much nicer to me. I avoided Gerta studiously. In the mornings, I rushed to dress and get to breakfast without walking near her. It was not easy. We sat at our tables according to dorm, floor, and room. Luckily, Louisa always sat between me and Gerta. In the evenings, after study hall, after free time, I rushed to get into bed before Gerta came to our room. I lay in my bed by the window hugging Teddy, curled against the cold, willing deep sleep to claim me quickly. Sometimes it did; most times it did not.

Over time, Gerta's insults, and perhaps her strong feelings behind them, eroded my self-confidence with a bitter, slow burn, like acid. I felt it happening, but I didn't know how to stop it. As I lay in my bed those nights, I forced myself to be quiet, to turn off my ears and shield my heart because I was afraid it was breaking. I thought it might be leaking out hurt that I would never be able to mop up. It was imperative that nobody see my hurt! I forced myself not to listen to anything Gerta said and not to react to her behavior toward me. I prayed for relief and promised all sorts of things to God if only I could get to sleep fast each night. In the mornings, I awoke exhausted and sad.

I went to my classes each day like everyone else. The only difference was that I stopped looking at anything with any interest whatsoever. I stopped walking with my head up. I watched my feet step by step in my penny loafers, on the ground, on the gravel, on the grass. I faithfully did my lessons and any extra-credit exercises. I sat in the classroom silently. I spoke only when absolutely necessary. I thought I might just possibly (Please God!) disappear.

I did my homework in study hall, rushed to my bed after free time, and awoke in the mornings more exhausted and more sad than the day before. I told myself not to be sad. I told myself nothing lasts forever, that I would not be at boarding school much longer. I cheered myself with small calendars in each workbook. I crossed off the day with relief when each day was done. Each day, I got better at getting through with less hurt in my heart and more hope for my stay at the alpine school to be that much closer to an end.

One day after study hall, during free time, we heard screams. They were frightened screams. These screams were quite different than the many kinds of screams one hears in a girls' dormitory. There were always screams. There were laughing screams, fighting screams, my-boyfriend-dumped-me screams, happy excited screams, and angry excited screams. The screams I heard now were frightened screams, and they were coming from my room. I rushed down the hall with all the other girls. We crowded in the doorway. Gerta crouched in a corner at the head of her bed, pressed against the wall. She had stopped screaming, but she was clearly terrified and nobody could see why.

One of the older girls, Magda, pushed her way past those of us wedged in the doorway. She tried to pull Gerta out of her corner, but the harder she tried, the louder Gerta's sobs became. Gerta pointed to the foot of her bed, and Magda went over. After a moment of staring at the pile of shoe polish and polishing cloths, Magda started to laugh. She laughed so hard that she had to sit down and hold her sides. Magda's laughing made Gerta quiet. She looked at Magda with such hurt, my heart felt sorry for her before my mind did.

Magda pushed herself off of Louisa's bed and stumbled outside the room. When she told the other girls what had happened, they laughed too. All you could hear for the next hour was laughing screams and shrieks of merriment in the hallway outside our room. Apparently, Gerta had planned to polish her shoes, and when she dumped her kit onto the foot of her bed she saw that it contained an unwelcome addition. Propped on its long-dead haunches, between tins of shoe polish and buffing cloths, was a white rat.

Gerta sat in her corner crying softly, clearly overcome with distress. We still heard the girls laughing at her expense. As ugly as she had been to me, I understood she that was devastated by her shoeshine kit discovery. I picked up the dead white rat by its long, thin, pink tail just as Louisa rushed into the room. I walked past her across our room to the big window by my bed, with the rat dangling from my fingers. I opened the window and threw Gerta's visitor out into the falling snow. It unsettled me.

Louisa stayed with Gerta at her bed. Gerta was still crying, and Louisa tried to comfort her. I picked up Gerta's shoes and her kit and took them to my bed. I sat there and polished and shined Gerta's shoes. When I was done, I set them at the foot of her bed the way she herself did. I folded her shoe cloths and put those and the polish back in her kit and set it on the floor next to her shoes. I left Gerta and Louisa in our room. Free time was almost over. I washed up and got ready for bed.

That night I slept curled up, hugging Teddy, but not so cold. I fell asleep quickly and awoke the next morning feeling better than I had since my first day at school. More importantly, I didn't dread what the day might bring. I still crossed that day off the calendars in each of my workbooks. I still spoke to no one, kept to myself, kept my heart shielded. Nothing much changed in my daily routine. As usual, after study hall, after free time, I rushed again to wash up and get to bed. Sleep was the only peace I enjoyed that I could discern in those days. When I got to our room, for the first time in months I was not alone. Gerta was there.

I stood in the open doorway of our room wondering what to do. I thought I would go sit in a shower stall until lights out. I did that sometimes to shield myself from the snickers and the onslaught of insults I didn't understand. Before I turned, though, Gerta looked up from where she sat crossed-legged on her bed. For the first time in our acquaintance, she smiled a friendly smile, with no guile in evidence. It was a powerful TKO. Was her Grinchness really gone? I didn't know. I stood silent and uncertain in the doorway. When my knees started shaking I went to the showers and sat in a stall until lights out.

That night, when I curled up hugging Teddy in my bed by the window, I fell asleep instantly. When I awoke in the morning I felt more peace. I felt more peace, and the sadness that shrouded my heart lifted a little. I felt a glimmer of hope that my remaining time at school might not be so harsh. I really missed mother, but I kept that to myself. I was supposed to be a big girl now, not a mama's girl. Still, I looked forward to going home. I knew mother would greet me with the warmest welcome.

Over a Clear Singing Stream and Through the Woods

I was surprised to discover that I liked the alpine great outdoors. I am still sometimes surprised about that, even though I have memories confirming that I liked it. Those memories are from the many walks we took at boarding school on half-day Wednesdays and Saturday afternoons. These walks were mandatory unless you happened to be dead. Even the students in detention had to get out into the fresh air and participate in the exercise. We walked in the rain and in the sun, in the cold and in the heat, but never in snowy weather conditions.

There was no way to get out of the walks. I suspect the reason was that it was a sure way to get all the students' restless energies fired up and bottomed out. Sometimes we walked down the mountain into the town. I didn't like those excursions much. It was hard for me to keep up. The older kids' interests were beyond my appreciation, and I didn't understand their jokes even when it was clear that I was the object of them, which was often the case. I knew I was not welcome. I was shunned by the townspeople as well as the students. Nobody wanted me with them, so even though I was there, I was not there. But our over-mountain treks were very different.

On our treks over mountains, we ran and walked and laughed and screamed. Sometimes we even yodeled. The walks began in the main courtyard of the school and went along a narrow mountain road into a whispering wood where a forest of feather-leafed evergreens grew. We walked along the road for unmeasured kilometers without ever seeing another soul. Then the path crossed over to the other side of the road, and by that time, our line of hikers was snaked out in twos and threes and ones and fours and me—straggling far, far behind the leaders of the pack.

I had discomfort on these walks because my legs got chafed and it was a long time before they felt better. As soon as they did, of course, we walked again. I got used to it, and before I knew it I liked the walks despite the discomfort. I liked them also because I could imagine I was a carefree goat in a herd of goats high on the hill, as in that song from *The Sound of Music.* I had not seen the movie, but I had listened to the album and knew all the songs.

I didn't sing much, but the other kids did and I liked to listen. I liked it when we reached a certain point on the mountain path where we could say anything in a voice soft as a sigh and it would echo back, echo back, echo back. Some of the kids would yodel. I didn't yodel, but I liked it when the other kids did. Sometimes we heard an alpenhorn. It sounded eerie and mysterious in the clear mountain air.

I kept apart. I didn't get too close to the other kids. If I did, they would notice me. Since my brother was on those walks, he would take the opportunity to tease me in front of an audience if he saw me. So I stayed by myself, alone. I studied the sky, breathed deeply of the air, and set each foot in front of the other with single-minded determination. I watched not to get too close to any of the other kids, and I listened to the birds and the goats and the cowbells. I was in a sea of sound and activity and was careful to keep my movements calm and unhurried while maintaining my emotional distance.

One of the most magical moments in our walk up the mountain happened when we got to a small footbridge over a clear singing stream and through the woods. It was a place where surely the fairies danced. Diamond streams of light laced through the trees, spilling their jewels on the forest floor where the fallen leaves softened all the footsteps into quiet murmurs lost among the moss-wood logs. And sometimes, if our procession was particularly quiet, we would not interrupt the n-n-n-knocking of a woodpecker drilling for its dinner way up high in the bark of a tree.

Occasionally we saw fish flying though the air several inches above the surface of the stream, like kites sailing on the wind. The sunlight caught in their scales, and they shimmered like broken bits of mirror scattered through the rippling stream, cresting on the water. I could stand on the small footbridge that spanned that section of the stream and watch the fish jump—and forget for a fleeting second that this forest was by no means enchanted, and a sleeping beauty I was not.

At the top of the mountain, we could see the entire valley below. It glistened like gems on a carpet of moss-green velvet or like ice crystals dancing in the light of a bright winter sun. Sometimes a thick and billowy gray-white fog lay over the valley like a fat, fluffy, eiderdown comforter. That is what I think I liked best. Even more than the fresh milk and hot chocolate at the farmer's inn on the other side of the ridge, I liked that spectacular view of the miniscule valley world far, far below.

In that spot on the mountain, looking at the tiny village, I could summon a recurring daydream in which I flew high above the clouds and looked down through them somehow. Through the clouds, I looked down and I saw myself as an insignificant speck of dirt on a whitewashed rooftop. But in my daydream on that mountaintop, I was free to float like a cloud.

From way up high I saw the bright green grass, the grazing cows, the grass-cutting goats, the yellow daffodils in the clover, and the patchwork of butterflies bobbing in the green for sustenance. If I was perfectly still, and if I turned just so, off in the distance I could hear the joyful peeling of bells in the valley and I was happy.

Sometimes, no matter how hard I tried to keep up, I would be the last to arrive at the farmer's inn. By that time, all the kids had had their first cup of hot chocolate and there were no seats free. I could usually sit at the table with my sister. Her friends would always make room, and one of them would get me a cup of hot chocolate. That was all I had time for before we were herded together like obedient sheep to hike back down the mountain to the school.

The downhill climb went much faster. Sometimes, I managed to keep up with the main body of kids. This was our Wednesday routine. We got walked for the exercise and fresh air to keep us strong and healthy. When we reached the school grounds, there was a head count and then we were dismissed to our dormitories to wash up for dinner.

That was Wednesday night dinner; my favorite meal of the week—even after I learned what it was I'd been eating. True, I gave up the main dish purely on principle, but I usually had enough warm bread and vegetables to fill me up fine. I rarely had trouble sleeping on those nights after a Wednesday afternoon walk, but often I was achy and my feet did sometimes get sore. Even with the aches and minor soreness, sleep kissed my eyes closed on those nights, and the next morning, if not the sun, then the bright white mountain light coaxed them open again to see a new day.

I think I learned to love those over-mountain hikes because for a short time I could go at my own pace, and if I was careful, nobody noticed me. In those quiet moments, I felt the magic of the earth. I felt it alive under my feet and it stirred with promise all around me. The walks helped to clear my little pigtailed head of all the nebulous fears and false starts that lurked in every hallway of the school and dormitory, which were the boundaries of my boarding school existence.

Sometimes, the creaks and moans of the old building were too loud for me. They shouted into the quiet of the long alpine nights. At those times, I found great comfort in the image of my feet walking the mountain paths. I imagined myself basking in the forest magic. I quelled my fears with images of the sun-dappled forest floor and bright flowers smiling at me through the trees from the hillsides. In those dark and lonely nighttime hours, I felt ever hopeful of finding a bright and welcome destination over a clear singing stream and through the woods.

Wednesday Night Dinner

Food ruled. In prison or not, we were fed like kings at boarding school. We got a hot breakfast of porridge, fresh-baked bread with butter, jam, eggs, ham, and sausage. At 10 o'clock, it was midmorning porridge with hot chocolate or strong tea with cream—real, fresh cream, not canned or powdered. Lunch was served at 12 noon. At 4 o'clock, we had a tea break with fresh-baked bread, butter, jam, and more hot chocolate followed by a huge hot dinner at 6. Five meals a day—pretty much all the food you could eat. I ate.

My favorite meal was Wednesday night dinner. It was the same menu each week, and in general, we ate a lot of venison, pork, and potatoes, peas and carrots, bread, butter, and gravy. We had other vegetables too, but I do not remember what they were. I liked most vegetables so I am sure I ate plenty. I remember the bread, the butter, the jams, and the delicious satisfaction of Wednesday night dinners.

At my first Wednesday night dinner, I asked Louisa what kind of meat we were eating. It was tender and tasty, and I had never seen that deep red kidney bean color before. Louisa and Gerta put their heads together and laughed and laughed at my expense. Louisa never failed to ask me if I liked it. Yes, I did like it. Very much. That meat made a rich red gravy just waiting for mashed potatoes, and there was nothing like it for rib-sticking, lip-smacking, hand-clapping taste bud satisfaction.

We also got a late-night snack of yogurt and hot chocolate around 8:30, just before lights out at 9. I sometimes saved my yogurt in the snow on the second-floor windowsill in my shared quarters. Louisa and Gerta always asked my permission to put anything out there. I think they felt guilty about having given me the bed by the window. I let them.

Well into the winter I still had no heavier clothes than those I had brought with me from Burkina. I remember that one day I struggled up the main road within the school grounds in my slippery penny loafers. I was so concentrating on not sliding back downhill for every three steps I managed to climb uphill, I didn't even care that the boy I had a major crush on stood watching from the window of my German language classroom.

Normally I would have waved, but not this day. It had started with fresh snow, and before leaving the dormitory I had had to put a piece of folded paper in the bottom of my shoe where the sole had worn away. That spot was cold and wet in no time at all. That foot was soaked, and the toes had begun to freeze. There was nothing to wave about.

Both of my feet were soon completely wet. I knew that later they would hurt bitterly from this bout with the cold. I looked forward to my next class because I thought it would give me time to dry my shoes and warm my feet. I sat near the radiator in that classroom. My feet would be warm and dry in time to get wet again during the trek to lunch in the main building at noon.

Luckily that morning, Louisa had given me a pair of white wool tights she said didn't fit her anymore, and I wore them under my navy blue knee-high socks. I could feel the cold chewing at my toes despite the extra layer. Maybe I would just put more layers of folded paper in my leaky shoe after dinner.

By the time I fought my way to the top of the hill, I was exhausted by the effort and my toes were stone-cold frozen. The new wool tights had a hole at the right knee that had originated when I fell on some ice in full view of Joseph, the object of my crush. As I struggled to my feet, I decided I didn't have a crush on him anymore. No, not with his presence right there at the window.

He was a witness to my hill-climbing trial of humiliation. I pretended I didn't see him; otherwise the embarrassment of it all would hurt too much. The cold hurt enough all by itself. I had thread and needles; I could mend the tights. I could bear mending my tights. I did wonder if I would be able to get the blood out. I hoped so, because if not there would be a rusty-colored stain on them.

At last, at the top of the hill, and so very late for my next class, I was surprised and dismayed to see both the headmistress and school administrator waiting there for me. I had never been so late for a class before. I guessed I was in big trouble. I had never had a visit from the Terrifying Twosome, the scary lady enforcers of all things scholastic and cultural in my tiny little boarding-school universe. They were mother and daughter, these two. They ruled the school with no tolerance for misbehavior; there was no hope of avoidance or escape for us because their eyes and ears were everywhere. My knees were shaking. I was afraid of them. They rarely smiled, and this day was no different.

Frau Ginsler spoke first and told me that I would not be attending the afternoon activity that day. Normally, I would have been pleased to miss our walk down the mountain into town, but I was too fearful at the time. She said that after lunch, I was to return to my room in the dormitory and wait there for her and Fraulein Ginsler. I didn't understand—was I getting detention? I didn't ask because I was too busy worrying. They walked me to the main hall and into the dining room; we were the only ones there besides the wait staff. As morning classes would soon let out, I was to stay in the dining room until lunch was served, then return to the dormitory after the meal.

When the other students began to arrive, Louisa, Joseph, and Gerta were among the first in the room. I looked up in time to see Joseph say something to the other two, and I quickly turned away. I had to shake off the shadow of shame that seemed to cling to me. It was like the smell of smoke that clung to some kids who sneaked cigarettes in the stone tunnel leading from the main building to the tennis courts. It wrapped around me like a heavy cloak. I could not shake it.

I wanted to forget that Joseph had seen me fall on the ice-slick gravel of the road outside the window of my German language classroom. I wanted to forget that I was afraid and had nobody to tell except my teddy bear. He was soft and accepting; he always comforted me. I kept myself turned away and told my eyes not to cry. At least this time they listened.

Both Louisa and Gerta were more attentive than usual, which made me think that Joseph had told them what he had seen. With Gerta knowing, now everyone in the school would know. Ah well, if I didn't think on it too much, the hurt and humiliation would not haunt me. Gerta gave me her mittens when lunch was over and it was time for me to go to the dormitory to meet the ladies Ginsler. It was so uncharacteristically generous of Gerta to give me something that I thought I would wait to put the mittens on. I figured I would check with her at study hall that night to make sure she meant for me to have them.

Gerta had once insisted that I take her gift of a little notebook, so I took it. Then I had to give it back to her when her parents came to visit. The notebook was a gift from them, and she didn't want them to know she had never liked it. She tore out the pages I had written on and threw them away and when her parents left, she tossed the little book in the bathroom waste bin. I thought the mittens were another gift like that, so although my hands would soon be cold, I didn't put them on but instead tucked them inside my math book.

After lunch, I walked back to my dormitory with much slipping and sliding. The Ginslers were talking with the house mother, and the moment I arrived they stopped speaking. They all looked at me with tight, fake, frosty smiles and we went straight to the room I shared with Gerta and Louisa, straight to my side by the window and to my assigned closet and drawers. Frau Ginsler asked me to unlock my closet and seemed surprised that I simply went over and opened it.

I knew that Louisa and Gerta carefully locked their closets each day. I never bothered to lock mine because I had so little and nothing of value. I already knew the other girls mocked me on this account. I had walked in on Louisa displaying my belongings to some of the other girls. They didn't even stop laughing when they saw me and they didn't put my things back either. They all just rushed out of the room.

Looking at the three ladies I wanted to rush out, and I did, for a short respite in the restroom. When I returned only Fraulein Ginsler remained. She told me that we were going into the village for the afternoon and asked me to dress more warmly. I pulled Gerta's mittens on over my gloves. I knew this was a fashion faux pas, but the mittens were the warmest articles of clothing I had. Fraulien Ginsler was visibly dismayed.

We went into the village, Fraulien Ginsler and I, and she bought me a carload of new winter clothes. Never had I been more surprised or embarrassed. We drove down the winding road into the tiny village in her little black car, with the heat on high. The first thing she bought me was a navy blue leather hat with fuzzy plaid lining and earflaps. Then, she chose a navy blue wool winter coat to match the hat and a sturdy pair of navy blue leather boots with deep snow-biting treads.

I had never owned boots before. I vaguely remembered wanting white go-go boots once. These boots were soft, supple leather with thick rubber treads and fluffy stuff on the inside, all the way to my toes! I didn't want to put them on over my torn tights and dirty socks, but Fraulein Ginsler insisted. I put them on, and as my toes began to thaw, I didn't mind the pain as much because I knew the new warm boots would keep my feet dry and toasty. We got more new winter clothes that day than I had ever owned.

We walked by a toy store, and I saw my reflection in the window wearing the new hat, coat, and boots. I didn't realize I had stopped until Fraulein Ginsler walked back to see what was keeping me. She looked in the window too. I think she thought I was looking at the dolls, because she asked me if I had one. I then saw that she was referring to the two dolls in the window.

The dolls were dressed in traditional Trachten outfits. They wore lace tights and tiny brown boots that looked like real leather. The skirts were made of wool to match the jackets, and tiny hats sat on their heads. They were the most wonderful things I had seen in a long time, even more wonderful than my new clothes. Well, the answer was that I didn't have a doll baby, and that is what I told Fraulein Ginsler.

Soon it was time to get back to school. Fraulein Ginsler's little black car was packed full of bags and boxes. She took me back to my dormitory and, along with Louisa and Gerta, helped me put all of the new clothes away in time for dinner. Now my closet and drawers were almost as fully packed as Louisa's and Gerta's.

That night I ate the most delicious meal I can remember. The bread was fresh and warm, the potatoes wallowed shamelessly in rich red gravy, and the meat was tender, filling, and tasty. And, as I had on a weekly basis since my arrival, I once again asked Louisa what kind of meat it was. This time she didn't laugh. Instead, she hesitated and then told me. Horse meat.

I sat in shocked silence. My hand was in midair; a tender morsel was poised on my fork, loaded with gravy, ready to pop into my mouth. I could not eat it. I set the implement of culinary doom down on the plate. My enormous appetite was immediately and completely quenched. I do not know why Louisa decided to tell me on that night. Was it because I now had warmth for the outside and maybe didn't need it so badly for my insides? All those weeks, of dining bliss, ended in that instant.

However delicious, however tasty and filling my dinner, I could not eat another bite. I still had to be sure about this terrible news so I went to the kitchens after dinner and asked the cook. He was very obliging. He showed me the halved horse carcasses hanging neck-down from gigantic metal hooks in the huge walk-in freezer. Skinless heads with hollow eyes stared out at us from cold metal shelves like gigantic frosted bookends as we moved closer to the big icy sides of meat.

It was true, then. No story, no lie. I recognized what I saw hanging on the hooks. I knew what I saw on the shelves. I looked at the long dark eyelashes framing eyeless sockets, the frozen flare of the nostrils, the familiar shape of the heads. I knew and loved that regal profile propped with a herd of others on a shelf. The hooks held shoulder, flank, rump, and shank for stews! I was heart-sore and heartbroken to find out that at my favorite meal of the week I had been eating the family pet.

Then and there I made a resolution: I had to stop. I didn't want to stop, but it was important. I had to. For the love of all the horses I had ever known or heard of—Black Beauty, Trigger, Comanche, Rebel, Cousin, Star, Penny, and National Velvet—I had to stop. I thought the least I could do, out of respect for my equine friends, and in true appreciation of my newfound warmth and winter-readiness, was to forgo, at once and forever, my beloved Wednesday night dinner.

A Lesson in Penmanship

I learned cursive handwriting with tremendous difficulty. In French school, we had withstood daily hour-long exercises, and our teacher would take every opportunity to make certain that each letter was placed securely within the confines of the squares on the grid paper we used for practice. In boarding school, it was much different. We didn't have a set time to practice. One had to practice however one could, so I spent much of my free time in the dormitory's great room filling my fountain pen to work on my penmanship. On the inside cover of one of my textbooks were examples of perfectly formed letters that I copied as best I could. For all my trouble I got blue fingers, and the paper featured many ink blotches that the blotter could not absorb.

These new letters were curly, rounded, and plump. They took up a lot of room on the page. The letters I had learned and practiced in French school were angular and spare, compact and efficient. It was hard for me to make the change, but I always tried. I had no friends and plenty of free time to practice as I sat by myself at the back of the great room in our dormitory. Some of the students were allowed to use ballpoint pens, but I was not one of them. When I wrote with a pencil, my penmanship was medal worthy; but if it was not in ink, it didn't count.

One day I lost my fountain pen. I looked all over the great room. This must have been quite a sight for the other girls. They rarely saw me move from my location at the desk in the back of the room. When a couple of them learned what I was looking for, they all took part in the search. They somehow made it into such a loud and unruly game that several of them got detention, and I never did find my fountain pen.

It was a bad thing, losing that fountain pen, because I didn't know how I would be able to get another. Most of the girls had special cases for their pens. The cases included extra ink cartridges, and some even had a matching mechanical pencil. I had just my fountain pen. I kept my pen and a couple of spare cartridges, with the ballpoint and the pencils, in the pencil case I had used at the French school in Bobo.

There was nothing special about my fountain pen. It was made of cheap plastic. It leaked, and I kept it in my green plaid, plastic pencil case, which closed with a snap and had a loop on one end. I never really knew what that loop was for. It was too small to fit any of my fingers comfortably, so it didn't seem to be for carrying. Was the pencil case supposed to hang on a hook? Anyway, I didn't find the fountain pen. I really needed it. For some reason, I kept looking in my pencil case as though it might magically appear there. If it did, I would be able to identify it without any trouble because it was as fat as my thumb and shiny black like Fraulein Ginsler's square little car.

For a week, I did my penmanship assignments with a ballpoint pen. The instructor told me that my writing had improved, but I still lost twenty points for each assignment I turned in that was not done with a fountain pen. I tried unsuccessfully to borrow a fountain pen. No one would lend me one since I obviously went around school misplacing fountain pens right and left. I even tried to borrow one just for our free time, with the idea of giving it back immediately afterward whether or not I was finished with the exercises. That didn't work either. It was my own fault though. I really had to take better care of my belongings. So I guess it served me right.

One day I went to the desk back in the corner of the great room where I always sat, and there was my fountain pen! Someone had found it and left it there for me. I was so pleased, I started on my penmanship exercises right away. I hoped that if I redid the old exercises, maybe I could get full points on them. But doing them over was more just something to keep me occupied.

I really didn't think my grade would improve, because I knew my fountain pen writing was not as good as my ballpoint pen writing. It never had been. But since I had nothing else to do during free time, I practiced my penmanship anyway. When the dinner bell rang, I carefully put my fountain pen in my green plaid pencil case and put my pencil case in my book bag. I was so glad I had the fountain pen back.

I turned in my old exercises with my new ones, and the instructor frowned over them. I think he was surprised I had made the effort to redo them on my own. Then again, it might have been that my penmanship was not that good with the fountain pen. I do not know. I had my fountain pen now, and I would take good care not to lose it again.

I soon lost it again. Or, to be more accurate, it was returned to its rightful owner. One of the other girls in the dormitory had lost her fountain pen. Hers was no cheap plastic thing. Hers was a fancy pen, very expensive. In study hall, we were all asked to check our desks and place our pens on top of our books. I did as we were all asked to do. I was so very glad to have my own fountain pen back. I understood exactly what this girl had been through.

The girl went up and down the rows. When she got to me, she picked up my pen with a shout of triumph. I could not believe it. She was taking my pen. Or so I thought. Well, I was wrong. I was very wrong. The pen was hers, and she could prove it. Her pen was engraved. Her name was on it. I had not even noticed. I was so sorry. I told her I was sorry. I had thought the pen was mine, and I knew firsthand what it was like to lose one's pen. My abject apology mattered for nothing. I guess I would not have believed me either.

From that day, I was known as a thief. My story, however true, was unbelievable. I understood everybody's skepticism. I didn't understand how they blamed me for what was my honest mistake. My new status landed me into a strictly enforced solitude in which I kept to my own company alone. It was not so different from before. Only now there was tangible hostility directed my way.

Frau and Fraulein Ginsler were very disappointed in me and, although my mistake was innocent enough, I didn't blame them either. I did protest my ignorant innocence profusely. Nobody listened and nobody cared. How could I blame them? My earnest protestations went unheard. Now, on a much larger scale, my isolation was impenetrable and more complete than ever before. So much for a lesson in penmanship.

The Gift of Great Surprise

When I left Upper Volta for boarding school in Switzerland, my trusted teddy bear was the only toy I brought with me. To tell the truth, I didn't stop to consider taking any of the others, because it was Teddy who calmed my fears at night; it was Teddy who was soft and smelled of Tide laundry detergent, and it was Teddy who kept my neck warm as though I was enfolded in mother's oh-so-tender, gentle, loving embrace. And, although he never had a proper name, it was Teddy who was always reassuring and faithful in his support of me. Actually, I didn't consider him a toy.

Boarding school life was well ordered, leaving little time for idleness and little time, if any, that was unsupervised. We did enjoy a tiny bit of free time in the great room of the dormitory to read or visit with each other, play board games, or knit. As long as one behaved and did what one was expected to do—did what one was told—it was okay. I didn't have a problem with any of that because I was used to following orders, taking direction, and making no waves.

I had no real friends at boarding school. I was isolated, but it was not an altogether unfamiliar situation. My two roommates had little time for me and I didn't blame them. The two-year difference in our ages made them young ladies, whereas I was clearly still a child. This meant that I spent every smidgen of our precious little free time alone. Yes, I was in the great room with all the other girls, but since they formed groups that excluded me, I sat by myself and they let me.

Normally, I would read ahead in my textbooks or make up crossword puzzles. Sometimes there was really nothing at all to do. I tried knitting and found it mind numbing, even though I managed to knit several long, long wool scarves with fringe. Knitting was not enjoyable. And, of course, sometimes I would practice penmanship. We mostly used pencils but were also learning to write with fountain pens, and since I often had spills and made blotches on my work I didn't mind practicing. Even so, my penmanship was never very good.

One day Fraulein Ginsler sent for me after lunch. Since our shopping expedition, I had not been afraid of her or her mother anymore. They had even brought me to their home for tea a couple of times. They were both extremely kind to me. We spoke almost exclusively in German for practice, and Frau Ginsler always took the time to coach me and compliment me on my progress. Frau Ginsler even found a young girl in the town, closer to me in age, with whom I was allowed to play on regular occasions.

On this day, Fraulein Ginsler met me at the foot of the steps outside of the main building. She wore a deep-brown fur hat with matching muff and stood by the school car with the medieval crest on the door. I wondered if I was being expelled. Then I guessed I was not, since she was smiling with a sincere and happy twinkle in her eye. In truth, I didn't know what was going on, and I would not give in to the luxury of wasteful speculation.

The chauffeur opened the back door and I climbed in. Fraulein Ginsler got in next and sat down beside me. We took the long, winding, narrow switchback of a road down into the tiny cobblestone town with the big gray stone fountain in the center of the village square. The streets were narrow, and the car bumped along rather slowly, finally stopping to let us out. The chauffeur would wait and we would walk to our final destination from there. For a second, I thought of Hansel and Gretel—I do not know why.

We walked into the labyrinthine streets of the crusty old town, and Fraulein Ginsler held my hand with hers inside her fur muff. It felt as if we were the only two people in the world walking hand in hand on the curvy stones steeped in the history of that ancient town. We stopped at a small bright shop with toys in the display window. Fraulein Ginsler opened the door and ushered me in.

She went straight to the counter, and the Gepetto-Man in lederhosen came from behind it to the front, greeting Fraulein Ginsler warmly. The man then turned to me, and I understood him to say there was a big surprise waiting. I looked at Fraulein Ginsler, and she just smiled with a twinkle in her eyes. The proprietor motioned me over to a long wooden table in the center of the shop, where there was a big white box. Pale pink tissue paper spilled out of the box, and as I got closer, I saw the most beautiful baby doll in the world fast asleep inside.

"She is yours" is what the shopkeeper said. I looked at Fraulein Ginsler, and she nodded her head in agreement. I could not believe it. I felt that if I touched anything it would all disappear and I would find myself sitting back in the great room at the dormitory, spilling ink and making wet blue blotches on wasted bits of paper. The baby doll, with eyes that opened and closed, was mine not as a loan, but to have! I could only stand and stare. Fraulein Ginsler showed me to a shelf filled with little tiny dresses and tights and smocks and slips and tops and coats and jackets and hats and shoes. I was to pick out what I wanted! I could not do it, though, because that is when I began to cry.

I never named the doll. I felt I simply didn't have the right. To name her, that is. That baby doll represented what I now know as validation or worth, or what you might call a certain acknowledgment of me as a person. That doll was a treasure for me and my tenuous little budding self during a period in my life when I felt very much forgotten and ignored and when I was more often than not treated like an afterthought or even an inconvenience. To name her would have made her ordinary like me, and that doll was extraordinary.

The doll was more special than any and every name because she was tenderness and joy, kindness and compassion. She had eyes that closed when you laid her down; and if you rocked her just so, she would cry. Fraulein Ginsler later knitted her a cap, a skirt, a jacket, and little yellow booties. That day in the shop she picked out an entire wardrobe, including socks and shoes. I will not easily forget the kindness both Ginsler ladies showed me during my dim and dreary alpine stay. After leaving the school I wrote to them both for several years, and they never failed to reply. Then, as often happens, time passed and I stopped writing. We moved again and again with my father's work, and I grew out of playing with dolls.

One year, on break from college, I decided it was high time I cleared my room of childish, girlish things. For close to a decade that most special gift of great surprise had lain on my bed among the pillows. Looking at her made my heart tender. Looking at her made me want to be kind. She was a good talisman. On that day, still remembering all of the joy she had generated in my life away from home and still feeling my heart brim with gratitude, I carefully packed her up.

I packed up my lovely doll with the long, curly eyelashes and all of her beautiful clothes, and even the pink and white and yellow hand-knitted treasures from Fraulein Ginsler. I carried her to the basement to go with the next donation to charity. It was one of the most difficult things I had ever done. I didn't dare look back. I knew I would see her standing there with the light glinting off her eyes. And I knew I could not bear it.

That evening, when I returned home after a full day of laughter and fun with friends, I went up to my room a little more slowly than usual, bracing myself for the empty space among the pillows on my bed. The room was dark, but silver-edged shadows spilled in through the undraped windows. I didn't have to turn on the overhead light to see that precious baby doll nestled among the pillows on my bed, as beautiful as she had been the day I first laid eyes on her. Just then mother came into the room. She said she had noticed the doll in the basement and had not wanted father to take her to the donation center by mistake.

I hugged mother and thanked her with a kiss. She left me standing in a moonbeam, looking at the doll on my pillows. I noted how my heart melted with tenderness and joy, kindness and compassion. I stood there and watched how the moonlight sparkled in her eyes, and it occurred to me that one cannot easily relinquish such a special gift of great surprise.

The Devil Made Me Do It

I was crazy. I was tempted. I was crazy tempted. I thought about resisting the temptation. I knew my parents had not raised me that way! I finally decided that I would resist. I decided to resist the considerable temptation. Then, quick as a snap, I gave in. I saw that I was tempted and I willingly succumbed. The temptation was to deliberately take that which I knew clearly and without a doubt was not mine. I was tempted to take, and did take, every glistening franc there on the bed.

For a moment, knowing full well I didn't believe it, I applied the philosophy of one of my brothers regarding right and wrong:

> If someone leaves money out and the money
> is taken, nobody but the person who left the
> money out is at fault.

There are so many things wrong with that philosophy. I never once believed it. I knew it was all kinds of wrong to take what didn't belong to me. At that moment in time, I didn't care. It is a hideously ugly fact of my life in social isolation—away from my parents, ignored by my siblings, and shunned my peers. I will never live it down. I stole money, and with it I bought a compass, a mechanical pencil, a Barbie, and some clothes for Barbie.

A special letter was written to my parents, and I had to sit in the headmistress's office while she wrote it. She frowned at me occasionally to emphasize the weight of her words on the paper. I knew I had done wrong, and I sat quiet and still while she wrote to my parents about the incident. She recorded, for their eyes only, her version of my crime. I had plenty of time to reflect on my wrongful act, and I had decided that it was true: it was a crime indeed, and I was going to pay. I was in prison, after all.

Frau Ginsler signed the letter with a flourish and blotted it. Then to the letter she applied the seal of the school with a heavy embosser. The embosser was kept locked in a brown wooden box on top of her desk. Frau Ginsler folded the single sheet of cream-colored paper into perfect thirds. After folding it, she put it into a matching cream-colored envelope. On the back of the envelope she dripped wax, and into the wax she set the seal of the school from the ring she wore on her smallest left-hand finger.

I was impressed. I think I was supposed to be. I then had the job of taking the envelope and, while Frau Ginsler watched from her office window, putting it into the mailbox. The big metal mailbox was on the side of the main building at the top of the wide, gray, stone steps. It stood to the right of the heavy, wooden, haunted door.

The haunted door led to a flight of stone steps that went down to the soccer field. The meadow beyond the soccer field was where the buried swimming pool lay. It felt ominous for me to be near the door. I wondered if the ghost of the child who had drowned in the pool would now taunt me. I wanted to get into the mailbox along with that letter and just go home.

I had to give everything I bought with the stolen money back to the stores from which they had come, and my sister was mad at me. I didn't blame her. My sister's world was a very different one from the one I lived in. I interrupted its smooth orbit with my transgression. I was sorry for that. My sister had to take me to all the stores to return my ill-gotten gains. She had to use her pocket money to reimburse the girl for the shiny silver coins taken from her. I felt sorry for that too. I wondered why I never got pocket money.

My sister had never noticed that I had no winter coat or that I had holes in my shoes or that I had only cotton dresses that winter before the Ginslers took me shopping. I didn't blame her. She was not interested in me; she was interested in boys. She was a teenager, after all. She was supposed to be interested in boys and fashion, hairstyles and cosmetics. I got a thorough scolding, which I deserved. She didn't speak to me often after that. To be fair, she rarely spoke to me before that. So not much had changed. Except that now I was, in fact, a thief. I kept my own company well, which was a good thing, because that was all the company I got.

As for my brother, I was lucky if I never saw him. He teased and terrorized me in front of any audience he could interest. It was best to keep well away from him, which is what I did. For my own comfort I often hummed "Jesus Loves Me" over and over. Jesus was my friend; the Bible told me so. What a friend I had in Jesus, all my sin and grief to bear, and did I not have the privilege of bringing them to him in prayer? At least, I told myself, I had a friend in Jesus.

The Sisters of Divine Intercession disagreed. They insisted that they were my true friends in Christ our Lord. However, because I was rebellious as to religion, they felt it their duty, as my friends, to school me in the most proper religious ways. I remembered reading how the champions of the Crusades tried that tactic too. The sisters instructed me that Jesus was not my friend, he was my Savior. They themselves were married to him and to the church in truth and in service. Because of this, they knew what was best for me. I was to practice the way of confession because they knew it was the best course of action for me.

I didn't understand the role of the priest in taking my confession. Sacrilege! The sisters were concerned. They whispered together about how many Hail Marys I might have to say and what other penance I must serve before I would be completely forgiven. I worried that the sisters didn't know that Jesus had died for all of my sins already. All of them, even ones I had not yet committed. That is what the Bible said. I thought the Bible was the only book those sisters got to read—why did they not know this? Well, it was a pretty big book, maybe they hadn't gotten to that part of it yet.

I didn't understand what were they reading if they weren't reading the Bible. Didn't grace and truth come to me from the Holy Spirit? I asked. Was it not correct that through Jesus, grace redeemed me the instant I confessed my sin of stealing to him? If I told a priest now what I had already told God months ago, was that not backward? Were the sisters saying that the priest was more important than Jesus? I could never believe that! I was confused.

Mother had explained to me when I was four or five or six that God was Jesus and Jesus was God's son and that when we accepted Jesus into our lives we got grace, and the Holy Spirit dwelled in us from then on. She said I could always talk to Jesus because even when nobody else did, He always heard me, even if I talked to Him only from my heart or in my head.

In Sunday school I learned that when Jesus died, the Holy Spirit was God's gift to us. It was Jesus who interceded on our behalf. This was not what the pure-hearted, faithful sisters believed. I didn't understand. How could the sisters not know about this? It was from the pages of the Holy Bible. They prayed just about every waking hour and The Holy Bible was their main book.

I resisted confessing and the Ginslers appealed to the sisters to teach me. They told me the sisters would answer any questions I had. The sisters had no answer to my question about why I needed a priest between the Lord Jesus and me. My way, I had a direct line. Their way, I had to wait in line. I refused to confess again because I already had to God. God already knew my heart was contrite. I had repented. I had confessed. They didn't take my confession on faith or accept the fact that I knew I would never steal again. Repent meant to quit it and do that thing no more. How did they not know this?

My refusal to confess to the priest tainted me with the stigma of religious insubordination. This was bad. Very. It meant no communion for me because I had not been absolved. I was a sinner. It also meant no participation in many of the children's activities at church. It meant that it was okay to punish me too. I didn't understand. I resigned myself to my lot. I was used to being made to feel I was wrong. I didn't expect this to change. If the sisters had to punish me, I must have deserved the punishment. I sometimes lay awake at night, wondering what exactly I was being punished for.

Left alone, the sisters likely would have whipped me white with their rosary beads, as well as with their words of fear and rejection. They took every opportunity to push, pinch, or pat me hard on my head as though I were a dog. Sometimes I got a quick pull on a braid when no one was looking. I thought that was wrong, to act one way in front of others and then another when we were alone. I think they knew it was wrong, I think that is why they had to pray so much.

After many tedious consultations over several months of warring, the Ginslers felt it best that I not attend church anymore. I didn't feel strongly about it one way or the other. The sisters vehemently disagreed. They insisted that all I had to do was confess to a priest who would tell God for me. Then all I had to do was confess to the Ginslers, to all the girls in my dormitory, and then, of course, to every student in the school. After that, God would forgive me and my heavenly slate would be wiped clean.

That was their way, and I could not do it. I would not do it. I knew it was backward. I believed it was wrong. God knew how sorry I was. Had I not told Him through thunderous tears of shame on my knees on the bare wood floor at the foot of my bed by the window in the room I shared with Gerta and Louisa? I had done that months ago, on the night of the day of my debacle. Was I now to make something up for the priest when my transgression was already over and done with?

Can a sinful child reason with clergy? I was relegated to keeping my own company because I refused to pretend with hypocrites. My insubordinate behavior, my argumentation, was met with the sisters' stony stares. They declared belligerently that many prayers would be prayed for me. They spit the words at me like snapping turtles. I thanked them. I told them I needed all the prayers anyone could pray.

Thank you very much, sisters divine. Lord knows I needed the prayers. No amount of Hail Marys or confessions or detentions would make me deny that, regarding my seduction by the shiny silver francs (and as God is my witness), the devil made me do it.

The Gift of Ann Elise

My fall into disgrace was a documented fact. Word of my sin and the details of my sentencing traveled quickly in our tiny boarding school community. Now even the students from different dormitories didn't speak to me. I also noticed that Louisa and Gerta, although always courteous, took every opportunity to keep their distance. I knew it was my own fault; and although it did bother me, this time I didn't let it hurt because my heart could not hold the humiliation. And besides, I had met Nancy Drew, and she had become my very best friend. This was important because my only other friend, Ann Elise, was not allowed to play with me anymore.

Ann Elise was of the village; she was a little less than a year older than I. She didn't attend classes at the boarding school. Frau Ginsler had found her. She was to be a friend for me, closer in age than any of the students at the school. Our first meetings were fun and filled with laughter. This was my friend

Ann Elise, whose mother greeted me on my first visit to their home with a big hug and a kiss on my forehead.

Ann Elise's mother gave us each half a Milka chocolate bar to share as we played on the living room floor. It was Ann Elise's father who did not allow me to come into the house when he met me for the first time, on my fourth or fifth visit. Ann Elise's mother protested right there in the doorway, where her husband stood to keep me from coming inside. She covered her mouth with both hands, and her face got red. She had tears in her eyes when she looked at me over his shoulder.

From then on, Ann Elise and I played outside and only for thirty minutes, not an hour like we had before. I thought my skin shade situation might be the reason, however, I really do not know. Ann Elise's father watched us play from the kitchen window. He came outside to tell me to get along back to the school when thirty minutes of our hour's time had passed.

I retraced my steps to the spot where a carved wooden door with a tiny sliding window was tucked into an arch of the centuries-old wall made of rough stone. I remembered to push hard to make sure it closed behind me. I walked slowly up the steep, narrow mountain road back to school. I wanted to use up as much of the time remaining as possible.

On another scheduled play date, I went to Ann Elise's house and knocked on her front door as always. This time Ann Elise watched through the kitchen window as her father stood on the step at the top of the stone pathway by the side of the house. He told me not to come there ever again. I told Frau Ginsler what had happened, and she said perhaps it was for the best. Her mouth was a straight line and she made her hands into fists. I never found out why the visits were to cease, but I think the fountain pen puzzle might have been the reason. It could have been the shiny silver francs or even my skin shade situation. I do not know. What I do know is that I was most recently the school thief, and that was one true thing I could not deny.

However innocent my mistake had been about the fountain pen, and however contrite my heart over the silver francs, however sincere my apologies, I was, after all, a thief. That was a good enough reason to keep me away from Ann Elise. I took to daydreaming more and more often in study hall. Usually, I was flying high above the clouds but able to look down through them somehow, and there, like a speck on a whitewashed rooftop, I would see myself standing alone. I was always solo, still and silent, stuck on doing nothing.

I rarely did homework in study hall. The homework assignments I got each day were easy, and I often had them finished before I left my last class. Since nobody noticed me, I sat in study hall and daydreamed. I was physically there. My mind, however, was far, far away. Or I did extra-credit penmanship exercises, for all the good they did me.

One day when I went to my desk, a small package wrapped in brown paper sat on top of it. I took the package to our house mother, who sat in the front of the room and monitored us from her wingback chair behind the heavy oak table with the lion's foot legs. Frau Bernhardt frowned at my approach, and everyone in the room stopped what they were doing to watch. I gave Frau Bernhardt the package and told her it had been on the desk that I used.

I could not claim that it was my desk because nothing there belonged to me, and I had to be careful not to make false claims. Frau Bernhardt didn't take the package from me, so I put it on the table beside her clasped hands. She waited until I had returned to the desk at the back; she waited until I sat down. Frau Bernhardt then called me back up to the front of the room. Some of the girls giggled.

I was not upset, or frightened, or anything. I had no feelings. I was not even curious. I stood in front of her where she motioned that I should stand. Frau Bernhardt asked me why I had brought the package to her, and I told her it was on the desk where I sat and I wanted to be certain I didn't take anything that didn't belong to me. She asked how I knew the package didn't belong to me. I told her it didn't have my name on it so I could not claim it. Frau Bernhardt dismissed me. All of the girls giggled. I sat at the desk at the back of the room and drew a tornado in the middle of my penmanship assignment. It seemed to need to go there.

Frau Bernhardt appeared at the desk I used, breaking my concentration. I looked up, and she handed the package to me. She said that she had put it on the desk and that it was for me. I opened the package. In it was a book with a single sheet of folded brown package paper on top. I unfolded the paper. It was a note from Ann Elise, asking me to read the book and return it to Frau Bernhardt when I was done. The book was, *The Hidden Staircase*, a Nancy Drew mystery by Carolyn Keene. I read the book during study hall that week. After finishing the book, I wrote "Danke, Ann Elise" on the blank side of her note. I wrapped the book up again in the brown paper and gave it to Frau Bernhardt.

The next day another book was on the desk that I used at the back of the study hall. The same piece of brown paper was inside the book, only this time it was not folded. The side on which Ann Elise had written was facing up. When I finished the second book I put two checkmarks under the "Danke" on my side of the note. Then I wrapped the book back up and gave it to Frau Bernhardt.

This exchange continued for several months, and my time of isolation in school away from home passed more quickly because of it. My friend Ann Elise loaned me all of her

Nancy Drew books. When I finished reading those, she loaned me a different book each week until I lost count of how many books I had read. With each one completed, I put a checkmark on the brown paper. I do not know how many checkmarks there were. We never got to talk about our favorite characters or any of the best Drew investigations.

When it was time to leave boarding school I managed to say good-bye to everyone who had been kind to me, even to some of those who had not. I wanted to say good-bye to Ann Elise. From the school I walked down the winding road to the spot in the curve of the third turn where I would find the carved wooden door with the tiny sliding window tucked into the arch of the centuries-old wall. I opened the door and took the worn stone steps, one by one, down to Ann Elise's side of the mountain.

I walked in the long grass, wondering what to do if Ann Elise's father was home. I knew I was not welcome at Ann Elise's house, and I prayed her father would not be home. He was home, though, and he would not even let me speak. His sputtering guttural rage pushed me away like a white-hot pillar of fire. I backed down the stone pathway because I was afraid to turn my back on him. That day I backed out of Ann Elise's life forever.

I did manage to get Ann Elise's father to take the note I had written her. He snatched it from me and balled it up in his big rough hands. I thought he might throw it at me. I do not know if he gave the note to Ann Elise. Something happened, though, because long after I began to trudge the mountain path, after I closed the heavy wooden door in the wall and started up the steep and twisting road to school, Ann Elise came running behind me calling my name. Maybe her father had given her the note, relieved to know that I was moving a continent away and thus was unlikely to ever taint his doorway again. I do not know, I didn't ask. I was overjoyed to see Ann Elise.

Ann Elise and I hugged our good-byes. There was nothing for either of us to say. And even though I had put my address in the note, Ann Elise knew she would not be writing to me, and I have to say, so did I. She left me with a lasting gift, though—the love of reading. I liked school fine, and I always read what I was assigned. Sometimes I even read the next chapter in a textbook out of general interest.

It was at this time, however, that I had the singular experience of reading strictly for pleasure. This kind of reading I learned alone, in a world apart, in a miniscule mountain village where I lived for a short time in near isolation in the company of my peers. I learned to read books and enjoy the small pocket of solitude; to live between the pages for a short time and to learn a few things. I was transported for a time into another place, entertained thoroughly, and given respite. I knew tremendous pleasure. That was the gift of Ann Elise.

Blacker Than the Plague

We were all forced to march. Every other week, weather permitting, and if we were not on an excursion to Salzburg or Liechtenstein or some other magical realm, we, as a school, trudged into town. It took a significant amount of time to walk down the wooden steps fitted into the mountain side. We never walked down the roadway because that was far too dangerous. The road had blind twists and crazy turns. Besides, straight down the steps was quicker by far. Quicker, but not all that easy.

As much as I came to love our treks high up into the mountains, I dreaded our trips down our mountain into town. I was a burden to everyone and an embarrassment to the entire school. It was my own fault; I had let the school down. Was I not a thief? None of the kids could afford to be near me. I knew their reputations would suffer. I didn't blame them. I didn't try and change things either because I felt I deserved my shunning.

As on the long mountain treks, here too on the steps, I found myself alone. I figured it was my punishment. I deserved no less. Had I not done this to myself? I would live through it. Unless God struck me down where I stood! I waited a moment, looking up at the cloudy sky with great hope. Nothing happened. I continued to walk down the steps in the long wake of my fellows. I have to say I was sorely disappointed.

My fellow boarders were well ahead of me. They laughed and rushed along in bright-colored coats, their cheerful voices carrying through the air. I saw my roommate Louisa's pink wool ski hat move down the mountainside. I plodded down step by step as slowly as I dared without drawing attention to myself. I didn't want to be reprimanded for dragging my feet. But I felt it important to keep my distance. Was I not the school pariah? It was only right to keep away.

One thing that can be said about my stay in the Swiss mountains is that I, along with the other students, got plenty of outdoor exercise. Whether we liked it or not. The old mountain town was tough, as were the townspeople inhabiting it. I am sure every single one of them knew of me. I am sure every single one of them liked me even less than my schoolmates did. I am sure it was due to my tarnished reputation. I didn't blame them. They were honest people who loathed dishonesty.

Our school treks into town had me trailing behind, much as on our mountain hikes. In town, however, it was impossible for me to go unnoticed. On cold days it was hard to loiter outside while the other kids were in a store. I knew they didn't want me tagging along, so I kept my distance. Ironically, the girl whose money I had stolen was extremely kind to me. She took me under her wing and made sure I sat next to her when it was time for tea.

At those times I tried to disappear, but it was not easy. Marlena was a very popular girl, and the other students were drawn to her vivacious personality. They tried their best to ignore me. I did my best to let them. Marlena, however, went out of her way to include me in conversations and make sure I didn't stay so far behind that she lost sight of me when we all walked outside. She was extremely kind to me.

I was extremely uncomfortable. I told myself that nothing lasts forever. I told myself that it was my duty to be cheerful and stay out of everybody's way. I told myself that I had gotten what I deserved and had better not be a crybaby. And I knew that all of what I told myself was true. I made sure I did as I was told. I stayed out of everybody's way, and I do not think I cried again for another five years.

One day, however, I almost broke into tears. My parents had come to visit and we kids were allowed to window shop near their hotel. The hotel where my parents stayed was close to the center of the town. In the center of the town was a beautiful stone fountain. A favorite trick for the boarding school kids was to hold back the water in the spout until the pressure built. Then they would let go and the water would shoot clear across the square. I had never tried it.

My siblings tried it and then everyone moved on. I wanted to try it too, so they said hurry up already. I put my hand over the spout and the water pressure built up. I waited until the square was clear and felt that the pressure was getting away from me. I could not control the water that was forcing its way out. Just as I let go, a man walked in front of the fountain. Of course he got sprayed.

The built-up pressure in the pipes shot the water out with considerable force. The man was soaked. He dripped from head to toe. I got sprayed as well, but that counted for nothing. The man was furious. I was petrified and "Sorry, I'm sorry!" was all that tumbled out of my mouth. He glared at me and then stalked away. I had to apologize properly. I went after the man to do so. The man moved quickly. He strode farther and farther away from me with every step. I rushed to catch up. He threw hot curses back at me over his shoulder. He didn't slow down.

When I finally caught up to him, he turned on me in a fury. I kept my mouth shut because he had so much to say. I put a hand out and touched his coat sleeve. His eyes shot icicles and slashed at me. His lips curled back thinly and his mouth turned down with disgust. He shook his arm, threw off my hand. I understood that my apologies were worthless to him. When he spoke, he said to get away. I should not contaminate his town anymore. He said to keep my blacker-than-the-plague hands off of him.

Blacker than the plague. What did that mean? How black was this plague that my hands were even blacker than? I stood in the narrow street, on the uneven cobblestones, and looked at the backs of my hands. I turned them over and studied my palms. They were pink with cold. I didn't understand. Black was a patch of cloudless alpine midwinter night sky. Deep winter, when it was so cold that even the stars forgot to twinkle. Blacker than that? I turned my hands over again, studying them for answers. They were shaking. Not with cold, with confusion.

I knew the man spoke from a very great anger. His bile spewed out and showered down on me, soaking my sadness with yet more shame. His words were harsh and ugly. I made myself look into his eyes. I needed to see the words come from him. I felt my heart's frantic beating slow, shudder, and thud hollowly in my chest. I wondered if it was breaking again.

On and on he raved. I wondered where my brothers and sisters were. Were they not worried about my being gone so long? I didn't dare take my eyes from the man's red, angry face. I stood and listened to the vile curses he heaped on my head. I worried about my ears stopping up from his curses, from the filth he shouted. There was much I didn't catch, but I am certain all the words had to do with pain and suffering. I gave the man my undivided attention. I figured I owed him that much.

However much I owed, I didn't have the emotion in me to produce tears. I was not able to produce tears of any kind. It would have been fitting for tears of shame to roll down my cheeks. If I could have cried, I am sure there would have been tears of hurt too. I felt hollowed out with sadness that what had seemed like such fun had put me at odds with an angry, ranting stranger. He leaned closer as if to study my eyes. I thought he was looking for evidence of tears. I knew there was none. He seemed taken aback, as if he thought, How dare I not cry?

Believe me, I wanted to cry, but all my tears were gone. I do not know where they went; they just left my eyes hot and burning, dry as a desert wind. Lord knows, I offered my apologies. They crashed up against immobility. They made no discernable impression on the man. His bile had not produced the result he expected. I think he needed to see me cry to feel that my apology was sincere. He didn't know my tears were all gone.

The man drew back, and quick as a blink he spat on me. It landed on my coat. He spat again and it landed on my shoes. He stalked away. I was taken aback. I looked at the spittle in shock. The shock went through me like I imagined a lightning bolt might. It seemed like a hard knock on my head that traveled through my body all the way down to the heels of my feet. When it got there, it sizzled out the tips of my toes. I thought I could feel it scorch them before it sank into the cobblestones on I which I stood. I smelled ozone and wondered why the ground didn't buck beneath my feet. I hoped the man felt better now for spitting on me. I hoped we were back to being even.

I left the spit on my coat and on my shoes as a reminder. I thought I deserved it. I know I would never spit on anybody, but I told myself that if I could not control my own actions and caused harm to another, spit on my shoes was the least I deserved. My shoes were forever changed, but not as much as my heart. My heart was bursting. It was bursting with confusion and shame and a deep sadness that no tears would ever soothe away. Nevertheless, I learned many things that day, not the least of which was to keep my blacker-than-the-plague hands off the stone fountain.

LADYBUG

Fraulein Ladybug's Lektionen
  von der Schule der harten Klopfen:

- Grinches are everywhere
- Food is good
- Thou shalt not steal
- Kindness matters
- God sees everything
- Keep your hands to yourself
- Love sustains us

MELANIE L. MARSHALL

TUNISIA

Brilliant blue - Carthaginian, Mediterranean, Phoenician, too.

New Kid in School

I was always the new kid in school. This was never more true than when my family moved to Tunisia, a country in North Africa on the Mediterranean Sea. This move was not like any of the others. It was not a normal move. This move was very disruptive to my tender heart and awakening consciousness. The normalcy I had known with all of our other moves was missing. It was missing because when we moved into our new house in the town of Carthage, mother was very ill. She had contracted malaria. There was little to nothing I could do to help her.

I was told to keep away from her but I didn't listen. I snuck in to see her more than I was allowed. My sanctioned visits included a quick morning visit and equally brief visits after school and before bedtime. I really missed mother in those first few months of our living in a new country.

One of the things I just could not understand was how mother got malaria and not I. We both took our quinine tablets regularly. They were nasty, bitter pills that caught in your throat and made you want to gag. We took them anyway to prevent ourselves from contracting malaria. What good were all those pills and the mosquito netting if you were going to get sick anyway?

I missed mother. She was in the same house, a room away even. Still, I missed her sorely. The days passed slowly and painfully. They passed slowly because much of my joy was leached away in the absence of mother's calm and nurturing aura. The days passed painfully because this was the first country, outside of the United States, where I encountered prejudice from my fellow Americans. That made the days long and the nights far too short.

LADYBUG

I knew what prejudice was; I had seen it before. I had been subjected to it before too. Knowing and seeing and experiencing didn't make this new encounter with it any easier. Several children in my new school called me foul names and treated me with contempt. These kids, to the one, were all from Texas. They were not the first Texans I had ever met, but they were the most ill-mannered. They were the most bigoted. Those kids didn't even know me! And I had no desire to know them.

What I learned was that this was the first time these kids had ever been away from home and they didn't welcome the experience. They spoke disparagingly of the local people and showed insolence and disrespect for the country, its culture, and the customs. They were disrespectful of our teachers as well. I do not know why I was surprised.

When the Texas kids got disciplined, they didn't reform. Their parents said they didn't have to. Their parents were the same way. The Texas parents cursed at our principal! They said he had no right to pull any of their children out of the classroom or hold them indoors during recess. The kids took great pride in the tongue lashings given to the principal by their parents. They gloated about it.

The Texas kids talked of watching television and cartoons in the early morning before going to school. I could not imagine that television before school was better than watching the sun rise and fill the sky with the promise of a new and glorious day. But I didn't know television, so how could I say? The Texas kids talked of television, cartoons, hamburgers, and McDonald's as though these things were the epitome of goodness. I grew up with none of those things, but I could see there was abundant goodness all around me. I didn't understand how they could not see it.

I did my best to keep away from those kids. I had met many people from Texas before; none of them had ever behaved so badly. Several of the other students befriended me. They were solicitous and very kind and often spoke up in my defense against the Texans. Still, it was a long time before I trusted any of them. It was unfair of me, but I was waiting for the nicer kids to become more like the Texans.

I had encountered such an intense essence of ugliness once before. It was in the United States, my own country, at the real American elementary school. There I was surrounded by racist children for several hours a day. I weathered their unkind words and ill intentions all by myself. I had been alone at that school.

I felt alone in this new school too, but it was a different kind of loneliness. This new loneliness came from living in the harsh reality of the present without the immediate buffer of mother's tender loving attention and bolstering embraces. Each day I was happy to get home from school so I could visit with her a short while before I did my homework and ate dinner.

After my bath and close to bedtime, I got to see mother again. She suffered from fever and chills and had trouble eating, but she always gave me words of encouragement and support. She always managed to say, "Sweet dreams, Ladybug." Although I hated to leave her, I would go to my room and say my prayers for mother to get well soon and then would get into my bed. Sometimes I lay there for a long time willing the sweet dreams to come so I could have them just for mother. I wanted to honor her wishes.

I began to dread school because of the Texans. But it was not just the Texans, two of my new teachers were prejudiced. I kept quiet mostly and tried to disappear because it was awful if either teacher decided to pick on any of us kids. One of the teachers was clearly a bully. It didn't help much that he was also a big, loud, strong man. Unfortunately, this man was our math and physical education teacher. However much I had loved math before, I now dreaded it because he took all the fun and wonder out of it. He made each class period his opportunity to direct personal verbal abuse against us kids.

One day he asked me what football team was my favorite and I told him I didn't have one. He said of course I did. He said that since I was from Washington, D.C., my favorite football team was the Redskins. I had never heard of them before; I thought football was soccer. That didn't matter, the bully-man called me "Redskin" after that. The first few times I didn't respond when he addressed me as Redskin, but he beat on my desk in front of all the other kids and said he was talking to me. After that, when he called me Redskin, I answered.

The bullying got worse when our math teacher became our physical education teacher. He was a mean person through and through, like the Grinch before he got his new heart. This man didn't get a new heart while he was my teacher. When we were supposed to be exercising, he never let go of an opportunity to be derisive or act superior.

If a kid missed hitting the ball in softball, he would demonstrate how it was to be done. He himself would then hit balls until there were no more in the big metal trash can that they were stored in. Then he would make the child he was "demonstrating" for go and collect all of the balls. Nobody else was allowed to help, so it usually took a very long time. With three or four of these demonstrations during our physical education period, it often took so long to collect the balls that class was over and we had not even played a single inning.

One day the class split into two teams to play kickball. It had been my favorite outdoor game. I was not so sure about that now, not with this new teacher and the Texans. In every game we had played so far, there had been no fun to be found. I had not had my turn to kick the ball even once. This game began no differently. I hoped it would be over soon. I wondered if our teacher would kick both balls if a kid didn't kick according to his liking. He appointed team captains, and it turned out that the Texans all ended up on one team. That left most of the least athletic kids and me on the other.

The Texans were up first and they took a five to zero lead. Then it was our turn. Although we didn't look like much, my misfit teammates were pretty athletic after all. We managed to eat away at their lead little by little until the score was five to three. Bases were loaded, and the kid two ahead of me kicked a high ball that was caught easily. Then the next kid kicked to left field and our runner on third made it to home plate just before the ball hit him. We all saw that he was safe—even the Texans groaned over it—but quick as a lie, the bully of a teacher called him out. There were now two outs and three kids on base, and it was my turn.

My team groaned—they were so sure I could not play. Our teacher waved the outfielders on the other team in. At one time I might have thought they all believed that because I was a girl, I could not kick. This time, looking at the Texans, I guessed it was more a matter of my skin shade situation. The Texans were joking with each other, seeing this as the endgame. The pitcher sent in a baby roll. He was laughing; they all were.

This was déjà vu for me. The ball came along and I waited. Then, just as it measurably slowed, I stepped forward and kicked it to the horizon. That brick-red rubber ball zoomed past the pitcher's mound and shot into center field. Nobody was there to get it. Third base came home, then second, then first, then me. We won the game seven to five because bigots and cheaters always lose in the end.

After that, even though I was still talked about and made fun of by the Texans, life in the classroom was a little more bearable. My new friends were true friends, and we spent many a recess in carefree laughter. My bully math/physical education teacher was still a bully, but a few of the parents had their eyes on him. The one other teacher who was a bully taught the grade below mine, so I had little contact with that teacher.

After a long while, mother recovered from her malaria attack and my world was immeasurably brighter for it. I made myself tougher in those first months. I made myself tougher in order to deflect the slights of prejudice and fits of bigotry I knew I would see again. I told myself I had to study them like a lesson. That way I could learn to make the best of it. The fact that some people didn't know how to behave didn't mean I had to follow suit. I accepted the fact that in the classroom of life, I would always be the new kid in school.

Swim With the Fishes

I learned to swim at an early age. It was out of sheer necessity. We were traveling from Nepal home to the United States, with a stop at the Dead Sea. I didn't know about taking a swim in something dead. I did know the sea had died a long time ago before we ever got there. Everyone acted as though a deceased sea was normal, so I took my cue from others. Mother told me that the sea was full of salt, so if I had any cuts or scratches they were going to sting.

I knew I had at least two or three. I was used to the stinging of cuts and scrapes. At the time, I didn't want them to sting, so I stayed out of the water. I watched my brothers and sisters frolic, and mother and I stayed on the beach. I actually wanted to go in the water, but I had never been in such a big expanse of water before. I was wary of it.

My sisters were close to the shore, and mother called them to get out of the water so they could get cleaned up before we left. They were young ladies and they took a long time to get presentable. My brothers wanted to stay in the water until the very last possible minute. Mother would help my sisters get dressed and my brothers were to watch after me.

My oldest brother asked if I wanted to come in the water just so I could say I had been in the Dead Sea. I thought that would be a good idea, so I went in despite my cuts. I waded into the water, and the cuts stung as I knew they would. I was ready to get out. My brother told me that the longer I stayed in the water, the less the cuts would sting. Besides, didn't I want to practice floating? Yes, I did, so he helped me and it was fun.

I was doing fine, my brother said, and he told me that all the salt in the water added buoyancy. *Whatancy?* It was one of those words I filed away for later. I didn't let my not knowing what it meant keep me from hearing what else my brother said. He said the extra salt made it easier to float and that the Dead Sea was probably the best place in the world to learn how to swim. I understood. Then he showed me how to crawl-swim, and I practiced with him for a while. I didn't like having my face down in the water. The salt burned my eyes. I practiced to my brother's satisfaction. He said I was a quick study.

When my other brother noticed us, he swam over. After watching a minute, he said he would teach me how to swim. I already knew his teaching tactics, so applying my lesson thus far, I swam away as fast as my crawling arms would take me. It was very necessary that I put considerable distance between us because my older brother liked to play mean. This was nothing new, just something to remember.

I swam closer to the shore where my feet could touch bottom. My arms were tired. I gave up crawling for my trusted dog paddle method. I could do that fairly well. I swam back and forth with an eye on my brothers, who were farther out in the water. I could not tell if the salt in the water made it any easier to swim or float. I was having so much fun, I didn't notice that my cuts no longer stung.

After that initial lesson, swimming became one of my favorite things to do. In Tunisia, we lived at the lip of the Mediterranean Sea in Carthage. Carthage was an old, old city, founded by the Phoenicians more than a thousand years before Christ. Our house was right on the water. I already knew I loved water. Now I learned to love the sound of it. There were so many different water sounds. I think I liked hearing waves run up the beach and away again, all day, every day.

Another favorite thing was to watch how light played on the water. I could do that for hours. I made myself learn how to swim under water. I made myself open my eyes under water too, so I could watch the sand dance on the bottom of the sea. Sometimes, when the water was calm, schools of fish rushed past and around me as I swam slowly. I tried not to disturb them.

Our house in Carthage was separated from a now unused port by a ribbon of a road. When the wind was calm, I could throw pine berries from the upstairs patio into the water. I loved to walk along the retaining wall that kept the sea at bay. I imagined how it might have looked those many thousand years ago as a bustling port of commerce. It fascinated me that Hannibal, the great general, had once been there.

One day, on the side of the bay farthest from our house, I found a beached dolphin. It was flailing on the sand, inches from the touch of the tide. I tried to pull and push the dolphin back into the water. It was less than a meter long, but too heavy for my efforts. I cupped my hands and kept it wet as best I could. Finally I raced home for supplies. I got a bucket and a towel.

By the time I returned, sadly, the dolphin was dead. Seagulls were circling, calling out to each other that dinner was ready. I shed a few tears then. Knowing that the laws of nature prevailed didn't make the death of the dolphin any easier to bear even when I realized the dolphin was, in fact, a shark. I gathered my rescue kit together and walked back home again along the beach.

In the warm months, one beach in particular was my favorite. I often got to play there with friends, and we stayed for hours. I liked to dig for clams. We always got to have lots of snacks, and lunch too, if we were lucky. Not only could I dig for clams and bring a bucket of them home for dinner, but I could walk out into the water forever and it never came higher than my waist! Then, just when I thought the water was like that all the way to the other side of the world, there was a dip in the sand where I had to sink or swim.

At this spot I liked to sink. It was like slowly floating downhill. I liked to open my eyes and put my hands over my head. My fingers poked out into the happy breeze above the waves. I walked a few more steps and the water receded so that it came up only to my knees. From there I climbed up onto a long, wide sandbar. At low tide, people brought their chairs and beach blankets to sit on the sandbar island and enjoy the fun.

I liked to sit still in water up to my waist and watch small fish come close to inspect the changes in their neighborhood. The water was so clear you would not believe it was there at all, except that you were wet. Sometimes, if I was very, very still, the fish would come up and kiss me! They swam up close and nibbled on me, right on my bare skin. Depending on where my sensibilities were at the time, this was either delightful or disgusting. Usually it was delightful.

The sandbar was my favorite place to be on that particular beach. It was a great place to catch clams. Clam digging on the sandbar was harder than on the beach, but the bounty was bigger so you didn't need to find as many. I often went to the beach with the Tómas family. This beach was also one of their favorites because of the sandbar.

On a particularly calm and clear day, they said you could see Sicily. I am not sure I ever did. In the atlas, Sicily was pretty far. I had seen it with binoculars once, but I am not sure I ever saw it with my naked eyes. Several times I know I saw something that looked like land. I guess it could have been Sicily, since that is what they said it was. I was learning that those "they" people were very opinionated in their proclamations and declarations. Those they people said many things. I was learning to believe sparingly what they said.

The sandbar was like a narrow island in the big blue sea. We usually headed straight out to it after we set up our spot on the beach. Mr. Tómas liked to snorkel in the trench that ran alongside the sandbar. He said it held a plethora of sea life at its best. That meant it was a veritable treasure chest of thriving marine diversity. I enjoyed snorkeling in the trench too. The biggest clams were found on the seaward rise of the trench. I often dug them up for Mr. Tómas to eat. He ate them right there on the sandbar.

Sometimes when I found the clams, their shells were open. If I was very careful I could catch them open like that and rinse them in the water to clear out any sand. Usually, though, they were closed, and Mr. Tómas would use his pocket knife to cut the ligaments and open the shells. I knew pretty quickly that I didn't like clams raw. I ate clams raw from the sea only a few times. I liked them best steamed with crushed garlic and served smothered with unsalted butter and fresh-squeezed lemon on a big steaming bed of basmati rice. As much fun as I had catching clams, fish watching was even more fun—the show was spectacular.

The day I remember most vividly was a day when I went to my favorite beach with relatives of a colleague of my father's. I didn't know these people, but they had a daughter and they were visiting from the United States. My father's colleague asked if I could come over and play with their girl. Of course I could. That sort of thing happened often where we were. The parents sent their kids off to play together (whether we liked it or not) because we were all Americans. There were problems every once in a while, but basically, we kids got along fine.

On this day, I met Audra, the daughter of Tammy and Donald, her parents. They told me to call them Tammy and Donald. I didn't know their last name, so I had to. Audra was younger than I and stayed close to her parents. We walked in the sand together, collected seashells, and dug for clams; but other than that, she didn't want to play with me, not even to build a sand castle. I didn't mind; I am not sure I would warm right up to a stranger either. Besides, she was really much younger than I was.

I felt much older than Audra too, because I was wearing a new, two-piece bathing suit mother had made for me. She altered a one-piece suit of my sister's and voilà, I had a brand-new suit. I loved my new suit. It was turquoise blue with three, shiny, black, shank buttons on the top. The buttons were in a straight line right down the center. I was lucky to have my new bathing suit because the one we had ordered from Sears would not be coming for another month. My body was rapidly changing, and the changes were out of my control.

I was just glad mother could make me a suit to wear. Mother said I was having a prepuberty growth spurt and since I was growing like a weed, there was a good chance that by the time the new Sears suit arrived it would be too small. I was not to get upset about it. I planned not to get upset about the new bathing suit. However, the prepuberty/puberty issue rather alarmed me. I noticed that I got upset over things that had never bothered me before.

I played in the water and walked out to my favorite sandbar. There was the usual dip, and I walked on the bottom. I always wanted to see as much as I could down in the trench before I had to come up for air. I knew that when I moved, the fish would race away. Sometimes they swam through my raised arms. I could feel the underwater waves they made.

I tried to prolong my sea-bottom visits as much as possible. This time there were not many fish swimming nearby, and the water was rougher than usual, but it was still very clear and I could see in all directions. Off to one side I noticed a dark shadow floating along with the current. I could tell it was not a big fish, so it didn't much interest me.

The day grew late and the tide started to come in. It was time to get to shore. I didn't mind; it had been a beautiful day even though Audra had not wanted to play very much. That didn't bother me. I was used to playing alone.

As I headed back to the beach, I had to go through a floating mattress of seaweed. It was the dark mass I had seen earlier. The mass had found its way into the depression at the edge of the sandbar and settled there. It was a long bed of sea grass, and there was no way to get around it. So, like everyone else on the sandbar, I had to swim through it.

The mat broke apart, and it was easier to get through than I had anticipated. Long green fingers of seaweed wrapped themselves around me. As I let the tide toss me shoreward, the seaweed waved behind like flags flapping in the wind. I didn't like the way it felt—it was slick and slippery. And it was impossible to avoid.

When I got out of the water, I soon knew I had brought more than slippery seaweed back with me. There were strange, whitish, jiggly things trailing down my front. I had not seen my favorite fish out on the sandbar, and these interlopers were the reason. Jellyfish. Unfortunately, the trailers of white tendrils down my front belonged to them. I had several jellyfish trapped in my swimsuit top, suctioned around my budding breasts. They stung.

Audra's dad helped me get the jellyfish out. We had to go back into the water and let it wash them off me. I wanted to just pull them off, but Donald said that anyone who touched them would get stung on the fingers and hands. Audra's mom ran back to the house to get the first aid kit. I had a total stranger washing off my budding breasts. It was beyond embarrassment. When Tammy got back, she gave me two aspirin and calamine lotion to rub on my chest. Still and all, despite the uninvited guests during my swim with the fishes, it had been a beautiful day.

Feet of the Baobab Tree

I fell out of a tree once. Considering that I had fallen down a flight of stone steps and fallen into raw sewage, I guess falling out of a tree was something just waiting to happen. My tree-fall happened on a day I was on a sleep-over at my friend Mia's house. Her house was in the city of Tunis, about a half-hour drive from where my family lived in Carthage. It was the first time I had visited overnight, and we were excited because our parents had said we could go to the zoo by ourselves.

Mia and I were tomboys but we still played with dolls, sure. That was expected—we were girls too! We didn't play with dolls on this visit because Mia didn't want her little sister to be around us. If we played dolls, they were half Alana's, so by default she got to play with us too. I didn't mind Alana's company, but Mia that said if I had to live with her, I would. I think I understood. After all, I was not the only child in my family either.

One thing we were allowed to do, that Alana was not, was leave the house and cross the street to visit the zoo. Of course we were not to feed the animals or stick our hands through the bars or do anything dangerous like that. We were thrilled because we loved the zoo! We never got tired of visiting. Sometimes it seemed as though some of the animals had disappeared because they stayed in their caves or under rock ledges for what cool or shade they could find. It was never a good idea to go to the zoo in the middle of the day. It was too hot then for the animals and for people.

We went over in the late afternoon. We could stay an entire hour. We promised to return in one hour; we'd keep time with Mia's watch. Mia's dad kept an eye on us as we crossed the wide avenue. We waved to him when we got to the gate and greeted the guard on duty. We knew Mr. Mouamir. His son, Kafir, was a grade behind us in the American Cooperative School of Tunisia ("A.C.S.T."). We asked Mr. Mouamir if Kafir could come with us. Regrettably, he said, Kafir would miss playing with us because he was with his grandfather and uncle at the Souk, the huge market in the center of town. Mr. Mouamir would tell Kafir at dinner that night that we had asked for him. We purchased our tickets, waved good-bye, and skipped on through the tall black wrought iron gates to our own private world of adventure.

Walking down the pebbled pathway as quickly as was ladylike, we hurried along to visit our animal friends. We didn't run because we didn't want to bring undue notice to ourselves. Because we were foreigners, it was important to act with circumspection and "politesse." We learned that from Mrs. Suliman, our art teacher. She had married a Tunisian man and said that as visitors, we were also ambassadors to Tunisia from our own respective countries. We had to be respectful. I knew that already—my parents said that as Americans, it was important that we approach different people and different situations with equanimity and good judgment. I had been reading the unabridged dictionary for years, so I knew what equanimity meant.

At the A.C.S.T. school, tomboys or not, all girls had to wear dresses or skirts. No girls were allowed to wear slacks except during physical education class. I was used to this dress code, but Mia was not. Nobody said that as girls, we could not wear shorts under our dresses or skirts. That is what I did all the time. Mia wore shorts under her dresses and skirts only at school; otherwise, she wore blue jeans whenever she could.

I was not even allowed to own blue jeans, or any clothes made out of denim. Ever. It was improper attire. My parents felt strongly about this. I didn't care—jeans were of no interest to me. I made most of my own clothes anyway. I liked light cotton fabrics; they were best for the climate. We lived in a hot place. That heavy denim would smother you for sure and give you heatstroke just for the fun of it.

Mia and I often thought alike, or maybe I mean we often had the same ideas at the same time. This day was no different. Our plan was to tour the whole zoo first; after we had seen all of the animals, we would go back and visit again with our favorites. We didn't even have to say it out loud. We just looked at each other, and that is what we knew. It was expected.

We made our tour and said hello to all the captives. We sometimes felt that the zoo was more of a prison than a home for them. We tried to imagine what it must be like for all the animals to be in their pens, cages, and caves away from their herds, flocks, and families. We knew we certainly would not like it very much. This was why all animals should be treated with care and consideration. That's what my mother always said; we were the caretakers, and we had to do our jobs well because animals in captivity were unable to care for themselves.

I knew about captive animals. We had dogs at home, and sometimes, even though they got food and water and love, they tried to run off. Mia didn't have any dogs. She had a parrot named Jake, a snake named Harold, a chameleon named Arthur, and a tortoise named Henry. I liked Arthur the best; he ate flies right out of my hand.

After our special visits to our favorite animals (the elephants and hippopotami this time), we hurried along the path to our favorite flora section of the zoo, which was far enough from the busy street that the traffic sounds were muted and less intrusive. We liked the spot because we could see the zebras and the sea from our favorite tree. It was a gigantic, rough-barked tree with thick-leaved, arching branches that made a canopy of green far above our heads. The tree had seen drought, which showed in the buckled roots that pushed up from below ground to run along the surface like knobby knees or crooked feet. Most of the roots looked like feet—big, tough, gnarled and twisted things that couldn't possibly wear shoes.

We imagined that our tree was the majestic baobab tree that grew in other parts of Africa. It was a very big tree; bigger than any other in the zoo park, and it fit in with our fun just perfectly because it was a great climbing tree. However, as much as we wanted it to be, it was not the titan baobab tree. Thinking about those trees reminded me of the brutal dust storms in Chad and the frying-hot-to-melt-your-brain days there too. That climate was nothing at all like the weather in Tunisia.

This day was fresh and bright, with a slight, salty breeze coming in off the sea. There was hardly a cloud in the Mediterranean blue sky above us. The gulls turned and wheeled on lazy air currents. Looking at them made me wish I could fly. Mia said we still had twenty minutes before we had to go home. We looked at each other and had the same thought. We would climb our favorite tree!

And climb that tree we did. It was fantastic. At the bottom were ripples and bumps in the ground where the roots came through. If you were not careful, you could really get twisted and trip on them. The tree's roots were lumpy because of many years of drought. The thick, twisted roots were now close to the surface in order to catch what moisture they could.

These roots were in all shapes, and quite a few of them looked like human feet—Jack-and-the-beanstalk-giant-sized feet, but unmistakably foot shaped. We liked to walk on them and say, "Sorry! Excuse me for stepping on your feet." We pretended that the tree said, "That's okay, if I could, I'd walk on them too!" No matter how many times we said it, we still laughed. We laughed a bunch that day.

We climbed up the trunk the way the date harvesters climbed date palms down in Sfax. It was easy; there were lots of cups and saucers for our feet and hands. We climbed higher and saw the city spill away from the tall zoo walls. We climbed higher still and saw the Souk in the west and to the north. We could see the sea! It winked at us. "Hello!" The sea was blue as an agate marble, and the wave tips glittered gold in the brush of the late afternoon sun. If this was heaven, we were in it! We also knew it was late, probably near time to head back. I looked at Mia and she nodded her head. We had to get home.

I was above Mia in the tree, inching my way back toward the trunk. Mia was at the trunk, stepping down to another level when she cried out. Her hair was caught in the branch above. She got it loose but lost her ribbon. The breeze pushed it away and up. It caught on a rough branch several meters out of reach.

It was a special ribbon, Mia's favorite from a silk factory in Milan. Her mother had brought it for Mia's birthday a couple of months before. Mrs. Horner said that at the factory they called it Botticelli blue. The ribbon was made of sheer aquamarine voile. There was a real gold filament woven through and through. Aquamarine or Botticelli, whatever you wanted to call it, the shade was the exact color of Mia's eyes. Mia loved that ribbon. She looked back at me. I nodded yes, I would get her ribbon.

The ribbon was caught on a branch a little less than directly opposite from where I stood. The wind had carried it a bit higher by the time I got over there, but I was sure I could reach it. I worked my way around the trunk. It was a big trunk. Rough and nubby, it caught at my clothes and scratched my arms as I hugged my way around it.

When I got to the other side, I saw that I was much, much lower than the ribbon. Or maybe the wind had pushed it higher again. In any case, my path from the other side had brought me down farther, much too far down now. I had to climb back up. I did, and I got Mia's ribbon. She did a thumbs up from where she stood on the ground below. There were giant cactus plants down there, taller than she was.

I looked down and stuffed the Botticelli ribbon into my shorts pocket. I didn't want to lose it. I turned to face the tree trunk, and my shoe caught on the knobby-nubby bark of the branch I stood on. Somehow I found myself holding on to nothing. In my turning, I had let go of the branch above me. My foot snagged on the rough bark. I was caught there with no anchor.

I tried to launch myself closer to the trunk. I stumbled. I made it! That was a really close call. My heart was racing. I think I was afraid. I stepped closer to the trunk and looked for a firm handhold. I had never climbed on this side of the tree before. We always did our climbing on the other side because it was clear of the giant cactus plants at the bottom. They had wickedly long sharp quills, just waiting to stick you.

What I noticed is that this side of the tree faced the zoo. From where I perched I could see the zebras grazing. Zebras. I loved them, but I would look at them more another day. I was ready to go home. I continued my descent until I was even with the second-floor level of the building adjacent to the zoo park. I could see in the windows. I wondered if anybody over there could see me. I should have been paying closer attention to what I was doing. I held on to a nub on the trunk as I stretched down to hop onto the branch below. It was a mistake, and I knew it immediately. But now I was on it. It was a twig, really, not a proper branch.

Crack! I felt the branch break under the soles of my feet. The force of it vibrated up to my knees before the sound of the crack reached my ears. Mia flew around the tree, and the astonished look in her eyes ignited the fear in me. I grabbed at the branch I had just hopped down from. It was a fraction too high; my fingers slid off. I felt the jarring pain of bark as it jammed up underneath my fingernails.

Wind rushed by, and Mia screamed. I knew it was bad. I thought to close my eyes, then it was over. I never had the chance. It happened so fast that my eyes stayed open as bark slashed and branches slapped against me. I watched as the ground rushed right up to smack me down. I wanted to scream during my fall, there just had not been time.

I was down! I landed on my feet and I teetered on my toes because my face was snagged in the long thorny arms of the viciously spiny cactus plants. My body shook all over. Then slowly, so I could feel the sharp spines stab deeper, my knees crumbled and gave way. I sunk those last couple or three feet right into the belly of the cactus plants. I was down. I was thoroughly ripped, stabbed, and punctured. I was on the ground. As I lay there, I felt nothing but surprise.

Mia was crying. She pulled me off the plants, and the thorns ripped across my skin. I saw delicate smears of pretty red on plush and luscious green. I saw the hurt with my eyes—

my body was not yet in any pain. I was on my side now, looking at scrubby dirt, pebbles, and burnt-brown grass. Tiny red ants marched toward me in single file. I could not tell if I lay in their path. I figured I would find out soon. I tried, but I really could not move. Even my eyes were stuck; they wanted to keep looking at the dirt.

Mia put her face down to my level. I saw her out of the corner of one eye. She seemed small and very far away. What were those things in my face? Those white things sticking out at different angles? I tried to tell her I thought I was still in one piece. I saw a dust puff rise up from where my breath hit the ground. I do not remember any sound coming out. I guessed that was why Mia's eyes got so big. She saw my mouth move, but no sound came out.

Mia didn't talk at first. She brushed at the ground under my face, and I saw the red ants scatter. Then she said all in a rush, "I thought you were dead!" I managed to shift my eyes a little better, and her image jumped from side to side as though my eyes were fastened to springs in their sockets and rocking wildly back and forth. Even so, I saw more clearly, and Mia looked horrified. Well, her expression was fitting, because that is how I felt—horrified. I guessed then that I couldn't be dead if I felt horrified. I had never been dead before, so I didn't know this for sure.

When I tried to sit up, Mia said to stay down. That was fine, actually, because I realized that I could not move, not even a twitch. Maybe my body was broken. Maybe that's why I couldn't move. Mia extended a finger and touched the tip of one of the white things coming out of my face. It hurt! That is what I thought; I still had no words. The red ants kept crawling and I lay there, an obstruction in their path, trying my best not to cry.

I began to feel again. I felt shaky, I felt smushed, I felt wounded. Those things coming out of my face told me I should be screaming. I think my eyes already knew that on their own; I think that's why they were jumping crazily in their sockets. I regarded Mia carefully. She looked gray. Even her Botticelli blue eyes had lost their color—they looked gray too. Mia said she was going to get Mr. Mouamir, but she didn't move. She stayed crouched down looking at me. She brushed the red ants off their path again; and this time, when she said she was going for Mr. Mouamir, she stood and backed away. I watched her shoes recede out of my line of vision and then she was gone.

I lay in my stinging bed, I felt my eyelids flip down and then up again as they blinked. They did it without any help from me. I was focused on the long, needle-thin, white things sticking out of my face. My eyes still jumped, but I could see fine. There was nothing wrong with my vision. It was as sharp as the long white cactus quills. There was one I could see out of the corner of one eye that was embedded in my neck where it met the curve of my shoulder. Whenever I inhaled, it scraped against my earlobe. I wondered, if it poked into my jugular, would I bleed my life away?

There were long, sharp quills in other places too. The one that sickened me the most was clean through the skin between my index and middle fingers. It was longer than a pencil. The tip of that one, and a few centimeters below it, were red and rough with my ripped and drying skin and blood. While I watched, a miniscule bright wave of color welled up around the point of exit, seeped, spread, and immediately began to dry. The part of the quill that had broken off from the plant was ragged and curled like the threads on celery stalks.

Seeing my hand stabbed between the fingers made me think and I didn't want to think. The cactus quills made me think that my situation was really, really bad. I still could not move, and I didn't want to see my skewered flesh anymore. I closed my eyes, and they jumped in deep orange darkness. I lay on my bed of thorns thinking I heard each slow second of time tick-tock slowly by. Tick, tock? Had Mia left her watch behind? Why would she leave her watch?

I knew it was not my watch, just as I knew that the red ants still marched along their path as though I wasn't even there and knew that the light breeze still floated in from the sea. I knew it was not my watch ticking because I didn't have one. I imagined that the zebras were chomping food in their pens. I imagined that I might successfully clear my thoughts. I did what I could not to think of the zebras or the quills or the red ants any more.

On the warm and dusty rock-hard ground, with razor-sharp cactus quills in my face, I thought it just too—too incongruent-incongruous. It was an "incongruality." I wondered, is that a word, incongruality? I told myself to use it in a sentence, but before I could, I got distracted by the smell of the dirt. It smelled hot and dry and sweet. Sweet? Oh, yes, sweet. It was sweet from the red ants. They gave off a burnt-sugar, rock candy kind of sick-sweet smell. It was mingled with a fresh blood, salty smell. I smelled that too. I knew it was my own blood and it frightened me, so I pushed that particular sweet smell aside.

The burnt-sugar, rock candy sick-sweet smell of the red ants made me drowsy. My thoughts drifted, and my body settled into a slow and quiet aching to the tune of gull talk high overhead. The gull talk floated on the lazy summer air, the sounds carrying toward me from the shores of the sea, the salty sea.

Salty like the big fat tear that leaked out of my eye and rolled over my nose and down my cheek. Salty like the tear that trembled at the corner of my mouth before it eased past my lips and dropped off my chin. I do not know where it went from there. A shadow of a shiver slid over me. An icy-cold finger touched my forehead. A coldness trickled down my spine and poured into the tips of my toes. I was cold through and through. Frosty cold. I let my eyes stay closed, thinking of incongruality. No, it was incongruity.

Use that word in a sentence?

Holmes said to Dr. Watson, "Yes, Watson, the situation smacks of incongruity."

Maybe Holmes would use inconguous.

I woke up and Dr. Watson, I mean Dr. Horner, Mia's dad, had his hand on my forehead. He was frowning and his head was turned to where I heard Mia's voice coming from. Her voice hitched, and she shook in her words and stopped talking right in the middle. Dr. Horner turned his head and looked at me. He smiled a big slow smile, "There you are, Tumble-Lena, you gave us quite a scare. How are you feeling?"

I thought I was okay, so that's what I said. My voice came out in a ragged whisper, I didn't recognize it as my own. It sounded w-a-a-a-vy and small as though it was shrinking. Dr. Horner said we would wait and see to be sure. I had no broken bones as far as he could tell, but my head was going to hurt. Mia threw herself next to the sofa where I was and grabbed my hand. I saw that it was bandaged between my fingers.

Poor Mia was a mess. Her eyes were red from crying and her face was puffy. Tears poured out of her pretty blue eyes. I told her it was okay, not to cry anymore. Her crying was making me remember. I wondered if the stinging on my face and neck was from red ant bites or cactus quills. Then I remembered how smushed I had felt and remembered the smell of the dirt and the red ants and my blood. I also remembered how fast I had fallen and, well, that it was actually kind of...thrilling. But I never told anyone that because it was really scary too. Dr. Horner said that I could have been killed and it was a wonder I had no bones broken.

Mia ate ice cream and I got to suck on an ice cube while Dr. Horner pulled the long white cactus quills out of my face with his fingers. He used tweezers for the smaller ones. I felt my skin tear. It hurt. There were tiny dark dots on a tissue by my right shoulder. I realized they were dried and dead red ants. I felt bad that they had died because of me but I was glad they were not crawling deep in my ears and laying scent trails inside my brain. Mia was feeling better. She said most of the quills were longer than chopsticks and some were as long as knitting needles—boy, were they sharp! Yeah, I knew that.

I didn't look at the quills, I tried not to cry. The quills still stuck in me were no longer than sewing needles. Dr. Horner had cut them shorter with scissors before I woke up. I wondered, what if they had gotten me in my eyes! I tried not to cry thinking about it. Dr. Horner said it was good for me to cry right then because sometimes tears just had to get out. He knew that we two, Mia and I, had tomboy reputations to maintain and that tears were not for tomboys, but this, he said, was a special exception situation. After he said that, my tears dried up all by themselves.

Later that night I did cry a little. Tears seeped out of my eyes; I could not keep them in. I was hurting all over. My legs ached even though they felt like jelly, and my head weighed a ton. Dr. Horner gave me two aspirin and said I would feel better in the morning. All I wanted was to sleep the aches and pain away. However, I was not allowed to. I was not allowed to sleep too long because I had had a concussion. Just when I fell into flying dreams, Mia's mother would wake me. I lost count as to how many times.

Each time I saw her, as much as I wanted to cry about being awakened, suddenly I didn't mind. Mia's mother looked like an angel, the dim light shining on her platinum hair made a halo around her head. Each time she woke me, she held up a finger. It may have been four. No, I it was three. Mrs. Horner looked at my pupils with the flashlight. Then she tucked me cozy and I fell into dreams again. She smelled like Chanel No. 5, just like my mother. I already knew that mother was an angel on earth. Probably Mia's mother was one too.

Dr. Horner walked us back to the zoo the next morning. Kafir ran to greet us. He asked why my face was cut up and bruised and swollen. What had happened to my hand? We told him and his father what had happened. Mr. Mouamir said he was so sorry he had left early for the day. I didn't understand why he should be sorry; my falling was not his fault. Mia and I both knew we were not supposed to have been tree climbing in the first place.

From the looks of where the branch broke, Mr. Mouamir said I had fallen about twenty-five feet. "Praise to Allah, you were not broken-bones dead!" is what he said.

I agreed. Praise to the mighty God of Abraham-Allah-Buddha-Jehovah-Moses-Fatima-Mary Mother of Jesus-Sister Moon-Brother Sun-Good Fairy-Tooth Fairy-Good Ship Lollipop! I thought, PRAISE THEM ALL that I was not broken-bones dead.

Mr. Mouamir made me and Mia promise not to climb trees any more. Not Kafir; he was a boy, after all. We both promised not to climb trees again. I have not climbed another tree to this day. I must say I missed climbing trees, but a promise is a promise. And I know how to keep one. To tell the truth, falling to the feet of our "baobab" tree was quite enough.

La Reine Didon

She wore a coat as black as a stormy monsoon sea, shimmering with stardust. She stood proud as Poseidon with fore- and fetlocks frothy as white-capped waves. She had a brilliant white star on her forehead, bright as the crystalline sand on the beach at Hammamlief on a diamond-hot summer morning. On a diamond-hot summer morning when the sun's light is shockingly white and eye-tearing bright, when it instantly brands those brave enough to bare themselves to its relentless intensity. She was, oh, so fine. She was a fierce and haughty thoroughbred filly. She was the Mithra of our Mediterranean paradise. Regal she was, and so very well appointed. She was Didon, in honor of Dido, Queen of Carthage. And, she too, was a queen.

The human Dido, Queen of Carthage, was a very smart woman. Legend says that after the defeat of her army, she was allowed to live on as much land as a goat's skin, "Byrsa" would cover. To the amazement of the conquering general, Queen Dido cut the skin into pieces as thin as thread and laid the strips end to end. In this way, Dido's space encompassed an entire hill. So impressed was he by her ingenuity that the general allowed her to keep the area known as the beautiful town of Sidi Bou Saïd. (The account has many versions in several different countries.)

The resplendent Didon of four legs knew that she was the boss of me. I tended to her as her supplicant. She let me. Barely. I accepted her near indifference with aplomb. I had the idea that I might atone for my sin of having eaten her equine fellows in my notorious past. I had once delighted in, yes, even looked forward to the eating of the equine. I believed, on some level, Didon knew this and that she merely waited in her midnight-clad majesty for the perfect moment to kick my head in. And I, in my jodhpurs, wearing guilt for a coat, cared for Didon meticulously and enthusiastically, knowing that if the kick came, it would balance the scales of my life thus far—fair and square.

I was ruled by Didon's every whim, striving never to displease her. I was always mindful and ever affected by her moods. I didn't doubt for a second that she merely tolerated my seat on her back. I knew I rode her on borrowed time. My ever-soft murmurings and sugar sweet treats eventually won Didon's forbearance. But that is all. It was our mutual understanding that I was inferior. I knew I was lucky to ride such a mount as she. I tried to be exacting and conscientious in my care of her. I hoped I would, yet knew I could never atone for my sin of equine consumption in my other life in a different world.

And so went my time with Didon. We trained for dressage in the ring pretending we rode famous Lipizzaner horses. The strength, grace and beauty of those horses was legend. I had even seen the Lipizzaners in a dazzling exposition of skill and training. The breed was descended from the Iberian Horse and, living in Tunisia, we knew the Phoenicians and the Carthaginians had probably ridden their ancestors. I thought they were worthy of worship. Having once seen the Lipizzaner horses perform didn't make me a better rider, but I was at an age where I appreciated their legacy.

One legacy from this equine chapter in my life had more of an impact on my physical fortitude than any other incident to date. That special inheritance was the advent of Sidi Anwar, the sadistic groom and right-hand assistant to our training instructor, Sidi Fahr. Sidi Anwar was king of the stables, or so he believed. He had the right to ride any of the horses, and this he did with impunity.

A few of my peers were peeved at how Sidi Anwar treated their mounts. It was rumored that Sidi Anwar was heavy with the whip, and short on temper, with even the most docile of mounts. Queen equine that she was, Didon had never favored Sidi Anwar with a ride. Sidi Anwar was as bitter a man as Didon was beautiful. Even had she not been mine, I think I would call her the most beautiful, albeit temperamental and haughty, horse I had ever met. (Sorry, Rebel.)

I won the right to train with Didon by default. She was an unfavored filly from the stable of a local sheik, and she was mine to exercise regularly until she was either reunited with her former stable mates or sold. It was never clear which fate she might enjoy. I was speechless with delight at my good fortune. Didon, the queen of horses, was mine! Well, except that her spirit belonged to no one. In my dealings with her, I quickly learned that I had to be calm and composed or she reacted with unpredictable moodiness and irritation. So, in my life with Didon, I existed only to do penance in every second I spent with her. I was a kid without a horse, and she was the only horse that fit the bill.

Most of my peers were in the same situation as I; only a couple owned their mounts. I won Didon in a coin toss. As it turned out, regardless of the result of the toss I would have chosen Didon because by the time I got to choose, the choice was between her and a severely swaybacked mare who was clearly lame and most likely a short stop away from the nearest glue factory. This poor horse was sweet as honey and blind in her right eye. I fell immediately in love with her against my will and all manner of reason. From what I had read about love, I was on the right track, though. Love was supposed to be unpredictable, upsetting, unreasonable, and unconditional.

Plain equine Jane was named Sofia. Her name meant wise; her demeanor was gentle. Even so, circumstances dictated, and I chose Didon. I chose Didon, who snorted when I got close. I chose Didon, who always snatched at the apple I would bring her and head-butted me for more. I chose Didon over Sofia, who always whinnied her thanks and blew softly, gently on my neck. Didon, I am certain, would just as soon have bitten my neck off my shoulders if ever she had the chance. She knew this and so did I. Yes, I chose Didon. Sofia had my heart, but Didon had my interest.

Sofia always favored me by shambling to her stall door when I entered the stable. I gave her rock salt and apples and sweet murmurings of affection. Didon had to be coaxed and cajoled—but gently—and she always seemed to present herself to me rump first. Yes, it was a fine rump, shapely and sound, sleek and firm. However insulting her intentions, I truly did admire Didon's beautiful horsy ass.

I often came early to train so I could groom Sofia, since nobody else did. Sofia swished and whinnied her thanks unlike the shiny black-coated queen who sidestepped with flared nostrils and pulled away from me at every opportunity. Didon tried to bully me, and a couple times she succeeded. I gave in because the guilt I wore like a lead vest made me.

Didon knew! Her knowing meant that we did everything her way, with me having to coax, beg, and plead to counter her snorts, rears, and head-butts. I was not afraid. Maybe I should have been, but I knew horses were people too. They all had their own unique personalities, and Didon knew how to play me. I let her. I let her because we both knew I was still doing paying for bad deeds.

One day I arrived at the stables a little earlier than usual and decided to groom Didon first. She was in her stall and facing the door—was she waiting for me? She was! Didon greeted me almost as affectionately as Sofia. I was so pleased, I thought that finally she had forgiven me. At last. We bonded that day, and every day after, Didon favored me more than the day before.

This newfound bliss continued for several weeks. I brought the treats of rock salt, apples, and sugar cubes for both Sofia and Didon. Our training in the ring progressed steadily, and the date of our exhibition grew closer. We all got new jodhpurs, and mother made me a classic tweed jacket with leather patches on the elbows. I got a new riding crop direct from Germany, hand delivered to me by the daughter of the military attaché who rode a feisty white Arabian stallion and was in my class at the American school. In honor of my first-ever new riding crop, I put a shine on my boots bright enough to start a fire. I was having such fun!

Our training started with simple tasks. We began with a series of jumps over bales of hay and fences. It was the kind of stuff you see in horse shows all the time. If Sidi Fahr had left it up to us, we would have just raced each other around the ring for as long as the horses could stand it. What he had us doing took more concentration and skill. We practiced controlling our mounts and getting used to the different jumps more than anything else. Sidi Fahr said we were to communicate effectively with our mounts, and they, in turn, would obey our every command. That's what Sidi Fahr said. I didn't make the mistake of thinking it was so. I knew Didon would be running my show.

Our course had the eleven of us trot and canter half-pass across the ring in a standard figure eight. We then switched to a full canter, split into two groups, and rode to opposite ends of the ring. There we turned to face each other trying to hold our mounts and trot in place. (The Lipizzaners would actually do so – theirs was called a sustained piaffe; ours was a crazy shuffle.) After a minute or so of this, we rode toward each other in as slow of a trot as we could manage. It was called "passage" when the Lipizzaners did it.

Our goal was to meet and to form one large oval. Once the oval was completed we cantered around the ring twice before each horse and rider executed pirouettes (a 360-degree circle, in place). From there, we formed two separate ovals, one clockwise, and the other counterclockwise. There was one tight four-horse circle inside a larger seven-horse circle. The inner circle would then piaffe, rumps center and the outer circle would rear. That was the goal.

After accomplishing this circusian feat, we then separated to opposite ends of the ring. With an about face and the execution of two tempi changes (skipping) at a canter, at just the right moment, one rider from the smaller group was to change direction in a hard about-face and join the larger group. This required meticulous precision and no one volunteered to be that rider, so we drew straws for the honor. Then, the smaller group was to tighten up so that there was only a pace between each horse, and the larger group would spread out so that there was a length and a half between the mounts.

When we accomplished two complete rotations, the smaller circle was to join the larger circle. This was done with the same hard about-face move of that first rider from the smaller group. Then, as one big group of riders, we were all to make a single large circle. When the circle was complete, another pirouette and a rear of all the horses together. Yeah, it required quite a bit of practice.

Oh, there were mishaps. We had occasional squishings, bumpings, and full body hits. We were kids learning to control hundreds of pounds of galloping muscle and sinew. For all our dreams, these were not Lipizzaners, and we were not of The Spanish Riding School. Our moves might have been choreographed with that in mind, but our horses hadn't been brought up in the tradition. We did the best we could.

None of us remained free of minor injuries. Neither did we sustain any dripping cuts or jagged broken bones from our about-facing routines. We all wore the bruises of our efforts, certainly, but that was the price to pay for riding a thousand pounds of muscle faster than you could run to save your life. And, for egging it on to canter or gallop, turn, stop or jump with a mere nudge of the knees, flick of the reins, click of the tongue, or pull on the bit.

Sidi Fahr scheduled a dress rehearsal the day before our flashy performance for the embassy community and invited guests. I wore my beautiful new tweed jacket and was the envy of my peers. When I arrived early to groom and dress Didon, Sidi Anwar was cursing and yelling in her stall.

I ran toward the commotion along with a couple of the other kids in my group. When we got there, Sidi Anwar was trying to catch hold of Didon's lead. She was rearing with defiance and determined not to let him. Without giving it a second thought, I slipped into the stall and approached Didon, within her line of sight. She came down on all fours and sidestepped to me, away from Sidi Anwar.

When Sidi Anwar saw me, he began a tirade about how bad Didon was and how he was going to teach her a lesson. One of the older kids who had come with us remarked that obviously Didon didn't like him and maybe he should just leave her alone and let one of the other grooms handle her. Sidi Anwar said he was the king of the stables and that every horse would obey him. I barely paid attention because I was busy calming Didon, glorying in the fact that she had come to me on her own to get away from Sidi Anwar. To me, this meant that I had finally been forgiven by the queen herself.

With a happy heart and whistling lips, I groomed Didon for the dress rehearsal and joined the other kids in the ring for our warm-ups. News of Sidi Anwar's battle with Didon had spread quickly, and Mrs. Beare, one of the parents, asked me if everything was all right. It was. My own parents would come to the event the next day, so at Mrs. Beare's insistence I promised to mention this incident to mother. Sidi Anwar was not in the ring.

We started our routine and it was going well. There was a certain wave of excitement that washed over us when we went through each part without errors, and our straggly audience was appreciative and generous in its applause. I felt flush with pride. Didon was a little more feisty than usual, but she performed beautifully and I was happy to be riding her. As we rounded the ring for our grand finale, a full gallop in a single line, I saw movement out of the corner of my eye. Before I had a chance to react and anchor my seat, Didon reared.

I managed to stay on with the rear, but I fell right off when Didon sidestepped and bucked at the sight of Sidi Anwar. My right foot slipped in through the right stirrup, and everything seemed to happen in slow motion from that point on. I lost my seat this time and slid off her back almost as an afterthought. I hit the ground hard.

I felt the wind being knocked out of me in a jolt to my right side where I landed on my hip. Didon continued to rear. She batted at phantoms in the air with her forelegs, her back hooves dug into the thick sawdust. My foot caught in the stirrup, and Didon jerked me along the ground in a jagged line. Lucy Beare finally held Didon steady, and Sidi Fahr knelt over me.

There was a sudden silence and I felt no initial pain. I looked up and saw millions of tiny dust particles dancing in sunbeams that sliced through the high vented ceiling. Clouds of dust swirled in lazy twists above my head. Then there came a ringing in my ears, which got louder and louder as a roaring thunder, drumming like pellets of hail during a heavy summer rain, rippled under me and shook the ground. My scalp was tender where my helmet hit at the back of my head.

That really didn't matter much as I concentrated on getting my bearings. Just as my mind connected with how unusual this seemed, I felt a steady burn along my back and right side near my hip and ribs. Then, as though suddenly finding a strong signal on a radio, I tuned in to shouts, yells, and the snorting of a frightened horse.

It registered that I was on the ground looking up. I watched with a great and detached fascination as the spinning roof of the riding ring came slowly to a stop. People rushed to me from all sides. I saw faces bending over me and heard shouting. Lucy kept Didon from bolting, but with each movement she made, my foot still jerked through the stirrup trapped at the end of my leg. My anklebones were screaming. Everybody talked at once and I could not make out any one word; it was all a jumble. My right hip hurt, and my back felt as though it was on fire. I thought with all the sawdust I might burst into flames. I closed my eyes. I just wanted to breathe.

Apparently Sidi Anwar's appearance had spooked Didon. Nobody knew what exactly he had done that afternoon when we all came upon him in her stall. Mrs. Beare told Sidi Fahr about it. We decided that I was not too badly hurt. I was bruised, certainly, and raw where the rough ground had shaved off skin on my back and side. It would continue to bruise and would scab over—nothing new to me. I was shaken and wobbly. My ankle was banged up and sore. I had had worse scrapes. I had never once, however, before this day, fallen off a horse.

I went home sore to the core and smoldering with anger against Sidi Anwar. He was cruel to animals but I was just a kid; there was nothing much I could do. My fall caught up with me later that night when I discovered a ragged tear in my new tweed jacket. That wrenched pitiful sobs of frustration out of me. But I should have known better. In her quiet and magical way (it was the angel in her), mother repaired the jacket while I slept, and in the morning my tweed riding jacket with the patch elbows was better than new. It was battle ready.

We gave a flawless performance the next day. I noticed an achy pain in my back that felt hot and sharp and then subsided to a dull throb. It was not enough to dampen the exhilaration of the moment. Well after our show we remembered some of the turns and jumps, and we rode like the wind on the beach north of town, racing the waves as though we were running for trophies. I had pain and soreness for months and months. I lived with it. I secretly thought it was my ego rubbing me the wrong way for having lost my seat that day in the training ring. If I had the chance I know I would do it all again, because nothing beat the honor of having won the favor—and the pardon—of the magnificent Reine Didon.

Kadijah's Victory

We had a mouse in the house! Or mice. Mother said we had to find out what was going on. She and Kadijah expected me to help. I didn't want to help, but that feeling was out of my control. The mouse problem was obviously out of my control; however, I was surprised that not wanting to help was out of my control. I knew I was changing; in fact, I had changed. My tomboy days had dwindled down significantly. With the mouse in the house, I realized they were over. In the previous few months I had noticed I was getting very girly, and it alarmed me. Not girly-prissy, but girly-squeamish.

This condition hadn't happened overnight; I did know that much. It had begun in Bobo Dioulasso and lain dormant in the tiny Swiss mountain village of St. Galen. Here in Carthage, where we lived in a Mediterranean paradise, my squeamishness was close to reaching full-blown, nearly hysterical proportions. I didn't know what to do about it. I believed I had to get over it, though, and fast, because our mouse infestation was an even bigger problem. We all knew it would not go away on its own.

LADYBUG

Mother expected me to help with mouse detection. Kadijah was helping already. And Kadijah was as much of girly-girl as anyone I had ever met. She was more girly than my sisters! I knew if Kadijah could hunt for the mouse, I had no good reason not to. And too, mother was still not feeling one hundred percent from her bout with malaria. I had to be the best mouse hunter possible if only to do my share. It was a horrible situation for me to be in, but a mouse in the house was serious. Mice ate everything they could, even things that were not food eaten by humans. More importantly, I knew from other encounters that it was important to eliminate mice because they carried disease and reproduced faster than rabbits.

I tried to be brave and to approach this task as I had so many years ago when I was curiously fearless and inquisitive. I knew for my own good that this was necessary. I knew it, but I was sick about it anyway and full of dread inside. We went about the hunt systematically. We searched room to room, top to bottom. We found much evidence, but no critters. The mice liked paper and cardboard, plastic and shoelaces. They left trails of droppings that we cleaned up as we went along. It was disgusting and tedious, but I did my best not to get upset over it. I was trying my best not to let the squeamishness take over. I filled my head with other thoughts while I worked in order to keep the mousemares at bay.

I thought about how happy I was that summer was coming and my siblings would soon return from boarding school. I liked to read the schoolbooks they brought home with them. I had already read just about everything I could get my hands on. I was looking forward to some new books. I once found a book I had not seen before at the very back of the one of the bookcases in the long front hallway. I started reading it. There was a word that confused me. Looking it up in the unabridged dictionary didn't help much. I asked mother.

"Mom, what is fellatio for?" She held out her hand for the book. I gave it to her, open to the passage. She read it and looked at me. She didn't give it back. I asked her why I could not read the book any more. She said to trust her, the book was not for me. I did trust her; she knew me like a book! Mother said that there was a time and a place for certain things and that neither was the case in relation to me and that book. I understood. I knew that she knew what was best for me. Mother knew everything. I had to find something else to read.

I went back to an old favorite, *National Geographic*. I had already read the most current issue cover to cover, but I read it again. I liked to read the English language articles to Kadijah. I had to read them into French, but there were some words I didn't know right out of my head. Kadijah usually figured them out with lots of back-and-forth questions and answers. Spot reading is what I like to call it, and that was usually what I did when there were no more books to read. I would find an old faithful like the *Geographic* or *Time* magazine and read the articles to Kadijah.

Sometimes I read Kadijah the newspaper *Le Monde*. It was written in French so I didn't have to translate it in my head. Kadijah often asked me questions about the United States, what it was like to live there, what the houses were like. Since I had been in the United States for only one year, and it was not the best year, I didn't have much to tell her. When I did find stories about something going on in the United States I always read them to her.

Kadijah was going to be married. She had not met her future husband yet, but her family had found him through a matchmaker and he was suitable. Kadijah's dowry was ready and she would be married within the next two years. She was very excited and wanted to know what American brides did. Well, even though I was not the tomboy I had been, my interest in things having to do with brides and weddings was nonexistent. I looked for the celebrity marriage announcements in *Time* magazine for Kadijah. She said those stories were a waste of time since we saw so many of the celebrities married, then divorced, and later married again to someone else.

I told Kadijah I was not going to get married, and she was incredulous. She asked how I would live without a man to care for me. I thought about that for a very long time. I didn't have the answer, but I did understand that we lived in two completely different worlds, she and I. She said she would like me to come to her wedding, I told her I would be honored. Then she said that her family's matchmaker would find me a husband when the time came, so not to worry. I didn't tell her, but I knew that was not going to happen. After being bartered for in the Bobo Dioulasso market, I knew that a husband was someone to get for myself if and when I was so inclined.

Mother found the mouse nest! My thoughts sprang back to the present and the probability that we were going to kill what mice we found. However true this might be, I tried not to dwell on the fact. I didn't want to think how we would kill the mouse. I knew a neighbor had drowned the puppies her dog had had. It broke my heart to hear her tell us about it. I knew that the fate of the mouse or mice would be bad for them and good for us. I was not looking forward to it.

I went with Kadijah to see the nest mother had found. It was in the dry storage pantry on the ground floor under the stone steps near the furnace room. We were all tired, but as it was the very last place to search, we did so. We went top to bottom, shelf by shelf. There was much evidence. We cleaned as we went. I was given the job of hot soapy water carrier. I had to go up and down the stone steps about a million times. I wanted to complain, but I didn't. I knew that my task kept me from any up-close mouse encounters, away from the front line, as it were. I dutifully prepared the cleaning water as mother instructed.

My job was to pour the dirty water down one of the downstairs toilets, rinse the container out with tap water, and pour that water down the toilet too. Then I went upstairs to the kitchen where we had our largest pot, filled with water, simmering on the stove. I dipped clean, hot water from the pot into the container and squeezed in a goodly amount of dish-washing detergent and a quarter cup of Clorox. After that, I added more tap water to the simmering hot pot of water and took the clean, hot, soapy Cloroxed water back downstairs.

Mother went upstairs to rest. She got tired more quickly since her malaria. I worried about her after her malaria attack. She told me not to, but how could I not? She said Kadijah knew what to do when we cornered the mouse and I was to do as Kadijah said. I told her Kadijah and I would take care of everything. I got cold water from the fridge for Kadijah. The pantry work was not easy, and she was parched. She sat on the bottom step of the curving stairs and drank her water.

I braced myself to pick up the cleaning where she left off. We were on the third shelf from the bottom, and I saw more mouse droppings there than anywhere else. Plus, it smelled. Ugh. I pulled the items off the shelf, wiping each separately before putting it on a portion of another shelf that had been cleared for that purpose. There was a hole in the plaster wall. I didn't know what to do about it.

I told Kadijah about the hole. I showed it to her. We decided we would clean the rest of the shelf as well as examine the remaining area for mouse trails. We did, and we hit the mother lode. The mice had made the pantry under the stairs their mouse headquarters. The evidence was obvious, and of course the nest mother had seen was in the section that was hardest to get to. It was in the far corner, where the fit was tighter the closer we got to the bottom shelves. Kadijah said we should clear out that entire side where the mouse hole was and below. It was a stinky mess, but I could honestly say I had smelled worse. Still, it was hard work.

We cleaned each item and put it on a clean sheet on the floor in the hallway. We found a rabbit warren of mouse holes! And we heard suspicious rustlings on the floor in that tight corner. As a practical matter, since Kadijah was a very large young lady, it was decided that I would do the honors. I tried not to think too far ahead. I didn't want my imagination to make things worse for me. Even though I had seen worse, done worse, I told myself to go one step at a time. As I was telling myself this, on my knees in the corner of the tiny below-stairs cubbyhole of a pantry, mother came downstairs.

Later we all agreed that the mouse made its desperate break because it knew it was cornered. All I know is that the mouse leaped at me and clung to my chest. It was so close I smelled it! I looked down, and the mouse twitched its whiskers and raced forward as though it was going for my face. That is when I let out the scream upon scream upon scream I had barely held in since our hunt started. I lurched back to get out of the corner. It was impossible to move. Kadijah had wedged herself into the pantry with me. She said not to let the mouse get out or we were sure to lose it! I do not know what she thought I could do pinned to my knees on the floor in the corner of the pantry.

We lost our chance. That mouse was small and fast and clever. It used me for a toilet as well as an escape route. The mouse climbed over my shoulder and right on down my back. I was in no position to see where it went. Besides, I think I was still screaming. Mother said it ran out of the pantry and into the furnace room through a narrow space between the molding of the door and the wall. We had spent almost the entire day looking for that mouse. And it had narrowly escaped our best efforts to catch it.

Mother and Kadijah laughed and laughed about my screaming. They said they would have screamed too. They were both glad the mouse got me and not them! How could I blame them?—I knew I would have felt the same way. While Kadijah and I finished cleaning the last pantry shelves and the floor; mother sat on the bottom step and kept us company. She pulled off bunches of steel wool from a big fat bale of it, and we packed the holes we found with that and mothballs. We did the same in the space where the mouse had made its escape into the furnace room.

I was secretly relieved that the mouse got free. I knew letting it go was not our plan. We had not discussed killing the mouse, and I had not wanted to ask how we were going to do so when we caught it. Now the problem was solved. I was relieved that my inconvenient girly sensibilities could finally take a rest. With the pantry back in order and cleaned to mother's satisfaction, we all trudged back up the stone steps to the kitchen. Kadijah set the simmering water to boil. Since we boiled all of our drinking water, we would use that big pot to fill our drinking water containers. There was no need to waste perfectly good water.

I didn't forget about the mouse. I am sure none of us did. We knew if it came back we would have to find it. I knew it would be another day of hard work; but mice carried disease, and you could not have them in the house. I almost let myself wish that if the mouse was found, it would be when I was not home. I almost let myself wish it, but didn't in the end because it meant more work for mother. I didn't wish more work for her.

More work came anyway. My parents were having a cocktail party. This was not unusual. They entertained; it was expected. It was also expected that I not only help with the preparations but also mingle with the guests and act like a lady. I was still tomboy enough to dread these parties. I could dread all I wanted, but I still had to participate and behave. Sometimes I was lucky enough to spend the night at a friend's. This was not one of those times.

Mother was making her famous and much-requested egg rolls. From scratch. Kadijah and I were sous chefs in her kitchen. We fetched and scrubbed, chopped, minced, and rolled. We cleaned and wrapped, soaked, dried, and stacked. I was on pantry-fetch duty. Anything needed from the downstairs pantry was for me to get. I didn't waste my breath complaining. There was no time to complain, it was a petty indulgence. I had read that in a book once. It stuck with me.

I was sent to the pantry for another can of bean sprouts. When I came back up, Kadijah was on her way down for heavy-duty foil wrap. We rolled our eyes at each other at the top of the stone steps. It made us giggle, and I was giggling while I opened the can of bean sprouts for mother. Then Kadijah screamed. Mother and I ran to the doorway at the top of the stairs. Mother held her rolling pin like a weapon, started down, stopped, pointed it at me, and told me to stay put. Kadijah was still screaming.

I heard cans fall, and cries from both mother and Kadijah. There was such a commotion down below. It was very upsetting hearing the sounds of bumps and crashes and Kadijah's shouts. I didn't hear mother's voice and I was afraid. I ran back to the kitchen and grabbed the six-inch cast-iron skillet off the stove. It was still warm but not hot. I held it with both hands and raced down the steps.

When I got to the bottom, I saw mother standing with a hand braced on the furnace room door frame. I didn't see Kadijah. Then Kadijah poked her head out of the small pantry.

She looked at me and mother. She stepped out of the pantry with a radiant smile on her face. In one hand, she held mother's favorite rolling pin. The other she raised up high for us both to see. Kadijah held the mouse by its tail in triumph! It was bashed-head dead and we were way behind schedule.

Kadijah disposed of the mouse and cleaned herself up. My job was to clean the pantry. Mother said I knew what to do, she would leave me to it. I stood in the doorway and surveyed my project. It was disgusting. There was brain matter spatter on the wall by the holes near the floor and on the underside of the bottom shelves. I forcibly pushed my girly, squeamish sensibilities away and got to work. I did a thorough soapy-hot-water Cloroxing of the entire area.

By the time I had finished, my fingers were waterlogged rubbery. My fingernails were sterilized and bleached white as chalk. I also cleaned mother's rolling pin carefully. I wanted to be certain not one smidgen of mouse brains was on it. I told myself it had to be so clean that I would not hesitate to lick it with my tongue as proof. Even though I soaped and scalded and Cloroxed that rolling pin, mother never, ever used it again. She gave her favorite rolling pin away. It was Kadijah's victory prize.

Pearly Whites
a/k/a Dangerous Dentistry by the Simple-Minded

My two front teeth stuck out parallel to the floor. They were eyesores. Why? I had sucked my thumb for many years. All I can say is that it was a habit I truly enjoyed. When I was a very small child my nanny, Ayah Lemah, tried unsuccessfully to get me to change from my left thumb to my right. I didn't want to change. My right thumb didn't taste the same. Ayah Lemah was persistent. So was I. By the time I decided on corrective measures, I had much damage to repair.

The damage to my teeth started back in Kathmandu, Nepal. I remember how hard it was to stop sucking my thumb. I remember waking up in the middle of the night, in my little bed at the back of the house, surprised that my thumb was back in my mouth. It thought it belonged there. I reluctantly put that hand under my pillow to guard against its happening again, but that didn't always work.

It was hard to stop. I slept curled on my side with Teddy tucked under one arm and the pillow plumped just so under my head. My left hand cradled my cheek through my pillow's tufty thickness. No matter, I still woke up in the drowsy folds of the night with that thumb stuck comfortably at the roof of my mouth. It was cushioned there by the tongue in my head that had grown used to its being there.

I think by now you know that I was a bit crazy. What I am about to tell you should not come as a complete surprise. I wanted to fix my teeth. They stuck way out, and I was ready for a new, less gopher-like look for my upcoming teen years. Straightening my teeth was to be my present to myself for my thirteenth birthday. I knew I had to work diligently if I was to complete my task before my birthday. As my brothers and sisters prepared to fly off to boarding school, I prepared to work on my teeth.

It had been a summer of many firsts. I had finally read the *World Book Encyclopedia* from volume A through volume Z. I had nearly conquered the entire embassy library. I read all the mysteries and the historical fiction and poured over the atlases. The only things left were the Westerns, which I had resisted for a couple of years, and the biographies, which I hoped would disappear before I had to turn to them. I also watched in nervous fascination as my body grew every which way without my input or consent. Thirteen was a tangible, looming presence. I had read that what my body was going through was called puberty. I knew I wasn't ready for it. Now, without my consent, I was living with another TKO.

I read everything I could get my hands on in our house and I borrowed books from friends. The embassy library was looking like my very last resort. I had little interest in reading about real people who were now dead, so I started with the Westerns. I fell in love with Louis L'Amour and Zane Grey. It didn't matter that had I lived back then, I'd have been a slave.

I read for the escape, the infusion of new ideas, and the chance to see the world through different eyes. In those western tales, I discovered Jack Schaefer's, "Shane." "Come back, Shane." That phrase took on a life for me well outside the pages of the story. That phrase symbolized my personal struggle to do what I had to do. I had to grow out of my childish ways.

Somehow, in my unconscious mind, the idea of Shane prompted the urgent need for me to correct the damage to my teeth. Shane represented my quest for straighter teeth. This strong compulsion became all-consuming. I didn't know how, but I knew I would do it. No matter how hard the task, no matter how painful, I decided my teeth were going to be straight. And, not just straight, I was going to close the big gap between my two front teeth, too, while I was at it.

The budding teenager in me saw no compromise. Each day, when I looked in the mirror, I saw buck teeth and a big gap. I could twist my tongue through the gap it was so wide. Two five-millième coins fit into that big gap. That is the size of two nickels and a penny, straight up, using the dinars-to-dollars money exchange. My lips didn't meet when I closed them because my teeth stuck straight out.

I had not seen a dentist in over four years. The last one I had been to had tobacco-smelly hands and stinking dead-fish breath and sprayed spit in my face when he talked up close. We were not due for home leave, so I knew I would not be seeing a dentist any time soon.

I also knew my teeth were not going to get straightened just by my wishing them to be. I would fix them myself. Physics and geometry applied here. I wanted to eat corn on the cob; I knew I could figure out my teeth-straightening problem. Remember, I was the adventuress—girl scientist, explorer, mud pie maker, slug eater, horseback rider, and shark rescuer.

I determined that my front teeth would be straight and gapless in honor of the thirteenth year of my life. No dentist, but why should that matter? I would fix them myself. I started reading those biographies. They were hardcover books with tough straight spines. That is why I read them. The spines were an integral part of my *dentological treatmentology*.

I read every single one of the thirty-two biographies in the embassy library. A handful stood out. I found I didn't like Thomas Jefferson as much after reading about Abraham Lincoln. Sure, I admired Jefferson, the inventor. He cleverly invented the lazy Susan and the dumbwaiter. I was disappointed in Jefferson the statesman. Although he advocated with passion that slaves were people and not animals, he still used slaves and sold his own son into slavery.

Now, Frederick Douglass, he truly inspired me. Slave, scholar, statesman, and educator. Reading about Douglass was very much an eye-opener. Frederick Douglass was a genuine self-made man. When he was a small boy, he learned how to read. When he got older, he worked on a farm where, during one period, he was whipped every single day.

Years later, he escaped his slavery. He rose to genuine acclaim from that point forward. He risked his freedom to write his autobiography. He traveled and lectured about his life as a slave. Frederick Douglass taught me that where you come from may try and hold you back, but you must keep moving forward, learn as much as you can because what matters is where you go.

Then I met Marie Curie. She was a woman scientist who broke into a man's world amid great resistance. She proved that knowledge through science and experimentation was invaluable. She conceived of the first portable X-ray machines, which were used to save many soldiers' lives. Curie was dedicated to science and research. She taught me that success can be won by anyone who but seeks and perseveres.

That is just some of what my reading taught me in the year I decided to straighten my own teeth without the expertise of an orthodontist. Perseverance. Yes, I knew the word back then. Remember, the dictionary was my rosary, and it was at my complete disposal. I understood that I needed to apply pressure of an opposing nature to that which caused the teeth to *plank,* or *board.* Those are my own clinical terms for the way my front stuck out like a platform that a fruit fly could take a dive off.

My corrective solution was to read. I read every book in the embassy library down to the last autobiography. We got several in while I was buried in the bowels of the biographies. I read the autobiographies because it was necessary in order to successfully complete my dental treatmentology.

I do not suppose many people know the value of books as orthodontic instruments for corrective dentistry. They are indispensable. The majority of the books I read were hardcover. I knew that part of the straightening process was by the application of pressure. That is what those miniature rubber bands did. I didn't have those tiny rubber bands. I had hardcover spines, and I used them to press against my front teeth to make them straight. I pressed until they were oh-so-slightly loose, and then I pulled them inward with my tongue and sucked clean the inevitable oozing of blood from around my gums.

This particular blood was not gushing blood like that which I had encountered in many of my other experiments. This gum blood was just a little bit of welling blood that first outlined the gum and then pooled up to frame the teeth like unshed tears. I studied it. I noted its special gum blood characteristics, you see. I knew that if I was not careful it would splash, and bright red drops would dot the white porcelain sink. I had learned all about this in previous bathroom-mirror gum examinations.

Sometimes the gum blood drops splattered so forcefully that tiny dots jumped onto whatever shirt I was wearing. When this happened the shirt was usually light colored. I got good practical experience in removing blood stains from my clothing. Lots of cool water quickly. Soak, blot, dab. Do not rub. Where was I? Oh. It was not the gushing type of blood that I had encountered in many of my other experiments; this was just a little bit of swelling, welling blood.

When this slow bleeding happened, I stopped applying pressure. It scared me, but not enough for me to stop completely. I do not know how many times I did this; it took several months over the summer and, I think, into early fall. Finally, my front teeth fit over the bottom ones when I closed my jaw. The gap between my two front teeth was still there, though. I didn't know how to close it. Then I discovered dental floss.

Ah, yes! That stringy, tough, girl-dentologist's tool—dental floss. I never once used it to actually clean between my teeth or gums back then. I found a much more immediate and results-oriented way to use this waxed, white filament of dental hygienics. Dental floss was the key to closing the gap between my two front teeth! I took a long, long piece, a little more than a foot's worth, and wound it around and around and around and around my two front teeth. I wound it so tightly that tears of pain popped right out of my eyes.

Often the floss broke off before I completed these many *circulations* of the two front teeth. But no matter, when I felt the two teeth loosen, I pushed them together even more with my index fingers. Or more often, on the binding of whatever book I was reading.

Every book I read had dents from my two front teeth. Those books were instrumental in my *denticular* rehabilitation. The problem I encountered was that with the blinding pain of it all, and the now freely flowing blood oozing from my gums, it was nearly impossible to locate the end of the floss and unbind my tortured throbbing teeth.

At these times of unforeseen *treatmentological* difficulties, I always went in search of mother. Through my tears of pain and with tissues to my mouth to blot the blood, I mumble-called out to her. And, as a ship in heavy fog off a rocky coastline travels toward a lighthouse, I stumbled, blinded by pain, in the direction of her answering voice and my salvation.

I think by now mother knew not to be surprised by anything I did. She met my never life-threatening, but most always peculiar, antics with utter calm and perhaps slightly raised eyebrows. Mother always tended to me lovingly and unhurriedly, which in itself let me know how stupid this, my latest experiment was, so of course she never needed to actually say it.

The dental floss ministrations were the exception. My application technique required countless loops around and around and around those two front teeth along with continual tight pulling on the floss. Mother often protested, but she knew I knew she knew I would not stop until my teeth were straightened to my singular satisfaction. So, when I came upon her in my twisting misery of self-inflicted pain, in tears because of the pain, mother paused. She paused until I stopped twitching and just looked at me.

Mother looked at me as though she had not seen the real me recently, or as though she was trying to confirm that my head was hollow behind the windows of my eyes. Or maybe she was just trying to find a simple intelligence in them. Just when I thought she was going to release the binding floss, she would say, in a very strong voice, "I WISH you would not do this." It always got my attention.

Mother always waited patiently for me to finish crying; sometimes she shook her head. And besides, we both knew I would not stop my treatmentology until the job was done. It was rare to hear that particular tone of exasperation in mother's voice. If I lost my teeth because of this foolishness, I understood it was on my own stupid head.

Although she always helped me, mother never started her rescue operations until I stopped crying, blew my nose, dried my eyes, and looked at her. When I looked at her I saw the fire in her eyes. That fire always squeezed another tear or two of self-pity out of me. I imagined mother's eyes saw the great fool in me.

That I was a fool was not anything I didn't already know. I knew I was a fool in many ways. I just didn't want to see the fool in me reflected in mother's eyes. It irked me that she saw the fool part of me so clearly, because during this same time period, mother often told me I had a good head on my shoulders.

By this time I shook from the pain in my teeth, so my tears of self-pity were not an aid in any way. Those tears sometimes gave way to pitiful sobs which, if I had been mother, I might have let me cry for a little while longer. But she didn't. Mother ministered to me with undivided tenderness. Still, I saw in her eyes a tiny spark of what might have been a look that said—that is what you get when you do stupid things. She never once said it.

At these times, it was very important for me not to move. You see, in order for mother to get the floss off, I had to be a statue of stillness and hold my lips open. Cutting the floss required a steady hand and a careful pressure. I had to keep my lips clear of my teeth and my teeth raised for inspection because mother had to cut the floss off with a razor blade. Although the razor cut right through the floss, the treatment was not finished.

After mother's careful and indulgent assistance, it took me another great while to clean my mouth. I had to rinse well with warm salty water and finish off with Listerine, as it was the definitive cure-all to any possible denticular infection. However, I could not properly clean my mouth until I had pried out all the cut bits of floss wedged snugly between my teeth and hitched up into my gums. This task was best done in front of the bathroom mirror because the light was good in there.

Picking the cut floss out from between my teeth took much longer than putting it there. I discovered that tweezers were good for this meticulous extraction operation. No matter how careful I thought I was being, the floss was slick and the tweezers hit my gums. I sometimes accidentally cut them and that really hurt, but I had to get every last piece of that slippery, stringy filament out from between my teeth; otherwise it drove me crazy. Some might argue that this was impossible as I was clearly quite crazy already. They may have already heard about how I once bit a burglar.

Ice-Cold Water

A burglar got in the house! It was the first time my parents had left me home alone. Well, not exactly alone. I was there with my school friend, Nina. Her house was a couple kilometers up the street. We were a telephone call away from her grandmother, who had come to visit from Mobile, Alabama. Our parents were attending an official dedication ceremony in another town, and we girls were at my house playing Julia and Barbie. If I stood on tiptoe on the front terrace, I could just about see the roofline of Nina's house behind the row of cedars along the street that curved around the bay.

It was springtime in Carthage, Tunisia. We lived on rue des Phoenicians, just down the hill from Sidi Bou Saïd, the area that Queen Dido won as hers for the measure of a goat's skin. We lived across the street from the Punic Ports, where Hannibal watered his elephants before he set off on his ill-fated journey to conquer Rome. I often imagined that I walked where he walked. I liked to think I could feel the tension and excitement that was buried in the banks of the Punic Ports. I fished for minnows in that water. That was where I had tried to rescue the beached dolphin—or rather, shark. The snout and jagged teeth had clued me in.

Our instructions that day were simple and clear. We were not turn on the stovetop. We were not to turn on the oven. Most importantly, we were not to leave the confines of the gated yard for any reason without express permission from Nina's Grams, Mama Nana. We could live with that.

The outer gates stayed locked. The brass plaque on the wall by the gates said, *Cave canem*, Latin for "Beware of dog." We didn't have a dog right then. The key to the gates was on a leather cord hanging on a hook by the refrigerator in the kitchen. Those were the days of marathon doll playing. Our dolls had mansions and magnificent clothes and the most fashionable accessories that could be selected from the order catalogue. We had the run of the house.

What a beautiful blue-sky day it was!—Phoenician blue, bursting with possibility and promise. We played outside and picked oranges and tangerines from the trees in the garden. We played kickball with the ball my sister had sent me all the way from the United States! It still smelled new and it was plump full of air. It bounced high and I loved it.

I loved the fact, too, that my parents trusted us girls to be home alone. We ate sandwiches for lunch and drank Fanta sodas. The sodas were a treat from Nina's Grams. I didn't often drink sodas, so it was especially nice to have one on this day. We also had plenty of delicious Phoenician mint tea to drink. Mother had made it especially for us. It was in the fridge for any time we wanted.

During our playtime in the garden, we both noticed a man walk up the street from the bay side. We also noticed that he stopped at the fence and looked at us. We saw him; we knew he was there. He looked tough and mean, so we didn't look at him too much, hoping he would go away. He didn't go away. He ran a stick against the metal bars of the car gate. It sounded loud and heavy and menacing in the quiet afternoon.

The man went to the iron entry gate by the fig tree in the corner of the garden and shook it. He pushed at it hard as though he might break it. We knew it was locked, but we didn't like his being there. The man started talking at us. He told us that he had been watching us for quite some time. He said he knew we were home alone and that he wanted water with ice, so we had better get him some! In French, and in Arabic too, so he was sure to understand, I told him to get away.

Nina thought there would be no harm in giving him ice water. I told her no, we were not going to give him anything. I said we should go inside until he left. Just then the man walked across the street. We hurried to the gate to see what he was up to. He stopped between two buildings, and we were shocked to see him relieving himself. He saw us and made lewd motions.

We fell over each other backing away from the gate. The man rushed back across the street to the gate without closing his pants. We ran for the front door of the house, which was up a long, steep flight of marble steps. There were twenty-seven of them, and getting up them seemed to take us forever. We heard him break the gate door lock; we didn't need to turn around and look for confirmation. Nina hesitated at the top of the steps and I pushed at her to get us both inside quickly.

Our front door was ten feet tall. It was an ornate, heavy double door—a traditional door, painted Carthaginian blue, with black metal studs in the wood. We still had the original wrought iron key, which was about a foot long and weighed a kilo. One side of the door had a sliding privacy window. It covered a wrought iron grill to look through so that one could see who was there. Nina stood on tiptoe and slid open the little window. She watched what the man did. She said he was at the faucet next to the gate and had turned it on.

Nina wanted to give the man the glass of ice water he demanded. She believed that if we gave it to him he would leave us alone. I reminded Nina that the man had just broken the gate to get onto private property. I reminded her that he was a total stranger who had just made crude remarks and lewd gestures. Hadn't she noticed he had just broken the gate to get inside our yard? I told Nina it was not a good idea to engage the man in any way. I didn't tell her I had seen horror movies that started out this way. More specifically, I had read every single murder mystery in the embassy library. It was a fact that stupid actions resulted in predictable injuries. Or worse.

We had this conversation at the front door. I stood there trying to think straight while Nina looked out the small window. I think Nina thought it was just another of our glorious and happy summer days. I think she thought that with his glass of ice water, the man would thank us and be on his way. I didn't have time to slap her back to reality as they do in the movies. I knew it would not work out that way. I believed we were in real danger.

Nina slammed the window shut and said the man had seen her. I didn't need to look out the window to know this was a bad thing. I told her to call Mama Nana and then to call the police. Call the police. Triple zero! She ran up the hallway. I got the door locked and the safety chain on. I could not find the night bar! We put it across both doors at bedtime, but it was nowhere in plain view that I could see.

Before I could look beyond the foyer for the night bar, the man was pounding on the door. He taunted us through it. He said of course we were home alone! He said he had better get his ice water. I told him he had better leave because we were calling the police! The man said all he wanted was cold water with ice, why would I call the police for that? When I looked, I didn't see Nina at the phone. Come to think of it, I could not remember if I heard her calling her Grams. I needed to find the iron bar. The man kept pounding, and the big wooden doors shook in the door frame.

I remembered that we sometimes kept the iron bar in the coat closet across the hallway from the door. I ran to the closet and rummaged inside. Although it was a walk-in closet, there was no light. I was feeling along the side of the walls when Nina came back up the hall. I saw out of the corner of my eye that she had a glass of water with ice in it. I could not believe it, but I was seeing it with my own eyes. I stood frozen in the closet. Luckily, my body reacted before my brain thawed.

I launched myself back across the hall to the front door. Nina got there before me and opened it! She held the glass out for the man to take, and he slapped it out of her hand. The glass crashed onto the marble steps. Shards sprayed along the top of the steps and inside where the door was cracked open. Before I could get there, the door burst open. The force of it knocked Nina off her feet. She scrambled up quickly and we both fought to close the door.

The man blocked our efforts. He managed to angle most of his body so that he was more in the house than out. We shoved hard, and he fell back so that only his leg and foot were in the doorway. I stomped on the top of his foot as hard as I could. He pulled his leg back, with a shout of pain and anger. Just then the latch on the right side of the door, which slid into the iron sleeve at the very top near the molding, fell down. This made that side easy to push open, even with the bottom latch secure in the hole in the floor. I prayed that the man had not heard the latch fall. I stood on my toes to push it back up. I felt my stomach fall into my feet as I carefully put the safety chain on. My hands shook. I knew that this battle had just started. We had to lock up the house.

Nina was across the hall crying and shaking with fear. She stood by the open closet door. I wanted to be over there crying too, but something told me that if I did so, that would be the last time I ever cried. I knew I could not let myself start. I was scared. And I was experiencing firsthand the fight or flight reactions we had studied in science class. I recognized the feeling. I had had this feeling before. This time it seemed much stronger. I was fighting, Nina was fleeing, and we were both in great danger. All I could think was that I absolutely positively had to pee.

There was shuffling and cursing at the door. I listened with my ear pressed close and heard the man stumble down the stairs. Nina was still frozen by the open closet door. I wanted to shake her but I thought she might break. Instead, I took her hand, and in as unpanicky a way as I could, I said, "Nina, let's close all of the shutters so the man cannot come into the house, okay? Nina?" Nina blinked and I repeated what I had said. She was to close the shutters upstairs and I would close all of the ones downstairs.

I suddenly remembered that the top half of the kitchen door was clear glass. That door, like the windows, had to be opened all the way in order for you to pull the back grill door closed. I ran into the kitchen and unlocked the back door. The man was at the bottom of the back steps! He bellowed with rage and rushed up them as I reached out. I had to step out onto the landing completely outside the house. I didn't want to do it.

There was no time to be timid. I stepped out onto the landing. I grabbed the heavy grill door and pulled it shut behind me. I knew I had to slide the bolt all the way to the left and then turn the key. It was a sticky lock. I knew I needed to use the strength of both hands together. I had to do it right the first time because I knew I would not have a second chance. I turned the key in the lock and it stuck.

I was frozen with indecision. Both my hands were on the key as I tried to turn it in the lock. And there was the man! He laughed. He knew exactly what my problem was! He pulled on the grill, and the key turned in the lock. That, he didn't expect. I slammed the kitchen door, and his fist shot through the space between the grill bars, right through the glass. He grabbed at me and caught my hair. I pulled the kettle off the low ledge by the stove and hit at his arm to get free. The kettle was heavy with water and he let go. I got sloshed with water and my scalp burned, but the man didn't get into the house through the kitchen.

I heard slamming around the house and realized, thankfully, that Nina was closing the shutters as I had asked her to. I remembered then that the furnace room door was unlocked. There were two doors to the furnace room. One led from the house into the furnace room, and the other led from the furnace room into the backyard a few feet from the back stairs. The man was still banging against the kitchen grill.

I raced downstairs. It was a long, tight, turning stairway with a small storage closet under the steps and the furnace door directly to the right beside the last step down. It was a heavy, reinforced door, and as I turned the key in the lock, the door handle moved. The man heard the bolt shoot through and pulled furiously on the doorknob. I left him banging on the furnace room door.

I ran along the north side of the house, closing the shutters in each room. The thing about the shutters was that you had to open the window access, then lean out as far as you could in order to catch hold of the shutters and pull them closed. And they would lock only if you did it right. The left-side shutter had to come in first, then the right one, then the latch. The latch had to go all the way down. All the way down. If it didn't sit in the base of the catch bar, a pull from the outside could pop it back up and the shutters could be opened. I did my best. I could not hear Nina running around upstairs any more, and that worried me.

The family room on the ground floor had French doors leading out to the garden patio. Same thing there. You had to open the doors and step out onto the patio and then pull in the shutters. The bars had to fit all the way down. There were two sets of French doors and more than ten windows to close. I was barely a window ahead of the man. I could hear him as he progressed around the house. He was banging against the walls and was trying each window, hitting at the shutters and pulling on them from the outside.

I fell up the back steps to the second floor and locked the door to the basement stairway. Nina was just finishing in the living room. She was hysterical and crying. I knew exactly how she felt. I hysterically needed to pee. We had to call the police! And I had to find the bar for the front door because I knew the man would be coming back that way.

I ran down the hall to the closet. I called over my shoulder for Nina to call the police. The number was triple zero, 0-0-0. She went to the phone. I had the baseball bat, but I was baffled at not finding the bar for the front door. Where could it be? The next thing I knew Nina was at the closet door. I asked her what the police said as I pushed it closed. Nina said the line was busy. I told her to get back to the phone and try again. She did and the line was still busy.

"The line was busy?! Nina! Keep calling until you get through! Call Mama Nana!" I yelled this at her in my own fear and frustration, and that was the last straw. Nina crumpled. I ran back up the hall to her. Nina was so scared she could not talk. She could not move. I didn't blame her; I was really scared too. Nina held the receiver out to me. She was shaking all over. It was Mama Nana. She told me to slow down, tell her what was wrong. I did. I told Mama Nana that we had locked all the shutters and the man was now outside. She said she would be right there and that when I got off the telephone with her I was to call the police.

The police station was closer to us than Mama Nana was. I got a dial tone. I dialed 0-0-0. The line was busy! I hung up again and dialed zero for the operator and was finally connected to the police. I told the officer our address and explained that we were two girls alone and a man was trying to break in. As I was talking with him, Nina was pulling on me. For some reason, what with the blood rushing in my ears, and talking as calmly as I could with the policeman, I didn't hear the pounding at the front door! I thrust the receiver at Nina and ran down the hallway.

My face was wet with tears, and I didn't even know I was crying. I was sorry I had yelled at Nina but didn't have time to tell her because just then the front door burst open. I do not know how. The man was in the house! I think he was as surprised as we were. Nina started screaming. It sounded horrific, and it stunned us both—the burglar and me. Then he lunged at me and I lunged at him. I tackled him at his knees.

The two of us fell to the hard tile floor. He was off balance, but I knew he would get the better of me as quickly as he could. Nina was still screaming. My arms slipped down his crusty legs to his ankles. My elbows banged on the floor. It really hurt, and it made me extremely angry with the entire business. I was determined not to let go. I held on. My funnybones were not laughing. We rolled up the hallway farther into the house. That was the wrong direction! Nina came to help and the man got hold of her. She screamed and she kept screaming. Nina's screaming made him crazy. Nina's screaming made me crazy.

The man twisted his hold on Nina and she fell, but she managed to scramble out of his grasp. When she started to get up from the floor he caught her by her long brown hair. It had come halfway out of the braid. I still had his ankles, and he held on to Nina with one hand while with the other he grabbed at the back my neck and tried to pull my head off.

For a wacky second I thought he was trying that *Star Trek* Vulcan pinch trick. Then I came to my senses. That was fiction, this was real. I thought that if we didn't get him out of the house, Nina and I were going to get hurt very badly. I thought we were going to die. Blame it on those murder mysteries, but I thought Nina and I were going to die in an ugly way. The three of us struggled on the floor, each of us desperately trying to gain an advantage.

I wondered why Nina was not screaming, I liked her screaming better than the silence. But actually it was not really silent. We were struggling hard, breathing hard, and reacting hard. There was a whole lot of noise going on, especially in my head. It was all I could do to hold on to the man's ankles. He stank and his skin was dirty, crusted with mud where he had splashed water from the faucet by the front gate. I certainly hoped it was water. I was losing my grip. I heard Nina whimper. All at once the man was roaring. He roared like an angry lion. We three were at an impasse. I knew something had to give.

Without another thought I opened my mouth and bit into the burglar's leg. I bit as hard as I could below his calf, near the back of his ankle just above his Achilles heel. I was going to pull a plug out of him. It might be the last thing I ever did, but I was going to do it. His roaring increased but I didn't let go. I heard Nina now; she had gotten free and was running away. I did not blame her. I would have run away too - if I could have.

My face stung from the man's slaps, and my lips were wet. It was his blood. The man hit me on my head and face open handed; he grabbed at my head and pulled my hair out of its braids. My scalp burned all over. I heard my barrettes skittle across the floor. He kept slapping me. My head bounced off the floor. I had a quick moment to find that really quite interesting. Extremely painful, but interesting.

My head bounced again and it was no longer interesting. I knew it was a good thing he could not reach me with his fists—yet. My arms were around his ankles and my eyes were shut tight. His slaps stung; I felt my eyes swell and tears squeezed out of them against my will. The man could not get turned around enough to get in better swings at me. I didn't think I could hold on much longer. Sweat was making him slippery.

The tile floor rumbled beneath us. It was Nina; she had the bat. She dragged it on the tiles all the way from the coat closet up the hall. It sounded like a train, and the floor thundered like an earthquake. The hitting on my head stopped because the man tried to grab the bat out of Nina's hands. He wrenched away from me and was free! I scrambled to get between him and Nina. I was next to her before he had a chance to get to his feet. He was saying, "Why? Why? Why?" over and over. He sounded pitiful. It made me want to feel sorry for him! I didn't like that. I had to fight with the energy of my anger. Why was he saying, "Why?"

"Why are you in my house? Get out get out get out," I screamed at him. Nina was shoving the bat into my hands. My hands closed over the wood as though they were not a part of me. I swung at the man, shouting, "Get out get out—get out get out" in French and in Arabic. I knew he understood.

He understood. He did not get out. Instead, the man lunged at us. I was not going to let him get close enough to touch us this time. I swung at him and the bat hit his hand away. He recoiled and looked baffled as he cradled his injured hand. I swung again and this time I hit his knee. I could not have made a better connection. The sound was awful. It was a thickly muffled *Pllomph* sound and I knew it was a really good hit. I felt the impact of it tingle into my fingers, ripple along my forearms and dance inside my elbows. He screamed in pain and I had to pee!

As his stream of obscenities ricocheted off the tiled floor and bounced at me from the wall in the long, long hallway, I felt an anger boil up inside like white fire. How dare you how dare you! I didn't stop to think, I rushed him intending to harm him. He managed to stumble out of bat reach. Then he lurched at me, trying to grab the bat and I hit his foot with it. I think it was the same foot I had stomped on when he had tried to get into the house the first time. He howled like a dog, shuffled out of my reach. I kept after him, pounding on the floor with the bat as though it was a pickax and I was digging in a hard rock wall, and he was it. He was the rock wall.

I backed the man all the way to the front door, but he did not want to leave. I hit him again on the same foot as before, I wanted him to leave! He looked at me with bewilderment. I was so shocked by the expression of hurt on his face, and by the pain I saw in his eyes, that I almost stopped. He was really hurt, and I had hurt him. I started crying again, the salt of my tears burned my eyes. I hurt him. I hadn't wanted to, but I had had to.

"Get out." I said it in a whisper. My voice was failing and I was very, very tired. Dangerously tired, I was drenched with sweat, thirsty and almost utterly exhausted. Time paused between heartbeats. The man's body was a big dark blotch in the tall outline of the doorway. The late afternoon sun poured in all around him where it could. Dust motes floated in the bright streaming light as though they had nothing better to do. I felt myself blink and in that instant, the man drew himself up and made a quick motion as if to hit me!

Blinking or not, I was ready for him. I sidestepped and used the big end of the bat to ram him out the front door. I hit him square in the gut and he lost his balance. He stumbled backward, backpedaling as though riding a bike. He may have even fallen down the first few steps, slipped on the water from the broken glass maybe. I do not know; I didn't care. I slammed the door shut and I did not look out the grill because I was afraid he would still be there.

The doors popped back open. I tried not to panic, I knew I had to make myself concentrate. I knew the doors had to be closed properly, so I pushed them carefully. My hands were shaking; I could not make them work. I said a quick prayer: God, please help me close the door right. First the right side, then the left side. The doors closed. Out of habit I reached for the broken chain. The chain was not broken! I didn't understand how it was not broken, I had no time to wonder.

I put the chain on very carefully. My hands were no better than before, they were cold and slow and still shaking. I held them together, close to my heart. It raced wildly. I leaned back against the front door for support. I stood there and tried to just breathe. And, out of the corner of my left eye, I saw it. Between the wood molding of the right-side door and the wall, where it had been all day, was the iron bar!

I picked up the bar and threw it across both doors. I pushed the stupid slipping lock back up into its slot. Then I tested it to make sure it was in tight. It was as tight as I could make it. My hands were still shaking. They hurt. My eyes were swollen, my nose ran. I wanted to look out the privacy window, but I just could not make myself do it. Instead, I hobbled down the hall to the phone. It was hanging by the cord; there was no dial tone, and I didn't see Nina.

I was ready to scream. Just as a wave of panic began to punch me in the throat, Nina came running into the hall from the living room. She grabbed my arm and pulled me with her to the window where we could see the road. I left the receiver dangling, I heard it crack against the wall. No time to worry if it got broken, a car was driving the wrong way down the one-way street!

It was Mama Nana. We recognized the car, we could see her behind the wheel. She kept her hand on the horn, it was a welcome sound even though it was still far away. We watched in hope and fascination as Mama Nana hopped the curb and drove straight through the park instead of driving on the road where it wound the circle around the park. People in the park jumped up and looked after her, pointing and shouting, waiving their fists. Nina and I jumped up and down and screamed with hysterical relief. We both stopped abruptly with the same thought—the man might still be out there. He might hurt Mama Nana when she came to the yard!

We heard loud talking and shouts from outside. We knew Mama Nana was still on the road and were afraid the man was back. I picked up the phone again and heard talking. We sometimes had a party line; we were not supposed to, but it happened sometimes. I asked the voices to please, please get off, it was a matter of urgency, we had to call the police! The voices didn't get off. They belonged to the police.

The police had never hung up the phone. They heard the whole thing and it was they who were at the front door. Nina would not go down the hallway with me beyond the kitchen. I didn't blame her; she was doing her best to keep her skin on. The policeman on the telephone said that Inspector Hassim was at the door with his men, we could let them in. I told him we could not, we were too scared. I told him Mama Nana was coming and he said to wait until we heard her voice at the door, then we could open it. He said we were right not to open the door to men's voices. He said to hang up the telephone and wait for Mama Nana, so I did.

I started down the hallway to the front door and now I heard Mama Nana. I knew her voice with her strong southern accent; Mama Nana didn't speak French. She was telling the policemen to move aside. They were trying to protect her from being first at the door in case there was trouble. I realized that they didn't know the man was gone. I looked back up the hall toward Nina. She was petrified.

I ran back to Nina where she teetered by the kitchen doorway and hugged her. She was white as bleached flour and her lips looked blue. I took her hand. It was ice-cold. I coaxed her to come with me to the front door. She really needed Mama Nana. I needed Mama Nana too. We were both doing our very best to keep our skin on.

When I got to the front door, Nina pulled away. I had to coax her to stay with me again as though she was a nervous filly. I told her to be calm, to take a deep breath. I told myself the same thing. I told Nina, "It's okay now, everything is okay, you did a really good job. I'm going to open the door 'cause Mama Nana is here, you want to see Mama Nana, I know you want to see Mama Nana." I opened the front door, and Nina stepped away. She stood across the hall out of my reach.

The three policemen and Mama Nana crowded into the doorway. For a long moment they all just stared at me. I stared back; I noticed that my eyes would not blink. I must have looked scary with blood on my mouth, my hair on end, and my eyes swollen. I am sure I had snot on my face too. I felt lopsided standing there and realized I had somehow lost a shoe. My cotton print shirt was torn; buttons grinned down the hallway like scattered teeth. I had no idea when they got there.

There was complete silence for a couple of heavy heartbeats, and then Mama Nana rushed through the door and hugged me tight. Nina came over and we grabbed her too. We hugged for a long time. Nina sobbed. I could not cry. I had not had a chance to pee, but it didn't matter. There simply was no more water in me. There was no water in me for tears or for anything else.

Our world quickly returned to normal. No sooner had the police taken a look through the house and the whole of the grounds than our parents returned. They were all very proud of us. The next day at school, everyone knew about our ordeal. One of our teachers gave a speech about how brave we girls were and said that we should be really proud. Nina told everyone I had saved us.

I could not stop thinking how none of it would have happened if Nina had not opened the door. Everyone said I was a hero. I certainly didn't feel like a hero. The last thing I wanted to do was to talk about it. Mother always said that one should err on the side of graciousness. Keeping this in mind, I kept my mouth shut and waited out the school day.

I was glad to be back home after school. I felt wounded and I was sore all over. Even my gums hurt. My face was swollen with deep, dark, painful bruises. There was a thick thumbprint bruise on the back of my neck, and welts had just begun to fade from where the man had scratched me. I also had odd button-sized fingerprint bruises on my throat.

Under one eye, the purple matched the color of the aubergine we had for dinner that night. My lips were swollen and fat like that eggplant too. It was hard to open my mouth; the corners were raw and sore. Salt in the eggplant made the cuts sting. I didn't feel like eating. I still felt exhausted and really just wanted to take a long nap or cry.

About a week later, the police caught the man. The police said they knew him. He had done break-ins before, but never break-ins with people in the house. The police said he had been in jail for burglary before. He was a vagrant, they said, a troublemaker. The police assured us he would not be doing any more break-ins. They identified him by his injuries, especially his bruised foot, and my bite.

Inspector Hassim said the man limped because of his knee injury. It was still swollen where I hit him with the bat. Knowing that didn't make me feel any better. The man's most glaring injury was from my bite. Inspector Hassim said my teeth marks were plain to see on his leg in back, just above his Achilles heel. I had to bite on a bar of castile soap for an impression comparison. The bite marks on his leg matched my teeth exactly.

Inspector Hassim and mother were the only ones who asked how I was doing. Mother knew I was having trouble sleeping. She sometimes sat with me and held my hand until I fell asleep. Inspector Hassim came by the house one day to visit. He brought me a Fanta soda. He was happy I was looking well. The last time he had seen me I had welts on my neck, a black eye, and a cut lip. My scrapes and bruises had finally almost faded away.

Inspector Hassim asked whether I was as healed on the inside as I looked on the outside. I didn't know what I could tell him. He told me I was a very brave girl. He said he would remember what I had done and always be proud of me. When it was time for him to leave, he shook my hand and said I was not to worry—the man was going to be in jail for a long time. I told him thank you, I was glad they caught the man. I tried not to feel one way or the other about the actual incident. That was impossible though. I felt frightened and bruised just about every second of every minute.

Normal creaks and noises in the house made me jumpy. I didn't like even being in a room by myself anymore. Mother told me that, as time passed, it would not seem as frightening. I tried to believe her. I was still very upset. I didn't even want to think about what had happened. I certainly didn't want to talk about it. I kept it to myself because I could see that mother was worried and I didn't want her to be.

All those Ellery Queen, Agatha Christie, Dick Francis and Ralph Ellison stories made me wonder about the bad side of people and things. I wondered what if. I never had before, not in relation to my own safety. My imagination ran away with me. I tried to catch it, slow it down, and stop it. I tried to turn it off; I tried not to wonder what if, but I wondered anyway.

The many possibilities of mayhem and more made my heart hop. The mayhem possibilities thumped and thrashed around in my chest, made it hard for me to breathe. I thought my heart might just stop altogether.

What if...

Horrid, ugly and violent variations crowded my mind, cramped my brain, stuffed my head up, and made it spin. It all made my stomach sick. My stomach was sick for a very long time.

I sipped on ice-cold water.

LADYBUG

Ladybug's Truth Knock Overs (TKOs):

- Love is best
- Jellyfish sting
- Red ants smell sweet
- Kindness matters
- Mice are everywhere
- People can be mad as dogs
- Reading is fundamental

Just a few favorites. Enjoy!

Alpine Hot Chocolate

1 dark Swiss chocolate candy bar
2½ cups whole milk
¼ teaspoon vanilla extract
1-2 teaspoon(s) sugar to taste

Melt chocolate in a double boiler or in a heavy-bottomed pot over low to medium heat. Add milk slowly. Stir with whisk or wooden spoon. Add sugar to taste. Turn up the heat. Ready when hot. Do not boil. Turn off flame. Stir in vanilla extract. Serve in mugs.

Ladybug's Bread With Chocolate

1 half-loaf French baguette fresh from the bakery
1 dark chocolate candy bar

Slice the half baguette lengthwise. Add chocolate. Wrap in a cloth napkin. Keep at room temperature. Eat when the chocolate is soft. If you leave your sandwich in too warm a spot, be careful because the chocolate will ooze.

Ladybug's Peanut Butter and Pickles

2 extra-thick slices of mother's heavenly buttermilk bread*
1 tablespoon crunchy peanut butter
1 teaspoon mayonnaise
1 big fat dill pickle sliced lengthwise**

Spread peanut butter on 1 slice of bread. Add pickle slices to peanut butter side. Spread mayonnaise on second slice of bread.

Press slices together. Serve with a glass of cold milk (not powdered milk from a box if you can help it).

*Substitute: There is no substitute. Try your favorite bread.

**Substitute: ¼ cup fresh clean begonia flowers for the pickles. (Smooth peanut butter works best with begonia flowers.)

Ladybug's Sardines and Crackers (before her tomato allergy)

6 or 7 of your favorite crackers
½ (3.75 ounce) can of sardines, drained
1 tablespoon mayonnaise
1 garden fresh, sun-ripened beefsteak tomato*

Mash sardines and mayonnaise together in a small bowl. Add Tabasco to taste. Spread sardine mash on crackers. Chase each mouthful with a bite from the tomato.

*Substitute: There is no substitute.

Mother's Heavenly Buttermilk Bread and mother's Famous Egg Rolls are Ladybug's family secrets.

Mother's Melt-in-Your-Mouth Butter Horns

1 cup milk
½ cup butter
1 yeast cake or 1 tablespoon dry yeast (dissolve in $1/3$ cup warm water with 1 tablespoon sugar)
½ cup sugar
3 eggs at room temperature
1 teaspoon salt
4-4½ cups flour

Heat milk to warm. Do not let it boil. Add butter. Let cool. Add in this order: sugar, salt, eggs, then yeast and flour. Mix with

Delectables

patience and love until flour is absorbed. Work the dough as little as possible. Roll into a round and set aside in a bowl. Let dough rise to double its size in bowl. Dust hands with flour. Punch down dough, clean sides of bowl. Let rise again. Dust hands with flour and turn onto lightly floured board. Shape as you like.

For crescents, pat dough into two or three rough rounds. Roll out in a circle onto lightly dusted countertop to ¼ thickness. Cut in wedges. Roll wide side to tip. Place tips up onto ungreased baking sheet.

For dinner rolls, pinch off small meatball-size pieces of dough. Roll into rounds. Place into nonstick muffin cups, three rounds per cup.

Bake in preheated 350°F oven 12-15 minutes or until golden.

Mother's Sardine Sandwich

½ (3.75 ounce) can of sardines, drained
2 thick slices of Mother's heavenly buttermilk bread*
1-2 teaspoons brown mustard (to taste)
2-3 thick slices of garden fresh, sun-ripened beefsteak tomato

Spread brown mustard on both slices of bread. Slice sardines lengthwise; remove most of the bones. Flatten fish. Arrange on first slice of bread. Add tomato slices. Top with remaining slice of bread. Remove crusts and feed to Ladybug.** Cut sandwich into wedges. Eat standing at the kitchen counter.

*Substitute: You'll have to use your favorite bread as there is no substitute.

**Eat the crusts yourself or save them to make bread pudding or croutons. Do not waste food.

Mother's Sweet Spice Shortbread

½ cup sweet cream butter, softened
¾ cup light brown sugar and 3 teaspoons set aside
1 cup all-purpose flour
¾ to 1 teaspoon cinnamon (to taste—less is sometimes more)
¼ teaspoon finely ground cardamom
1 teaspoon finely grated fresh ginger root

Preheat oven to 325°F. Blend together butter, sugar, and spices in a medium-size bowl. Beat with a wooden spoon until creamy. (Or use an electric hand mixer.) Add flour and mix well. Place in round ungreased cake pan; press evenly. Prick thoroughly all over with a fork (make a picture or a design).

Bake 18-20 minutes until just turning golden. Cool; sprinkle with remaining sugar and cinnamon. Cut into wedges.

Mother's Wish-There-Was-More Peach Roll Pie

1 (21 ounce) can of sliced melba peaches*
½ to ¾ cup granulated sugar
4 or 5 tablespoons sweet cream butter
⅛ teaspoon, or less, freshly grated nutmeg to sprinkle
1 to 1½ teaspoons ground cinnamon to sprinkle

Prepare pie crust for a single 9-inch pie (a butter recipe is best). Roll dough in an oblong as you would a jelly roll (about 13 inches long by 9-10 inches wide), about a ¼ inch thick, onto lightly floured surface. Prick dough all over with fork. Cut butter into bits and sprinkle over pie dough. Sprinkle on the tiniest bit of nutmeg, then several pinches of sugar. Sprinkle on cinnamon. Add a handful of peaches. Roll them like a jelly roll in the dough. Repeat this until all the peaches are enfolded.

LADYBUG

Delectables

Pinch ends and fold under to close (not too thick, just to keep the peaches in). Sprinkle top with cinnamon and sugar.

Bake at 350°F in a preheated oven on an ungreased cookie sheet, 30-35 minutes or until it turns golden. Remove from oven; cool out of reach of little Ladybug hands. The roll will bubble and cook a while longer until it cools. Ladybug loves it warm!

*Drain liquid and set it aside for Ladybug. (She does not have to share.)

The Painter Dorian Gray's Sardines

1 (3.75 ounce) can of sardines in oil*
1 Swiss army knife**
Lots of crackers

Open can with the can opener tool of the Swiss army knife. On top of sardines in oil in the can, lay as many crackers as will fit. As crackers absorb the oil, smash into sardines as desired. Eat out of the can with the point and blade of your Swiss army knife.**

*Substitute a bowl for the can.
**Substitute a fork for the Swiss army knife.
Cleanup: Wipe knife blade on your pant leg or sleeve; toss can into a corner.

Phoenician Mint Tea

1 medium-size lemon
1½ cups water and 1 ice tray
4 tea bags (1 tea bag for every two servings, adjusted as desired)
2 cups boiling water
4 cups room-temperature or cold water
¾ cup honey (to taste)

Delectables

3-5 mint leaves fresh from the garden (cleaned)

The night before: Squeeze the juice out of 1 lemon; take out any seeds. Keep the pulp. Add lemon juice and pulp to 1½ cups water. Pour into ice tray. Freeze.

Steep tea in 2 cups boiling water. The longer it steeps, the stronger it will be. Add honey to taste before it cools. Stir in crushed fresh mint leaves. Add remaining water. Chill thoroughly. Remove mint leaves before serving. Serve in a glass over lemon ice cubes. Add fresh mint as garnish if desired.

Recipe for Disaster

Eating flora like Ladybug. Do not do it. Doing so can make you sick or worse. You do not want to get sick. And nobody wants to get worse.

You may wonder why recipes for Ladybug's mud pies, Azmadou's dinner, Kalima's cooking, and Wednesday night dinner are not included. Snap out of it.

Recipe for Success

Sow kindness, cultivate love, practice peace.

Glossary

board
(bôrd) v. A dentological term meaning to stick straight out parallel to the floor.

circulations
(sûr-ku-lay-shunz) adj. Entwining and continuous motions to effect a particular outcome specifically related to dentological treatmentology, in Ladybug's case, using floss or floss-like apparatus on her two front teeth.

circusian
(sûr-kes-sē-in) adj. Of, or characteristic of, circus-like acrobatics in an obviously non-circus venue.

denticular
(den-ti-cue-ler) n. Any part of, about, or having to do with, teeth; not gums, just teeth.

dentological
(den-toe-la-ji-kel) adj. Pertaining to the denticular aspects of dentistry as practiced by the simple-minded.

Dido
(dī-dough) n. Queen of Carthage. Legend has it that she was allowed to live after the defeat of her army. Dido was allowed to live on as much land as a single goat skin would cover. To the amazement of the conquering general, she cut the skin into pieces as thin as thread and laid the strips end to end. In this way, Dido could occupy an entire hill. So impressed was the general by her ingenuity that he permitted her to

keep the area we now know as the beautiful town of Sidi Bou Saïd.

horriphology   (ho-ri-fo-lo-gē) n. The science of horror and its attendant phenomena. Specifically, the avid and objective study of things that are creepy-crawly,   slithery-slimy,   and otherwise frightening and / or disgusting.

incongruality   (in-con-gru-al-i-tē) n. The condition of being out of place yet being clearly experienced; therefore, a reality; a puzzle much like that in a Sherlock Holmes mystery. For example, the needle-sharp and viciously long cactus quills in Ladybug's face presented a startling incongruality.

plank   (plănk) v. A dentological term meaning to stick straight out like a flat board parallel to the floor.

peckful   (pek-ful) adj. Deliberately intending to puncture or poke (not to be confused with *peckish*).

TKO   (tē-kay-o) abbr. Truth Knock-Over. In the case of Ladybug, undeniable reality. When reality finds you, face it.

treatmentological   (trēt-men-ta-lo-gi-kol) adj. Of, or having to do with, treatments; in the case of Ladybug, the dentological aspects of straightening the teeth. See *treatmentology*.

Glossary

treatmentology
(trēt-men-ta-lō-gē) n. The science of treatment, as well as the practice of treatment. In the case of Ladybug, the straightening of the teeth and the associated mental preparation for the pain and suffering of the entire process, including the spiritual acceptance of the stupidity of one's act even though it is for the good of all of the teeth.

un[bug]eevable
(un-bu-gē-va-ble) adj. A fantastic, odd occurrence that has no practical explanation and is impossible to substantiate even when witnesses are in agreement. For example, an unjumpeevable distance is a fantastic distance, but Ladybug jumped it with ease and alacrity. Thus the term refers to a jump greater than an Olympian could accomplish or greater than ever previously recorded.

311

Last, but not least, I would like to thank three men of quiet strength and excellent character:

My father, Herman Oliver Marshall, Sr., without whom these stories could not have been written. A hardy pioneer and frontiersman, an educator, and a renaissance man; he has been the epitome of discipline, duty, loyalty and success. His grace and dignity in some of the most difficult of situations, his steady force of will and personal discipline have been tremendously inspiring. I hope I might one day be even half as accomplished as he.

My brother, Herman Oliver Marshall, Jr., whose unwavering faith in me is largely undeserved. Our visits together over the years have helped me become a kinder and more gentle person with a keener interest in repairing my many character flaws than caring about anyone else's. His careful reading of my work and considered comments have also made me a better listener, and hopefully, a better storyteller.

My heartfelt thanks to Michael Eli Davidow, whose frank criticism, generous encouragement, and brutal honesty kept me focused and kept me writing. But for our many conversations and his hefty pushes, "A Clean Heart," "Blackie and I," "Kalima's Cooking," "Numéro Sept Avenue Rapp," "Feet of the Baobab Tree," and "Out of Order" would not have been written.

LADYBUG

The author and her mother, Catherine.*

About the Author

Melanie Marshall was born in Washington, D.C. The youngest of five, at three months of age she moved with her family to Kathmandu, Nepal, and lived there for seven years. After returning to the United States for a year of home leave, she moved with her family to Upper Volta, now known as Burkina Faso, where her father, a career foreign service officer, had been newly assigned.

While in West Africa, Ms. Marshall traveled extensively throughout the region with her parents in Bertha, the family's trusted Ford station wagon. Soon, boarding school in Switzerland intervened and the family subsequently moved to Chad. Their next post was Tunisia where she went to school and lived for several years.

Although raised primarily overseas, Ms. Marshall now lives in Washington, D.C. and considers herself a faithful Washingtonian. She would be the first to say that writing about her experiences has taken her by surprise and she hopes you enjoy these stories. As they are all true, please be mindful when reading them to children, and caution them not to attempt to replicate these outstanding adventures.

CPSIA information can be obtained at www.ICGtesting.com
Printed in the USA
LVOW070023070212

267379LV00002B/1/A